Zvi Halevy

JEWISH SCHOOLS
UNDER CZARISM
AND COMMUNISM

A Struggle for Cultural Identity

Foreword by George Z. F. Bereday

SPRINGER PUBLISHING COMPANY
NEW YORK

CREDITS

Pages 22-23: Quotation from *The Brothers Ashkenazi* by I.J. Singer, translated by Maurice Samuel, pp. 24-26. Used by permission of Alfred A. Knopf, Inc. Pages 193-195: Quotation from *The Jews in the Soviet Union* by Solomon Schwarz, pp. 135-137, printed by Syracuse University Press in 1951 and reprinted by Arno Press in 1972. Used by permission of Syracuse University Press. Pages 237-238: Quotation used courtesy of YIVO Institute for Jewish Research, 1048 Fifth Avenue, New York, N.Y.

Springer Publishing Company, Inc.
200 Park Avenue South
New York, N.Y. 10003

76 77 78 80 / 10 9 8 7 6 5 4 3 2 1

Library of Congress Cataloging in Publication Data

Halevy, Zvi
   Jewish schools under czarism and communism.

   Bibliography: p. 276
   Includes index.
   1. Jews in Russia—Education—History. I. Title.
LC746.R8H34   377'.96'0947   74-79410
ISBN 0-8261-1740-6

Printed in the United States of America

Contents

Introduction 1

Chapter 1 Russian Jewry: Origins and Socioeconomic
Status since the Polish Partitions 7

Chapter 2 Traditional Jewish Education 36

Chapter 3 The Secular Yiddish School Movement
before and after the Russian Revolution 58

Chapter 4 The Secular Hebrew School Movement
before and after the Russian Revolution 101

Chapter 5 The Rise and Development of the Soviet
Communist School in Yiddish 146

Chapter 6 The Curriculum of the Soviet Communist
School in Yiddish 215

Chapter 7 Yiddish Schools in Annexed Areas,
1939-1940 258

Postscript 268

Bibliography 276

Index 294

ACKNOWLEDGMENTS

I wish to thank Professor George Z. F. Bereday of Teachers College, Columbia University, under whose direction the doctoral dissertation on which this book is based was written. The many long and interesting discussions between us on this and related topics have always been highly enlightening to me. The source material was located mainly in the Columbia University Library, the Jewish Division of the New York Public Library, the Library of the Jewish Theological Seminary, and the Library of the YIVO Institute of Jewish Research. Like all authors I am indebted to those who helped me obtain the books I used.

I shall always be in the debt of my late father, Max Lipset, with whom I discussed the topic of this book many years ago. His encouragement and example were all-important in enabling me to finish the book.

Foreword

The rich literature and culture of Yiddish—the language that once linked Jews of all the East and Central European nations in a communality of consciousness in the Diaspora of modern times—may be destined to recede into history. The decimation of Eastern European Jewry by emigration and the tragedies of war, and the valiant rebirth of Israel, have restored Hebrew to the center of Jewish life. This book by Dr. Zvi Halevy is designed to capture a glimpse of Yiddish education during its final stages under Czarist and Soviet Russian rule.

Some inroads on the prevalence of Yiddish in Jewish schools came from the aspirations of Russian Jews who wished to develop Hebrew as a common language in anticipation of a national Jewish state. A number of Jewish socialists, especially in urban areas, advocated Russian as the language necessary for all Jews as the basis for full participation and economic opportunities in the increasingly industrialized society of Russia.

The main impact, however, on the fate of Yiddish education and culture came from shifting government policies. The tragic pogroms of Czarist antisemitism frequently resulted in destruction of Yiddish schools and deaths of leading educators. The Bolshevik Revolution first promised respite with the principle of free development for national minorities, but this principle did not extend to religious culture. Thus the traditional Yiddish schools, oriented toward the Jewish religion, were doomed to total destruction.

The Soviet government, under Lenin as well as Stalin, promoted the growth of a network of Yiddish public schools, vocational institutes, and cultural centers devoid of religious elements but amply propagating Soviet political teachings. This policy of educating the nearly 3 million Yiddish-speaking Jews for Soviet citizenship was maintained until the mid-thirties, when Stalin, with intensified nationalistic goals, began to abolish and finally destroyed all segments of Yiddish-language education in Russia.

The author has produced a thoroughly documented chronicle of these developments. Dr. Halevy combines immersion in the Yiddish culture of Europe with American upbringing and extensive university teaching experience in Israel. This book originated in doctoral research at Teachers College, Columbia University, where Dr. Halevy specialized in the study of education of Soviet nationalities, an integral part of his concentration on the U.S.S.R. in particular and on comparative education in general. The book has emerged from this remarkable set of unique qualifications of the author. The publication had the benefit of a small subsidy from the Center for Education in Industrial Nations at Teachers College.

George Z. F. Bereday
Professor of Comparative Education
Columbia University

Introduction

THE "JEWISH PROBLEM" in the Soviet Union is a very old one. For hundreds of years it obsessed Czarist regimes which attempted to apply a variety of solutions, few of them liberal. Their policies of economic, legal, and political discrimination — including pogroms — produced Jewish opposition, and the Russian rulers could claim that resistance and subversion gave credence to their original assumption that Jews were alien to Russia and had to be rooted out.

Count Sergei Witte, the greatest of all prerevolutionary Russian statesmen, recognized that if the liberal policy of Tsar Alexander II had been followed, the Jews would not have become such a factor in "our accursed revolution" and the Jewish problem would have become just what it was in all countries with a large Jewish population,[1] — that is, that the

Jews were there, a separate entity apart from and often disliked by the rest of the population, but not a force working actively against the regime.

In his memoirs the Count relates that the Czar once asked him, " 'Is it true that you are in sympathy with the Jews?' 'The only way I can answer this question,' I replied, 'is by asking Your Majesty whether you think it possible to drown all the Russian Jews in the Black Sea. To do so would, of course, be a radical solution of the problem. But if Your Majesty will recognize the right of the Jews to live, then conditions must be created which will enable them to carry on a human existence. In that case, gradual abolition of the disabilities is the only adequate solution of the Jewish problem.' "[2] Witte's counsel was never heeded by any Czarist regime.

After the Czarist regime fell, enlightened people throughout the world hoped that the new government would abolish oppression and discrimation and institute the democratic freedoms that the peoples of Russia had never enjoyed. The democratic revolution of February, 1917 was followed by the Bolshevik revolution later that year, and its leaders promised to wipe out past evils and build a just society.

One of the most difficult problems they faced was the national minorities' question, a hornet's nest that contributed substantially to the downfall of the Empire. Recognizing its strategic importance, the Bolshevik regime issued "The Declaration of Rights of the Peoples of Russia" on the seventh day of its existence.[3]

The nationalities question was dealt with on different levels corresponding to the population of each group and the degree of territorial concentration. Thus it was relatively easy to implement new policies for Ukranians, Georgians, Armenians, and White Russians: they were substantial in number and were concentrated in one area. Separate Soviet Socialist Republics, theoretically independent, were set up, and their languages were officially authorized for government, public affairs, and culture.[4] In the case of minorities concentrated in one area but not numerous enough to assume the financial and technical responsibilities of self-government, Autonomous Soviet Socialist Republics were established. They were much more limited in their rights than the Soviet Socialist Republics, but nevertheless had their own Councils of Ministers and Supreme Soviets. Among those who were granted status of Autonomous Soviet Socialist Republics were the Germans, Tartars, Kalmucks, Bashkirs, and Mari.

A level of government similar to that of the Autonomous Soviet Socialist Republic was the Autonomous Province. There were relatively few; some of the peoples inhabiting them were the Circassians and the Khakass.[5]

The third type of Soviet minority consisted of peoples either so scattered that cultural institutions would not have been practical or so few in number that large-scale investment in separate cultural institutions could not be justified. The Jews, Greeks, Poles, Bulgarians, and Hungarians belonged to this category. Only a minority of these peoples resided within the borders of the Soviet Union. For these groups, and also for the more scattered members of larger peoples, a lower level of autonomy was devised: the national district, comprising five to ten villages, and the national village Soviet and national collective farm.[6] A large number of these were Jewish: three Jewish National Districts were established in the Ukraine (Kalinindorf, Stalindorf, and Novo Slatapol) and two in the Crimea (Fraidorf and Larindorf).[7] In the early 1930s there were 12 Jewish village Soviets in the Smolensk province of the RSFSR,[8] 168 in the Ukraine,[9] and 27 in White Russia;[10] and there were 500 Jewish collective farms in the Soviet Union.[11]

These institutions were part of the attempt to implement the vaunted Soviet formula for solving the dilemma of minority culture: "national in form, socialist in content." Another major means for the realization of this policy was the school system, and this study will report on the schools of one of the Soviet minorities, the Jews.

Although the situation of the Jews must be viewed in the light of the overall Soviet minorities policy, Jewish cultural institutions are interesting and unique for several reasons:

1.   Jewish cultural life, noteworthy for its internal vigor throughout the millennia, was especially persistent under pressure. In this respect the Jews differed very much from the other nonterritorial minorities. The Poles, Greeks, Hungarians, and Germans who resided in the Soviet Union existed in cultural backwaters: the center of Polish culture was Warsaw; that of German culture, Berlin and Frankfurt; of Greek culture, Athens; and of Hungarian culture, Budapest. In contrast, Russia was the cultural center for all Jewish people. Every important national and cultural movement among the Jews originated in Russia and found its greatest advocates there. The world centers of Hebrew and Yiddish scholarship and writing in the pre-World War I period were in Odessa, St. Petersburg, Warsaw, and Vilna. If any nonterritorial minority could reach cultural self-fulfillment in the Soviet Union, it would have been the Jews, with their long tradition of learning in the Russian environment.

2. The Jews are one of the largest of the Soviet minorities. According to the 1959 Soviet census, there were 2,267,814 Jews. The 1970 census showed 2,151,000 Jews,[12] but it is generally believed that the actual number is higher. The Soviet government itself, in a report submitted in 1959 to the United Nations Subcommission on the Status of Minorities, estimated the number at 3,000,000.[13]

3. The status of Jews is frequently a gauge of the liberality of a government's policy toward minorities. Thus by examining the Soviet government's Jewish policy as it manifested itself in the fate of the Jewish schools, this study hopes to shed light on the character of that government, and to enhance the reader's understanding of Soviet minorities policy in general.

Notes

1. *The Memoirs of Count Witte*, edited by Abraham Yarmolinsky (New York: Howard Fertig, 1967), pp. 377-378.
2. Ibid., p. 376.
3. William Henry Chamberlin, *Soviet Russia. A Living Record and a History* (Boston: Little Brown & Co., 1932), p. 213.
4. An excellent survey of the formation of the various constituent parts of the Soviet Union is Richard Pipes, *The Formation of the Soviet Union: Communism and Nationalism, 1917-1923* (Cambridge, Mass.: Harvard University Press, 1954).
5. Walter Kolarz, *Russia and Her Colonies* (New York: Frederick A. Praeger, 1952), p. 22.
6. Ibid., p. 23.
7. Ibid., p. 172.
8. Yakov Kantor, *Natsionalnoe stroitelstvo sredi evreev SSSR* (Moscow, 1934), p. 28.
9. Solomon Schwarz, *The Jews in the Soviet Union* (Syracuse: Syracuse University Press, 1951), p. 151.
10. Kantor, op. cit., p. 27.
11. Kolarz, op. cit., p. 172.
12. *Narodnoe khoziaistvo SSR v 1970 g.* (Moscow, 1971), p. 15.
13. United Nations Commission on Human Rights, Subcommission on Prevention of Discrimination and Protection of Minorities, *Study of Discrimination in the Matter of Religious Rights and Practices* (Conference Room Paper No. 35, January 30, 1959) (New York, 1959), p. 4.

Chapter 1

Russian Jewry: Origins and Socioeconomic Status Since the Polish Partitions

Origins

THE RUSSIAN JEWS had first been Polish and came under Czarist rule at the time of the three partitions. Originally they came from Germany at the end of the twelfth century as a result of the Crusades.[1] Immigration continued on the crest of the general wave of German settlers into Polish lands, and gained momentum during persecutions in the fourteenth and fifteenth centuries.[2]

At the end of the fifteenth and the beginning of the sixteenth centuries, a huge wave of Jewish immigrants poured into Poland, primarily from Bohemia. When the immigration was basically completed in 1572, Sigismund II, the last of the Jagiello dynasty of rulers of Poland and Lithuania, issued a decree several months before his death permitting the settlement of Bohemian Jews yet stipulating that no more Jews be permitted entry into Poland.[3] A small additional number of

German Jews did come to Poland at the time of the Thirty
Years War, but, on the whole, it can be said that the Jewish
population at the end of the sixteenth century was the ances-
tor of modern Russian Jewry.[4]

Jewish immigration into Poland was encouraged by the
Polish kings who were anxious to build up a countervailing
force to that of the Shlakhta or nobility. The motives for
encouraging the immigration of Christian tradesmen and
handicraftsmen from Germany also applied to the settlement
of German Jews, who brought not only capital, but also the
ability to handle capital.[5]

Legal Status

Jewish life in Russia did not basically change for several
hundred years. Economically, socially, politically, religiously,
culturally, and intellectually, the status of the mid-nineteenth
century Jew was the same, or in many cases worse, than it had
been at the time of the Polish partitions in 1772, 1793, and
1795, or even in preceding centuries when Jews enjoyed
internal autonomy under the kingdoms of Poland and
Lithuania. Before we consider how Jewish life changed, we
need to understand how the Jews lived for the centuries
preceding the 1860s.

Old Russia — before the acquisition of Poland in the
three partitions — had no Jewish population.[6] The Jews who
came under Russian rule were almost all small town dwellers;
only 10 or 15 percent lived in the cities. There was not a
community in all of Russia with a Jewish population of
10,000.[7] The entire Jewish population of the Russian Empire
in 1815 amounted to only 1,200,000 persons.[8]

The Jewish population which had accrued to the Russian Empire at the time of the Polish partitions was restricted as to where it could live. From the outset, the policy of the Czarist government was to keep the Jews strictly confined to the newly acquired Polish and western provinces and to prevent their spreading out to other parts of the Empire.[9] And even within this area, the Pale of Settlement, there was an effort to narrow the sphere of Jewish economic life. Christian merchants and small burghers were none too friendly to their Jewish competitors, who were placed in a special category and paid twice as much in taxes as their Christian counterparts.[10]

Under Paul I (1796-1801) several commissions were established to investigate the situation of the Jews. On one occasion when the Polish landed aristocracy was convened at Minsk to inquire into the poverty of their peasant serfs, they made no objective inquiries that might have resulted in some blame being laid on themselves, but instead accused the Jewish tavern keepers of being responsible. In fact, the landed aristocrats were eager to retain their monopoly of the manufacture and sale of spirits. At the same time they wanted the Jewish internal organization to be broken down so as to bring about an amalgamation of Jews with the rest of the population — the Russians in Russia and the Poles in Poland. Friesel, the governor of Vilna, was convinced that the root of the evil lay in the outlandishness of Jewish religious customs. In 1800, Derzhavin, a poet and senator, wrote an elaborate memorandum to the Czar on the "curbing of the avaricious pursuits of the Jews" and their transformation into an element "useful to the government." Two projects had been submitted to the governor by Jews: Nathan Shklover, a wealthy St. Petersburg merchant, counseled that the Jews be drawn to manufacturing enterprises and to agriculture in colonies near Black Sea ports, and a physician named Frank proposed that the Russian public schools be opened to Jewish children.[11]

Paul died before the report could be acted upon. In 1802 his successor, Alexander I (1801-1825), appointed a commission for the improvement of the conditions of Jews in White Russia and in the other provinces acquired from Poland. When the Jewish deputies, summoned to receive the plan, were unable to accept certain "correctional measures," they were dismissed and ordered to submit their suggestions for effecting the reforms.[12] In the commission itself Count N. Speransky was the only statesman who pleaded for a maximum of liberties and a minimum of restrictions, emphasizing the futility of reforms from above. He believed that if the Jews were left to themselves and all avenues of success became open to them, they would accomplish their own improvement. However, the contrary opinion prevailed: the statute submitted to the Czar and approved in 1804 provided that Jews be kept out of Russia proper and confined to Poland and thirteen other provinces — five in Lithuania and White Russia, five in the Ukraine or Little Russia, and three in New Russia. In addition, future Jewish agriculturists might settle in two eastern provinces, Astrakhan and the Caucasus.[13] In the economic sphere, article 34 of the statute ordered that within three and, in some cases, four years Jews should be deprived of the right to lease and manage taverns and inns in villages and thoroughfares, or even to reside there.[14] This stipulation meant potential ruin to 60,000 Jewish families, about half a million persons.[15]

Thus while the law permitted a small group of Jewish farmers to exist, it brought disaster to the greater part of the

Jewish people. Those expelled from the villages had no place of refuge. A Russian writer described their expulsion:

> Jews pleaded for extension of time, they cried and groaned, but to no avail. They were mercilessly driven under a guard of peasants and, in some cases, of soldiers! They drove them like cattle into the towns and hamlets, and there on open lots under the sky, they were left to contemplate the vicissitudes of fate.[16]

An official historian, friendly to the reign of Alexander I, records the tragic results of the evictions:

> In the dead of winter half-naked Jews, driven from their domiciles into the towns, were crowded together in quarters that gave them no breathing space, while others, ill-sheltered, were left exposed to the bitter cold . . . . There developed among them disease and death.[17]

The ruthless and unsystematic dislocation of such large numbers of Jews created a serious problem for non-Jews as well. From a report of the Jewish Committee submitted to the emperor we learn that many local authorities complained to the central government about their inability to take care of the refugees who swarmed into their towns. They were afraid "that these people, because of poverty might even cause riots or take to looting or murder."[18] There were also protests from landowners, whose sources of income were depleted through the evictions.[19]

Complete expulsion from the villages was temporarily postponed because of unusual circumstances. The Czar was fearful of Jewish susceptibility to the Napoleonic spirit.

Because he interpreted Napoleon's convocation of the Jewish Notables and the Grand Sanhedrin as a maneuver to win hegemony over the Jews of Prussia, Austria, and Russia,[20] the Czar ordered the governors in 1807 to convoke provincial assemblies of Jewish representatives. But after the Peace of Tilsit, when Alexander and Napoleon came to an understanding, the ruthless expulsion of the Jews from the villages was resumed. It was scheduled to be carried out in three installments and completed by 1810; but in 1809 a new commission worked on the problem and after three years returned with a report, one of the most remarkable documents in the history of Russian-Jewish relations. Pointing out the absurd logic of the expulsion idea, the report stated that it would not benefit the peasants but only hasten the ruin of the Jews. The government submitted; the expulsions were halted. Very rarely did the Russian government take such a liberal attitude toward the Jews.[21]

This is not the place to detail the history of the Jews in Russian legislation. It will be sufficient to say that the "liberalism" of the report was never again repeated and the history of the Russian Jews was a succession of hundreds of repressive laws accumulating over the years until the March Revolution of 1917.[22]

We shall deal here with only one aspect of the status of the Jews in Russian law: the Pale of Settlement. As has been mentioned, the area of the Pale where Jews were permitted to live was defined in a preliminary fashion in 1804. In 1835 a law was passed codifying the earlier law and subsequent restrictive amendments. Minor changes and further restrictions were made until 1917, but basically the law of 1835 remained intact. As of 1904, the Pale included the following areas:

1.   In the Kingdom of Poland: the provinces of Warsaw,

Kalisz, Keltsy, Lomzha, Lublin, Petrokov, Plock, Radom, Suvalki, and Siedlce.

2. In Lithuania: the provinces of Vilna, Kovno, and Grodno.

3. In White Russia: the provinces of Minsk, Vitebsk, and Mohilev.

4. In Southwestern Russia: the provinces of Volhyn, Podolsk, Kiev (except the city of Kiev), Chernigov, and Poltava.

5. In southern Russia: the provinces of Bessarabia, Kherson, Ekaterinoslav, and Tavrida (except the city of Yalta).[23]

At various times many modifications of the absolute prohibition to enter the interior of Russia were made. Since Russian legislation regarding the domicile of the Jew was very complicated, only the main features can be stated here. Its essential principle was that, while the general prohibition remained in force, the following specified classes of Jews were given the privilege of domicile throughout the Empire:

1. Merchants of the first guild — that is, merchants paying a very high business license — after having paid that license somewhere within the Pale for five consecutive years. This right to live anywhere in Russia outside of the Pale lasted only as long as the payment of the license was continued. After ten annual payments, a permanent right of domicile within the city in which the payments had been made was acquired.

2. Professional persons, such as physicians, lawyers, dentists, graduate engineers, army surgeons, midwives, and graduates of universities and higher institutions of learning in general, as well as students in such institutions.[24]

3. Master-artisans working at their trades when admitted to their artisan guilds, or possessing the necessary legal

evidence of proficiency in their crafts.[25]

These restrictions were extremely effective. According to the census of 1897, only 314,765 (6.07 percent) out of a total Jewish population of 5,189,401 lived outside the Pale of Settlement. The census figure appears larger than it actually is because it included many native Jews of the Caucasus and Central Asia who were not of Polish origin and did not speak Yiddish. They had the right to live outside the Pale. Table I lists the Jewish population of the Russian Empire according to the 1897 census:

Table I

Jewish Population of the Russian Empire in 1897[26]

Pale of Settlement

Northwest Russia	1,410,001
Southwest Russia	1,418,279
South Russia	729,780
Total Pale in Russia	3,558,060
Poland	1,316,576
Total Pale of Settlement	4,874,636

Outside the Pale of Settlement

European Russia	207,706
Caucasus	58,471
Central Asia	12,729
Siberia	34,377
Finland	1,382
Total Outside the Pale	314,765
Total Jewish Population of the Russian Empire	5,189,401

Economic Status

At the beginning of the nineteenth century, Jews lived in abysmal poverty. The famous Yiddish writer Mendele Mocher Sforim said, "We are a community of moths that, one like the other, are all equal."[27] More than 30 percent of Russian Jewry were innkeepers or lessees of property; more than 35 percent engaged in commerce or trade, mostly as small shopkeepers, merchants, or peddlers. If we add to this group a host of religious judges, beadles, ritual slaughterers, and managers of various religious and community institutions, we can safely say that more than 80 percent of Russian Jewry belonged to what is technically called a petty bourgeois mass. Artisans and their workers accounted for 17 or 18 percent and 2 or 3 percent were upper bourgeosie or rich merchants and lessees.[28] The occupational distribution of the Jews in Zhitomir, a typical Russian Jewish town, in 1789, is interesting.

Table II

Occupations of Jews in Zhitomir, 1789[29]

(Total population, 3,690; Jews, 882 (23.9%)

Occupations	Number	%
Inn and tavern keepers	345	39.1
Trade and shopkeepers	219	24.9
Craftsmen	187	21.2
Servants and maids	58	6.6
Poor people	73	8.2
Total	882	100.0

The onset of Russian rule meant economic disaster for the Russian Jew. His traditional economic base was destroyed and he descended into even greater depths of poverty.[30] The situation continued to deteriorate throughout the first half of the nineteenth century. A Russian scholar who made a special study in the 1840s of the Jewish communities in the Pale concluded that only three out of a hundred Jews possessed capital of any consequence, with the rest leading a half-starved, miserable existence.[31] A government committee appointed in the 1880s to investigate the condition of the Jews reported that 90 percent constituted "a proletariat living from hand to mouth, in poverty and under the most trying and unhygienic conditions."[32]

Because of the smaller population and more favorable natural conditions, the economic situation was always somewhat better for Jews in the Ukraine than in the Northwestern provinces — but even here, poverty was the common lot. A Russian economist and statistician reports that in the Chernigov Province most Jews lived in poverty and squalor, their food consisting generally of bread and vegetables.[33] According to the testimony of a landowner in the Province of Kiev, most of the Jews of that territory were poorer than the peasants, and their existence was a precarious one.[34]

The Impact of Emerging Russian Capitalism on Jewish Life

The freeing of the serfs in 1861 marks the beginning of the growth of modern capitalism in Russia. Russian society began to develop in a totally new direction, and the life of the Jews was greatly affected by the change.

The view that the growth of capitalism and urbanization in the Czarist Empire was responsible for the change in Jewish life should of course be put in perspective. The belief that economic causes are the primary determinants of changes in society and ideas is generally termed the economic interpretation of history. Russian Jewish life from 1860 until the First World War illustrated both the strengths and the weaknesses of this theory. Certainly the growth of capitalism in Russia caused profound changes in Jewish life. But the nature of those changes was shaped by the Jewish historical, social, religious, and intellectual tradition. In the succeeding pages, when the growth of capitalism and its effect upon the Jews is recounted, it should be kept in mind that if we limit ourselves to economic explanations, we will not fully understand the story of what happened to the Jews.

One of the most graphic indicators of Russia's economic growth was the rapid extension of the railway network in both European and Asiatic Russia.[35]

In addition, the value of industrial production grew as follows: 1870 — 500 million gold rubles; 1890 — 1.5 billion gold rubles; 1912 — 5 billion, 738 million gold rubles, a twelvefold growth since 1870. Foreign trade amounted in 1886 to 914 million gold rubles; and in 1913 it reached three billion gold rubles.

Russian economic development was especially rapid after 1905. For example, in 1905 sugar production totaled 51 million pud and in 1913, 93.5 million pud. Not only did the export of sugar grow but the domestic consumption also rose: in 1905 it amounted to 14 pounds a year per person, and in 1913 it had grown to 18.2 pounds.[36] Russia had the second largest number of sugar refineries in Europe (288 as compared with 324 in Germany). One half were in the southwest

(Kiev Province alone had more than a quarter of the Empire's refineries), one-quarter in Poland, and most of the rest in southcentral Russia.[37]

Those industries which before 1861 had relied on free wage labor profited from the emancipation. The influx of labor from the villages to the industrial centers was facilitated by the removal of the personal restrictions of serfdom. Moscow's textile industry made great progress. After experiencing some difficulty with raw cotton supplies during the Civil War in the United States, it went rapidly ahead. Another important textile center grew up in and around Lodz, in the west of Russian Poland. Some indication of the progress of the industry (including both these areas) is given by figures for Russian imports of raw cotton (in millions of pud): 1863, 1.1; 1877, 5.2; 1881, 9.7; and 1894, 15.4.[38]

The railway boom spurred the rise of a metallurgical industry. A large new industrial area developed in the south — in the coal mines of the Donetz basin and the iron ore of Krivoi Rog — and soon outstripped the old metallurgy of the Urals. The production of pig iron in Russia grew as follows (in millions of pud): 1862, 15; 1866, 32; and 1896, 98. Production figures of crude oil were 5 million pud in 1875, 116 million in 1885, and 348 million in 1895.[39]

The number of factory workers also increased rapidly: 356,184 in 1870; 482,276 in 1879, and 738,146 in 1891.[40]

The effect of this economic development on the Jews was enormous. Jews participated both as capitalists and workers. Starting at the top of the social pyramid, banking and contracting Jews played the most important role in railway construction in Russia and Poland in the nineteenth century; it may be assumed that not less than three-quarters of all railways were built by Jewish contractors. The Poliakoffs,

Kronenbergs, Nathansons, the bankers Efrosi and Co., Rafalovich, the Gunzbergs, etc., were the most prominent railway builders in the second half of the nineteenth century. Since Russia possessed no capital of her own for railway construction, it was necessary to secure long-term foreign loans. Of all the strata of the Russian population, the Jews had the most suitable connections abroad and were best adapted for the purpose. The French-Jewish firm Periera Freres and the German-Jewish firms, Bleichroeder, Sulzbach and others had, through the medium of the Russian-Jewish bankers, a very great share in the construction of the Russian and Polish railways.[41]

Jews laid the basis for and promoted the further development of Russian and Polish banking. Steiglitz, the first prominent banking concern in Russia (in St. Petersburg), played the pioneering role. Its founder was a baptized German Jew. In 1859 the Gunzbergs opened a bank in St. Petersburg, which very soon became active in various projects. The bank of Meyer & Co. was opened in 1861. A comprehensive banking activity was pursued at the same time by the Wawelbergs, the Kronenbergs, and the Fraenkels in Warsaw. In Odessa the Efrosi Bank played an important part in the grain export trade. A decade later the Poliakoffs founded the Moscow Agrarian Bank, the Don Agrarian Bank, the Azov-Don Bank in St. Petersburg, the Moscow International Bank, and others. During the time of Finance Minister Witte, toward the end of the nineteenth century, Jews obtained larger access to economic activity, and their participation in the banking business and in Russia's foreign trade increasingly gained in importance. In 1916, among the 70 members of the boards of the 14 largest joint-stock banks in St. Petersburg, 28 were Jews. But Jews still had no residence rights in that city.[42]

Although railroad building and finance played a very important role in the economy, only a small number of Jews were involved in these industries. On the other hand, the foreign trade of Odessa, the small industry in the White Russian and Lithuanian provinces, and the textile mills of Lodz and Bialystok employed many thousands.

Odessa had a Jewish population of 17,000 in 1855. By 1897 it had grown to 138,915 and in 1904 it numbered 152,364.[43] The growth of sugar and grain export, the foundation of this expansion, was largely a Jewish activity. The sugar industry, which was closely bound to agriculture, had been in the hands of Russian great landowners who lacked a commercial and entrepreneurial spirit. It was the Jews who introduced the capitalist mode of operation into this undertaking. On the eve of the First World War, Jewish factories turned out 52 percent of the production in the Ukraine, the center of the industry. The Jewish share in the export of sugar reached 60-70 percent.[44]

As for grain export, it rose from about 15,500,000 pud in the years 1836-1846 to 75,000,000 pud in 1910.[45]

Jews were occupied in every step of the export process. Odessa, Nikolaev, Kherson, and Kremenchug were the sites of the central offices of firms employing thousands of agents and brokers who scoured the countryside to purchase produce from the Ukrainian peasants.[46] In Odessa a Russian economist noted:

> The exporters, that is, the commercial houses which concerned themselves with grain export, belong now by a majority to Jews. At any rate the largest firms belong to this people. This situation newly exists since the Jewish houses used to hold second place to the older established Greeks who have now for the most part gone

bankrupt. There is not one Russian among the expor-
ters . . . . At the summit of the grain export trade in Odessa
stood two Jewish firms, Efros and Cohen.[47]

Out of 55 export firms in 1910, 46 (81 percent) belonged to
Jews; but the Jewish firms exported 89 percent of the total.[48]

It should be pointed out that the export trade not only
employed Jewish brokers, commission merchants, agents,
and factors. Jews also worked in offices as managers and
clerks, and were also port stevedores (in 1884, there were
1,709 Jewish stevedores in Odessa).[49] The standard of living
of these port workers was very low. A Russian investigator
reported:

> From their external appearance it is difficult to guess at
> their nationality, so strong, rough and muscular do they
> look. Their wages, besides being very low, rarely more
> than 50 kopeks (25.8 cents at the end of the nineteenth
> century) for a whole day's work, are seldom regular,
> their employment almost accidental, and the large num-
> bers of these laborers anxiously waiting for an opportun-
> ity to earn a few kopeks, and crowding the so-called
> market (or the open public ground) is one of the most
> distressing pictures of each and every Russian Jewish
> town.[50]

Odessa was not only a trading port, but a vital industrial
center with many Jewish workers. As in other parts of Russia,
Jews were concentrated in several specific occupations and
hardly worked at all in other fields. For example, 96 percent
of tobacco production workers, 66 percent of paper production workers, and 61 percent of match production workers
were Jews. But Jews constituted only 4.3 percent of metal
industry workers and 3 percent of sugar industry workers.[51]

The textile industry occupied the greatest number of Jews. Concentrated in the Pale of Settlement, it was a source of livelihood for scores of thousands of Jews in all categories — from the richest capitalist to the poorest worker. Centered in Lodz, Bialystok, and Warsaw, textiles came to be the most characteristic Jewish industry in that era of industrialization.

Nowhere is the effect of industrialization upon the traditional Jewish life in the Russian Empire so well described as in the following quotation from I.J. Singer's Yiddish novel:

Like a river in thaw, bursting its banks and carrying before it the dams and barriers which had long held it in, the Jewish population of Lodz and the surrounding country swarmed to the weaving trade, overthrowing in the rush of their hunger all the barriers, the special laws, ukases, prohibitions which a hostile government had erected against them. Thousands of country innkeepers, peddlers and village merchants had been ruined with the ruin of the nobility. In the general movement which ensued — the search for bread — it was Lodz which sucked in the largest part of the unsettled population. In the little towns the Jewish dry-goods stores either were closed or stood empty from morning to night; young sixteen-year-old wives, the supports of scholarly husbands who gave all their time to study the Talmud, sat there waiting for customers who came no more. For the nobility was either impoverished or exiled, and the liberated serfs were as poor as ever. Steadily the weaving business spread out of Lodz, and looms were set up in the townlets and villages; but Lodz remained the metropolis and chief centre of attraction. The Jews of the villages, long accustomed to the meanness and brutalities of the nobility and their servants, made light of the obstacles which the Germans and the officials placed in their way in the city; they came pouring in, setting up their looms everywhere . . . .

Steadily the number of Jews who could work a loom increased. Fathers brought their sons in from the villages to learn the trade. Barefoot they came on all the roads leading into Lodz. They came with sticks in their hands to beat off the village dogs, and on the outskirts of the town they put on their boots, which they had been carrying all the way. It was the custom to apprentice the boys for three years. A sum of money, the savings and scrapings of God knew how many seasons, was paid into the hand of the master weaver. The boys would receive no pay during the apprenticeship. They would get their meals and a place to sleep in, and from morning to night they would learn.

They stood in the hundreds at their looms, their skull-caps on their heads, the ritual fringes hanging over their cheap canvas trousers, pieces of colored thread clinging to their curly hair and sprouting beards, while their hands flew swiftly over the looms, weaving from before sunrise till long after sunset the piece goods which were to be made into dresses and women's handkerchiefs. As they worked they sang snatches from the synagogue services, trilling the bravura passages like real cantors, pausing with special joy on the sacred words of the high festivals. The master weavers paraded up and down the aisles, keeping an eye on the heaps of merchandise, urging the workers on, infuriated if one of them stopped to wipe the perspiration from his forehead or to roll himself a cigarette.[52]

In Warsaw, at the beginning of the nineteenth century, 8,000 Jews constituted about 8 percent of the entire population; in 1914 there were 337,000 Jews, or 38 percent of the population. In 1882, 43.1 percent of Warsaw's Jews were engaged in commerce and 29.7 percent in industry and handwork. On the eve of World War I, these figures had changed dramatically: only 36 percent were in commerce and 40.2 percent in inudstry and handwork, a vivid testimony to the process of proletarianization. At the turn of the nineteenth century only a few score Jewish families resided in Lodz, a village where Jews were not permitted to live. By 1910, some 200,000 Jews lived there, forming a third of the entire population. In 1860, 11.8 percent of all Lodz textile factories belonged to Jews; and in 1910, close to 60 percent did. In 1885, there were almost no Jewish workers in factories with more than 25 workers, but at the end of the century Jews made up 20 percent of the labor force in this type of factory.[53]

The extent of the proletarianization of the Jewish population is further illustrated by Table III which gives the occupational distribution of the Jewish population of Kovno Province in Russian Lithuania.

One of the large Jewish industries in the northeastern provinces was the leather industry based in Shavli, Kovno Province. It was begun in 1894 by Chaim Frankel, whose plant had grown tremendously by 1914. In 1908 the Nurock brothers founded their factory, which was about one-third the size of Frankel's. Under their leadership Shavli attracted many smaller firms and by the First World War was one of the world centers of leather manufacture.[55]

The data in the 1897 census show the central occupational makeup of the Jewish population:

These workers were, of course, employed primarily in small factories or workshops. Centers of heavy industry and large factories, such as St. Petersburg, had few Jewish workers.[57] That does not alter the fact, however, that a basic

Table III

Occupational Structure of Various Nationalities in Kovno Province (1897)[54]

Occupation	Lithuanians		Jews		Poles		Russians	
	numbers	(%)	numbers	(%)	numbers	(%)	numbers	(%)
Agriculture	210,433	(73.0)	3,270	(4.9)	22,880	(44.9)	6,252	(18.8)
Industry and craftwork	22,075	(7.6)	22,024	(33.3)	6,780	(17.3)	2,373	(7.1)
Commerce and credit	1,724	(0.6)	17,821	(26.0)	621	(1.2)	297	(0.8)
Transport	1,423	(0.5)	2,628	(4.0)	1,173	(2.3)	774	(2.3)
Liberal professions	2,893	(1.0)	3,018	(4.6)	1,757	(3.4)	2,344	(7.1)
House servants	33,104	(11.5)	7,355	(11.1)	10,570	(20.7)	1,789	(5.4)
Without occupation*	8,635	(3.0)	6,171	(9.3)	4,718	(9.3)	1,279	(3.8)
Military service	672	(0.2)	1,934	(3.4)	1,210	(2.4)	17,549	(53.1)
Indefinite	7,560	(2.6)	1,911	(3.4)	1,251	(2.5)	509	(1.6)
TOTAL	288,519	(100.0)	66,132	(100.0)	50,960	(100.0)	33,266	(100.0)

*This rubric includes elements that live on capital, reside in old age homes, are in prison, etc.

Table IV

Percentage of Jews in the Russian Empire Engaged in Each Group of Gainful Occupations (1897)[56]

Occupation	% of Jewish Population Engaged
Manufacturing and mechanical pursuits	36.3
Commerce	31.0
Personal service	11.5
Professional service	4.7
Communication and transport	3.0
Agriculture	2.4
Miscellaneous	7.6
Military service	3.5
	100.0

economic transformation had taken place in Jewish life: from a nation of innkeepers and merchants they had turned in great part into members of the working class.

Cultural and Educational Conditions

Jewish culture before 1860 was shaped by religion to an extent that is difficult for us to imagine today. Pauline Wengeroff, whose *Memoiren einer Grossmuter*, written in German, is one of the our most valuable sources of information on Jewish life in this period, wrote of the scrupulous adherence to ritual that was typical of the Russian Jew and the dominant role which religious observance played in his life:

> Upon rising in the morning he [her father] strictly observed the rule not to walk four cubits [about six feet] without first washing his hands. Before taking the first bite, he leisurely recited the introductory morning prayers, following which he would repair to his study.

Time in her father's house was measured by references to the three daily prayers: it was either before or after the services, before or after *mincha*, or between *mincha* and *maariv*. Similarly, the time of the year was referred to in relation to the festivals: it was either before or after Chanukah, before or after Purim, etc.[58]

Secular education was practically unknown among Russian Jewry before 1860 and was confined to a few intellectuals scorned by the Jewish masses for their modernism. Although modern education was regarded as heretical there was practically no illiteracy among Russian Jews; almost every male —

and many females as well — could read the prayer book and the Bible. Learning was a universal pursuit in the Russian ghetto, where there was neither a time nor an age limit to the study of Torah.

The importance of education is illustrated by the following selection from the autobiography of Abraham Paperna, a Hebrew-Russian writer and an advocate of secular education for Russian Jews. His description of the cultural life of his native town can be taken as typical of Jewish life in Russia, particularly in Lithuania during the reign of Nicholas I:

Educational institutions in the modern sense of the word were conspicuous by their absence in our town. There was no government or public school of a secular character in Kopyl. The Christian population was without exception illiterate. The Jewish population, on the other hand, had an overabundance of schools, though of a special type. First, there were the *chadarim* — about twenty of them. Kopyl had a population of about three thousand souls: Jews, White Russians, and Tartars. Jews constituted the majority. All Jewish male children from the ages of four to thirteen were taught in *cheder*. Although education was not compulsory for girls, they, too, in most cases could read the prayers and the Pentateuch in the Yiddish translation. A Jew of Kopyl spared nothing for the education of his children. It was not rare for a poor man to sell his last candlestick or his only pillow to pay the *melamed* . . . . With the single exception of Meerke the idiot, who was both stoker in the bath house and water-carrier, there were no ignoramuses in Kopyl. And even this moronic water-carrier somehow knew the prayers and could quite satisfactorily recite the blessing over the Torah.[60]

M.J. Berdichevski, the famous Hebrew writer, gives the following account of life at one of the famous Russian yeshivas at Volozhin:

> He who walks along the yeshiva square on a winter night will behold a wondrous sight. Lamps shed their light on the white snow. The voices of the three hundred students studying with ardent devotion are heard from one end of the square to the other. Here a comely youth, a volume of the Talmud under his arm, hurries by; his soul thirsts for the Torah. Some students turn their steps homeward; weariness has overtaken them, yet it is with reluctance that they have interrupted their studies. It is here that Jewishness is revealed in all its majesty. It can truly be said that he who has not witnessed this sight has never witnessed beauty.[61]

A late-nineteenth-century historian asserted that the successful transition from religious to secular education on the part of Jewish youth in modern days was due to their Talmudic training. "When the emancipation came," he declared, "the Jewish intellect, exercised for centuries in this dialectical training school, readily mastered the difficulties in various branches of learning in the universities."[62]

Every modern Jewish educational system has been engendered by the social and political movements of the last 70 years. Great social movements do not arise without cause; they are a response to major dislocations in the cultural, religious, economic, political, or psychological state of a nation. The traditional fabric of Jewish life was destroyed in Russia after 1863.[63] As a desperate answer to the pressing problems of the day, several solutions were proposed,

Zionism and Socialism being the best known and most influential ones.

Subsequent chapters will discuss these movements and show their relationship to the educational movements that arose at the same time.

Notes

1. Simon Dubnov, *Divrei Yimei Am Olam* (6th revised edition; Tel Aviv: Dvir, 1958), vol. IV, p. 151.
2. Israel Friedlaender, *The Jews of Russia and Poland* (New York: G.P. Putnam's Sons, 1915), p. 28.
3. Ibid.
4. Ibid., p. 29.
5. Ibid., p. 30.
6. In the mid-eighteenth century, when the Senate recommended that the Jews be admitted into the Ukraine and Riga in order to spur the development of commerce, Empress Elizabeth adamantly refused: "I seek no gain at the hands of the enemies of Christ" (V. Levanda, *Polny Khronologicheskii Sbornik Zakonov i Polozheni Kasaiushchikhsia Evreev* [St. Petersburg, 1874], p. 19). The best history of the Jews of Russia and Poland is S.M. Dubnow's *History of the Jews in Russia and Poland* (Philadelphia: Jewish Publication Society of America, 1916-1920), 3 vols. Notwithstanding its age, it has not been surpassed.
7. Yaakov Lestshchinsky, *Dos sovetishe yidntum* (New York: Yiddisher Kemfer, 1941), pp. 30-31.
8. Yaakov Lestshchinsky, "Evreiskoe naselenie rossii i evreiskii trud," *Kniga o russkom evreistve* (New York: Union of Russian Jews, 1960), p. 183.

9. Levanda, op. cit. p. 19.
10. Ibid.
11. Dubnow, *Divrei Yimei Am Olam*, vol. I, pp. 322-328.
12. The Jews were shocked when the Russian government actually consulted them. One historian wrote: "The population was stirred. It was the first time that the Russian government wanted to listen to the Jews themselves" (I. Gessen, *Evrei v rossii* [St. Petersburg, 1906], p. 77).
13. Levanda, op. cit., pp. 55-56.
14. Ibid., pp. 54-55.
15. *Russkii Arkhiv*, vol. I (1903), 258.
16. V.N. Nitikin, *Evrei zemledeltsy* (St. Petersburg, 1887), p. 16.
17. N. Golityn, *Istoriia russkago zakon odatelstva o evreiakh* (St. Petersburg, 1886), pp. 686-687.
18. *Russkii Arkhiv*, loc. cit.
19. Simon Dubnov, *Divre Yimei Am Olam*. vol. I, p. 346.
20. Simon Dubnov, "Subdy evreev v rossii v epokhe zapodnoe 'pervoi emansipatsii' (1789-1815)," *Evreiskaia starina*, vol. V, p. 120.
21. The Report stated: "It is not true that the village Jew enriches himself at the expense of the peasant. On the contrary he is generally poor, and ekes out a scanty existence from the sale of liquor and by supplying the peasants with the goods they need. Moreover, by buying the corn on the spot, the Jew saves the peasant from wasting his time in traveling to the city. Altogether in rural economic life the Jew plays the role of a go-between, who can be spared neither by the squire or by the peasant" (quoted in Dubnow, *History of the Jews in Russia and Poland*, vol. I, pp. 353-354).
22. There are several studies of the situation of the Jew in Russian law. Besides the above-cited study by Levanda, mention should be made of M.I. Mysh, *Rukovodstvo k russkim zakonam o evreiakh* (St. Petersburg, 1914).
23. Jewish Colonization Association, *Sbornik materialov ob*

ekonomicheskom polozhenii evreev v rossii (St. Petersburg, 1904), vol. I, pp. xviii-xx.

24. It should be pointed out that the right of Jews to practice these professions was severely restricted. For example, an imperial order, issued on November 8, 1889, stipulated that in the future the application of every non-Christian lawyer for permission to practice his profession must be confirmed by the Minister of Justice. Although this order was not specifically directed against Jews, it was applied to them only. During the first six years of its operation, not one Jewish attorney was admitted to the Bar. (Mysh, p. 490).

25. Jewish Colonization Association, vol. I, pp. xx-xxii. The many limitations, exceptions, sudden changes, and odd interpretations of these laws frequently made it very difficult to take advantage of them. Thus, the important city of Kiev was removed from the Pale, and even merchants of the first guild could live only in certain districts of the city. In 1893 the city of Yalta was removed; the cities of Rostov and Taganrog, by being transferred from the gubernia of Ekaterinoslav to the Don Army Territory, were also excluded from the Pale. (Mysh, pp. 104, 164).

26. *Jewish Encyclopedia*, vol. X, pp. 529-533.

27. Quoted in Lestshchinsky, *Dos sovetishe yidntum*, p. 19.

28. Ibid., p. 20.

29. Yaakov Lestshchinsky, "Di sotsial ekonomishe antviklung fun ukrainer yidntum," *Yidn in ukraine* (New York, 1961), p. 166.

30. Simon Dubnow writes that "the poverty of the Jew was the artificial result of the fact that the cities and townlets were overcrowded with petty tradesmen and artisans, and this congestion was further aggravated by the systematic removal of the Jews from their age-long rural occupations and the consequent influx of village Jews into the cities. (Dubnow, *History of the Jews in Russia and Poland*, vol. I, pp. 361-362).

31. Quoted in Jewish Colonization Association, vol. I, pp. xxi.

32. Quoted by A. Subbotin, *Evreiskaia biblioteka*, vol. X (1880), pp. 76-77.
33. Prince Demidoff San Donato, *The Jewish Question in Russia* (London, 1884).
34. I. Orshansky, *Evrei v rossii* (St. Petersburg, 1877), p. 141.
35. P.I. Lyashchenko, *History of the People's Economy of the U.S.S.R.*, tr. from the Russian (New York: Macmillan, 1949), pp. 115, 502.
36. Nikolai A. Bazili, *Rossiia pod sovetskoi vlastiu* (Paris: Imprimerie "Val," 1937), p. 10.
37. Hugh Seton-Watson, *The Decline of Imperial Russia, 1855-1914* (New York: Frederick A. Praeger, 1952), p. 283.
38. Ibid., p. 115.
39. Ibid., p. 116.
40. V.I. Lenin, *The Development of Capitalism in Russia*, tr. from the Russian (Moscow: Foreign Languages Publishing House, 1964), p. 601.
41. Yaakov Lestshchinsky, "Di ekonomishe evolutsie fun yidn in 19tn un onheib 20tn yorhundred," *Algemeine entsiklopedie*, Series "Yidn," vol. I, p. 396.
42. Ibid.
43. Yaakov Lestshchinsky, *Dos yiddishe folk in tsippern*, p. 71.
44. H. Landau, "Der onteil fur yidn in der russish-ukrainer tsuker industrie," *Shriftn far yiddishe ekonomik un statistik* (Berlin, 1928), p. 102.
45. Dr. Otto Friedel, *Der Handelshaften Odessa* (Leipzig, 1921), pp. 14-15.
46. Lestshchinsky, "Di sotsial ekonomishe antviklung fun ukrainer yidntum," p. 203.
47. I. Yanson, *Statisticheskoe isledovanie o khlebnoi torgovlie v odesskom raione* (Moscow, 1870), p. 234.
48. Lestshchinsky, op. cit.
49. Ibid.
50. A.P. Subbotin, *V. cherte evreiskoi osedlosti* (St. Petersburg, 1888), vol. II, p. 228.

51. Yaakov Lestshchinsky, *Der yiddisher arbeter in russland* (Vilna, 1906), Table XXV.

52. I.J. Singer, *The Brothers Ashkenazi*, tr. from the Yiddish by Maurice Samuel (New York: Alfred A. Knopf, 1936), pp. 24-26.

53. Yaakov Lestshchinsky, *Di ekonomishe lage fun yidn in poiln* (Berlin, 1932), pp. 133, 127.

54. Yaakov Lestshchinsky, "Di ekonomishe lage fun di yidn in Lite," *Lite* (New York, 1951), columns 849-850.

55. The development of the leather industry of Shavli by Jewish entrepreneurs is described in Jacob Frankel, "Di Pioner fun der leder industrie in Lite, Chaim Frankel," *Lite*, columns 941-971.

56. Boris Brutskus, *Professionalnii sostov evreiskago naseleniia rossii* (St. Petersburg, 1908), p. 8.

57. For a description of the employment of Jewish workers in one large industrial center, see A.S. Hershberg, *Pinkas bialystok* (New York, 1950), vol. II, pp. 49-53.

58. Pauline Wengeroff, *Memoiren einer Grossmutter* (Berlin, 1908), vol. I, pp. 5-6.

59. For a description of the importance of education in traditional Eastern European Jewish culture, see Mark Zborowski, "The Place of Book-Learning in Traditional Jewish Culture," *Harvard Educational Review*, vol. XXX (1949), pp. 87-107.

60. A.I. Paperna, *Perezhitoe*, vol. II (1909), pp. 31-32. Quoted in Louis Greenberg, *The Jews in Russia* (New Haven: Yale University Press, 1945), vol. I, p. 59.

61. Quoted in Abraham Menes, "The Yeshivot in Eastern Europe," *The Jewish People, Past and Present* (New York, 1948), vol. II, p. 113.

62. D. Philipson, *Old European Jewries* (Philadelphia: Jewish Publication Society of America, 1894), pp. 218-219.

63. In 1882 the Russian government proclaimed the so-called May Laws, one provision of which forbade Jewish settlement in the villages. Unlike the law of 1804, these laws were

enforced and caused a sharp exacerbation of urban poverty by driving the former village Jews into cities where there was no room and no work for them. A non-Jewish observer writes of the effect of the expulsion on the town of Berdichev, which had a Jewish population of 60,000 before the May Laws:

> It was then an overcrowded place, made up for the most part of old and unsanitary rookeries, in which was huddled one of the poorest populations to be found anywhere in Europe. By August, 1891, it was said that fully twenty thousand additional Hebrews had been driven in from the surrounding country. The spectacle of their poverty and squalor was something too sickening for words. The whole place, with its filthy streets, its reeking half-cellars under the overhanging balconies, and its swarming throngs of unwashed, unkempt wretches, packed into the narrow thoroughfares on the lookout for food, made a picture scarcely human. Mr. Pennell tells me that when he was there in November he was assured that instead of the sixty thousand Jews of August, there were then in Berdichev no less than ninety thousand . . . . There are over a hundred towns in that hell called the Pale where the same causes operate which have made Berdichev such an unspeakable charnel-house, and in each one the Russian police have done their brutal best to reproduce the conditions of Berdichev (Harold Frederic, *The New Exodus: A Study of Israel in Russia* [New York, 1892], pp. 260-261).

Chapter 2

Traditional Jewish Education

The Cheder *and the* Yeshiva

THE NEW TRENDS in Jewish education in Russia in the nineteenth and twentieth centuries cannot be understood without reference to their origins. Prerevolutionary Jewish education in Russia was a continuation of a tradition dating back to Biblical times and was developed under the conditions of internal autonomy which Jews enjoyed throughout the diaspora. As the Jewish immigrants began to pour into Poland from Germany and Bohemia, they brought not only their cultural and educational traditions but their language, as well. In Poland the Jews increased in population and developed their culture to a high level. Russia acquired most of Polish Jewry in the three partitions of Poland (1772, 1793, and 1795). Since the entire tradition of the Russian Jews developed under Polish rule, we shall survey in detail the conditions of Jewish life in those areas of Russia which had been Polish territory.[1]

Under the peculiar political and legal organization of the

Polish state, the Jews formed a separate class and enjoyed liberal autonomy within the sphere of their communal and spiritual interests. This status was promulgated on August 13, 1551 by the Polish King Sigismund II in an edict that came to be known as the Magna Carta of Polish Jewry.[2]

The Jewish delegates usually met at Council meetings during the Lublin spring fairs.[3] At first known as the Council of the Three Lands — Poland (Great and Little), Lithuania, and Polish Russia (Podolia, Volhynia, and Galicia) — it shortly became the Council of the Five Lands — Great Poland, Little Poland, Russia, Lithuania, and Volhynia. From 1623, when Lithuania formed its own Council, until 1764, when Jewish autonomy in Poland and Lithuania was abolished by the Polish Parliament, the Jewish self-governing organization was known as the Council of the Four Lands — Great Poland (with its capital, Poznan), Little Poland (Cracow), Polish or Red Russia (Podolia and Galicia with its capital Lvov), and Volhynia (capital Ostrog, or Kremenetz).[4]

The Council's annual session at the Lublin spring fair lasted about a month. Another meetingplace was the Galician town Jaroslav, during the chief fair at the end of the summer. Soon after the beginning of the seventeenth century, it became customary to hold two meetings annually, one at Lublin before Passover and the other at Jaroslav before the autumn holidays. In exceptional cases sessions were held in other localities.[5]

The powers of the Council of the Four Lands were extensive: it judged disputes between communities and exercised considerable authority over individuals.

The leaders of the Four Lands... had authority to judge all Israel in the Kingdom of Poland, to establish

safeguards, to institute ordinances, and to punish each
man as they saw fit. Each difficult matter was brought
before them and they judged it. And the leaders of the
Four Lands selected judges from the provinces to relieve
their burden, and these were called judges of the provinces. They attended to cases involving money matters.
Fines, titles, and other difficult laws were brought before
the leaders of the Four Lands, may their Rock and
Redeemer preserve them. Never was a dispute among
Jews brought before a gentile judge or before a noble-
man, or before the King, may his glory increase, and if a
Jew took his case before a gentile court he was punished
and chastised severely.[6]

The Council's activities can be divided into four divisions: legislative; administrative; judicial; and spiritual and
cultural.

Its legislative activity consisted in working out regulations and rules for various institutions of Jewish self-
government in Poland.[7] The administrative activity was, of
course, closely linked with its legislative work. The Council
took whatever steps it could to watch over the general status
of Polish Jews. It sent its agents (*shtadlanim*), representative
men, whose wealth and station afforded them access to the
court or to the magnates, to watch over Jewish interests
during the sessions of the Polish Diet at Warsaw. It was
especially imperative to be in attendance during the "Corona-
tion Diet", when a new king ascended the throne and pressure was likely to be exerted by anti-Jewish elements to annul
or curtail privileges previously conceded.[8] The judicial function was extensive: every town had a local court, and the
capital of each of the Lands had the equivalent of an appeals
court.[9] It should be noted that each of the Four Lands had its

own Council and self-governing organization on the provincial level. Each locality had its own community organization, the *kahal* which might also include small villages in the surrounding countryside where the Jewish population was too small to establish its own *kahal*. The *kahal* was the unit of local self-government which operated the large number of agencies and societies organized by the Polish Jews to take care of their needs. The spiritual and cultural activity of the Council was very important; its regulations and interpretations of religious and educational practice were strictly enforced.[10]

Supervision over education was one of the most vital activities of Jewish self-government. Education was of extraordinary importance to the Polish Jew. Forced to live in an alien environment, his education was designed to permit him to live a complete and knowledgeable life in that milieu. The base of Jewish culture was the school, but the child received his first instruction in the home. When a boy learned how to speak, his father taught him the principal prayers. At the age of three the child began to familiarize himself with the Hebrew alphabet. At the age of six he was put in elementary school, the *cheder*. School instruction was not obligatory for girls, but they were required to learn the many laws concerning the work of the Jewish woman. A father who did not want to pay for his son's *cheder* instruction was forced by the *kahal* to do so under threat of confiscation of his property to pay the teacher. Each community, no matter how small, had a *cheder*. The language of instruction was Yiddish, the spoken tongue of Polish and Lithuanian Jewry. Students were taught the Hebrew Bible, the easier tractates of the Talmud with commentaries, and, in certain schools, Hebrew grammar, reading, the writing of Yiddish, and arithmetic. There were two levels of *melamdim* (teachers), each with his own cheder. The *dardeki melamed* taught the elementary subjects up to the Bible; the *gemora melamed* taught the rest.[11]

To institute compulsory school attendance at that time was extraordinary, as evidenced by the low educational standard of the Polish society in which the Jews lived. "The great body of the Polish people at this time were in a state of ignorant servitude; only the nobles, the merchants, and a very small proportion of the peasantry were instructed."[12]

The task of founding the schools was left to the individual *melamed*, but he was strictly supervised. He had to possess a certificate of competence to teach and a special license to collect fees from his pupils.[13] The community (*kahal*) directly operated only the Talmud Torah, a school for poor students and orphans. For the purpose of supervision and inspection the *kahal*-appointed school commission worked out the program of studies, fixed the salaries of the *melamdim*, and watched over the application of school rules.[14] The record book of the Chevrat Talmud Torah (Education Society) of the Jewish community of Cracow for the years 1551-1639 offers valuable insight into Jewish education of that period. It includes the following regulations:

1. Members shall have general supervision over the teachers and shall visit the Talmud Torah every week to see that pupils are properly taught.

2. No melamed shall teach the Pentateuch except with the translation *Be'er Mosheh* (Yiddish translation by Moses ben Issachar, Prague, 1605) which is in our vernacular; for the advanced pupils he shall use only the Rashi commentary.

3. A melamed in the primary class shall teach not more than 25 pupils and shall have two assistants.

4. One melamed shall not compete with another during the term of his engagement, and shall not seek to obtain a pupil in the charge of another teacher, even at the expiration of the term, unless the father or the guardian of the pupil desires to make such a change.

5. Members of the Talmud Torah Society shall hire a competent and God-fearing melamed, with an assistant, for poor and orphaned boys at the House of Study.

6. The melamed and assistant shall teach pupils the alphabet (with the vowels), the Prayerbook, the Pentateuch (with the *Be'er Mosheh* translation), the Rashi commentary, the order of the prayers, etiquette, and good behavior — every boy according to his grade and intelligence; also reading and writing in the vernacular (Yiddish). The more advanced shall be taught Hebrew grammar and arithmetic; those of the highest grade shall study Talmud with Rashi and Tosafot.

7. Boys near the age of thirteen shall learn the regulations regarding phylacteries.

8. At the age of fourteen a boy who is incapable of learning Talmud shall be taught a trade or become a household servant.

9. The income of the Society shall derive from the following sources: (a) one-sixth of the collections made in the synagogues on Monday and Thursday mornings; (b) at each birth, the *Mohel* (Circumciser) shall request from the guests alms for the Society; (c) the Society shall send one of its members to all marriages to request from the bridge and groom gifts in its favor; This member shall likewise hang up, in the room of the marriage, a collection box for receipt of alms; (d) all gifts given to the kahal by anonymous donors shall be set aside in favor of the Society.[15]

The election of officers was by ballot—three directors,

three assistant directors, and a treasurer. Only learned and honorable men over 36 were eligible. The rules regulating these sources of the Talmud Torah Society's income dated back to 1551. Joel Sirkes, Rabbi of Cracow, endorsed these regulations in 1638 and added many others, all of which were confirmed at a general assembly of seventy representatives of the congregations that year.[16]

Community supervision over education was comprehensive. In 1639 we find a provision in the record book of the Principal Communities of the Province of Lithuania (Brest, Grodno, Pinsk, Vilna, and Slutsk) in which the rabbis are enjoined to examine the young men in the community to see whether they are continuing their studies. The students are advised that even after they start to study Talmud, they should not cease to study the Bible until they know it thoroughly.[17] Teachers are also warned against proceeding to teach Talmud before the children know the Bible.

For advanced pupils there were academies of higher Talmudic studies, the yeshivot, supervised by rabbis but financed by the communities. From 1530 to 1580 the most famous Polish yeshiva was at Lublin. It attracted the greatest Talmudic scholars, and its prestige was so great that the Polish king conferred the title of "gymnasium" on the institution and the Rosh Yeshiva (Head of the Yeshiva) was entitled to call himself "rector."[18] Yeshivot arose all over Poland and Lithuania. The functions of rabbi and Rosh Yeshiva were combined in the smaller communitiess, but in the larger ones they were held separately. One historian has likened the contemporary rector of a Jesuit college to the Rosh Yeshiva: he was absolute master within the school walls and exercised unrestricted control over his pupils, subjecting them to a stringent discipline and dispensing justice among them.[19]

Our best source on the Polish yeshiva is the memoirs of Nathan Hannover, published in 1653:

> Throughout the dispersions of Israel there was nowhere so much learning as in the Kingdom of Poland. Each community maintained academies, and the head of each academy was given an ample salary so that he could maintain his school without worry, and that the study of the Torah might be his sole occupation. The head of the academy did not leave his home the whole year except to go from the House of Study to the synagogue. Thus he was engaged in the study of the Torah day and night. Each community maintained young men and provided for them a weekly allowance of money that they might study with the head of the academy. And for each young man they also maintained two boys to study under his guidance, so that he would orally discuss the Talmud, the commentaries of Rashi, and the Tosafot, which he had learned, and thus he would gain experience in the subtlety of Talmudic argumentation. The boys were provided with food from the community benevolent fund or from the public kitchen. If the community consisted of fifty householders it supported not less than thirty young men and boys. One young man and two boys would be assigned to one householder. And the young man ate at his table as one of his sons. Although the young man received a stipend from the community, the householder provided him with all the food and drink that he needed. Some of the more charitable householders also allowed the boys to eat at their tables, thus three persons would be provided with food and drink by one householder the entire year.

There was scarcely a house in all the Kingdom of Poland where its members did not occupy themselves with the study of the Torah. Either the head of the family was himself a scholar, or else his son or his son-in-law studied, or one of the young men eating at his table. At times, all of these were to be found in one house. Thus they realized all the three things of which Raba spoke in Tractate Sabbath, chapter I: Raba said: "He who loves the rabbis will have sons who are rabbis; he who honors the rabbis will have rabbis for sons-in-law; he who stands in awe of the rabbis will himself be a rabbinical scholar." Thus there were many scholars in every community.[20]

The pogroms in the Ukraine in 1648-1649 brought a terrible dislocation in Jewish life. Many communities were physically destroyed and it took many years before they could restore the level of prosperity they once had.[21] Although the search for learning and the operation of *chedorim* were as widespread as ever, many communities could no longer maintain the large yeshivot.[22] In the wake of the national tragedy many Jews lost their faith in rational Talmudism and turned to messianic movements like that of Shabetai Zevi and Jacob Frank.[23]

In the middle of the eighteenth century the Chassidic movement swept through Polish and Ukrainian Jewry. The protest against the exalted position of Talmudic study found forceful expression within Chassidic circles, which stressed the precedence of prayer.[24] As a result, Talmudic study was no longer so widespread. A great scholar of the period complained that in some communities the state of learning had sunk so low that even in the Houses of Study a complete set of the Talmud could not be found.[25]

The Chassidic movement, with its emphasis on ecstatic joy rather than learning, did not penetrate Lithuania, which became the new center of study of the Talmud. The great Talmudic scholar of Lithuanian Jewry was Elijah of Vilna, known as the Gaon (genius). His *kloyz* (study room) became a higher academy for Talmudic study.[26]

Under the Gaon's influence the Volozhin yeshiva was founded; for over a century it was the outstanding center of Talmudic learning in Eastern Europe. In the middle of the nineteenth century, at the peak of its development, its enrollment exceeded 300. The students at Volozhin all studied in the same hall. The Rosh Yeshiva usually opened the day with a 60- to 90-minute lecture designed to introduce the students to the deeper meanings of the texts, after which the students studied alone or in pairs. Usual hours of study were from nine in the morning to nine in the evening with a break for the midday meal, but many students began much earlier and ended late at night. The study hall was never empty.[27]

Another famous yeshiva was located at Mir in White Russia. Thanks to L.I. Mandelstam, the noted educator and Bible scholar, an account of life there has been recorded. In 1840, on his way to Moscow University where he was to be the first Jewish student, Mandelstam spent a few days in Mir.

This school, which has become famous among Jews, is located in a rather large though old and dilapidated building not far from the synagogue. The building includes a large hall and a room where the students congregate for the entire day, from five in the morning until ten in the evening. Altogether there are about one hundred students, almost all of them striplings. Almost all are very poor and are maintained by contributions

collected for the purpose in numerous Jewish settlements. . . . Of these funds each registered student
receives seventy-five kopeks a week. With this allow-
ance he has to maintain himself the entire week with the
exception of Saturday, since on Sabbaths and holidays
students are invited out for meals by the local residents.
Their daily routine is as follows: at five o'clock in the
morning the students are already at work preparing their
morning service and have their breakfast consisting of
bread and water. At eleven o'clock begins the instructor's discourse, which lasts around two hours. Then follows lunch, consisting of the so-called *krupnik* — grits
cooked in water. At three o'clock there is a review of the
discourse. At six — mincha (the afternoon service) followed by a study of *Yoreh Deah*(Teacher of Knowledge). Although the *maariv* service (evening prayer) at
eight or nine o'clock officially concludes the day's work,
the students usually remain over their books til ten and
twelve o'clock. The greater part of the student body
sleeps in the school.[28]

Another well-known but quite different yeshiva was at
Eishyshki in White Russia. This yeshiva did not raise funds
from other communities, but depended on local Jewish community support. When they did not have enough themselves,
the yeshiva students were provided for. Even the *maskilim*,
who advocated enlightenment and the abolition of traditional
religious practices, were impressed by the dignified devotion
to learning of the people of Eishyshki.

Most yeshiva students studied at Vilna, Kovno, Minsk,
Slutsky, Grodno, Bobruisk, Slonim, and other towns where
"eating days" were available. This custom provided that
Jewish students eat with a different family every day.[29]

Many full-time students in this later period did not study

in yeshivot. They spent their time in the local synagogue, which was as much a house of study as a house of prayer. One of the learned men in the community served as a teacher; he received no pay, but great prestige was attached to the position. Since the teacher's role in advanced study was minimal, the learning neither lagged nor suffered.[30] This pattern of every community supporting full-time students in a local synagogue was a reversion to the period before the massacres of 1648 and 1649 when every community supported a yeshiva. Higher Talmudic studies also began to return to the areas where Chassidism was strong after the Chassidic movement began to temper its former bitter opposition to Talmudic studies. At the end of the nineteenth century, yeshivot even began to re-appear again in Chassidic areas. The Lubavitcher sect of the Chassidic movement opened a number of yeshivot.[31] In 1939, just before the German invasion destroyed Polish Jewry and its institutions, Lublin had once again become the site of one of the leading yeshivot.

Cheder education gradually reached its former level and structure after the Jews recovered from the massacres of 1648-1649. After the abolition of Jewish autonomy by the Polish government in 1764, the *cheder* became more and more private — organized by individuals, its supervision by the community continued to decline and finally ceased altogether. This lack of supervision undoubtedly resulted in the deterioration of the *cheder*. The care with which manners, morals, and upright behavior, as well as grammar and the four fundamental operations of arithmetic were taught and the provision made for those who were unfit to pursue Talmudic studies, serve as an interesting contrast to the educational conditions in Russia and Poland after the decline of Polish Jewish autonomy.[32]

Even though the Jews were no longer forced to send their sons to school after the abolition of autonomy in 1764, almost all of them did so; illiteracy was almost unknown in the Pale. The Czarist Ministry of Education kept records of the number of *chedorim* and their pupils and published the figures in its annual reports. In 1899 there were 7,915 *chedorim* with 154,613 pupils.[33] These totals probably grossly underrecorded the actual number. For example, the Vilna educational district listed 3,318 *chedorim*, the Warsaw district, only 134,[34] a preposterously low figure.

The *melamed* led a quasi-legal existence, many were unwilling to expose themselves to the law by registering.[36] An investigation conducted by the well-known Imperial Russian Free Economic Society in 1894 fixed the number of *chedorim* at 14,740, with 202,000 pupils, an average of 13.7 pupils per *cheder*. This gives us an idea of the widespread nature of the school. The Jewish Colonization Society collated data from 507 localities with a Jewish population of 1,420,000, and found 7,145 *chedorim*: their estimate of the total number of *chedorim* was 24,000. Taking the average number of pupils per cheder as 13.7, these 24,000 *chedorim* evidently taught about 329,000 pupils.[35]

The investigation of the Russian Free Economic Society showed that, in 1894, out of a total of 201,964 pupils registered in the 14,740 *chedorim* reported, there were only 10,459 girls, or 5.2 percent. Apparently, almost every boy of school age attended *cheder*, but only a few girls did so.[36]

The nineteenth-century *Haskala* (Enlightenment) movement bitterly attacked traditional Jewish education as a source of ignorance and backwardness. An article in the *Voschod*, organ of the Russified Jewish intelligentsia, said:

Our *chedorim* with their *melamdim* represent a copy in miniature of the medieval inquisition applied to children. There are no rules and no system. . . . Our Talmud Torah makes an even sadder picture. . . . Its program consists of cold, hunger, corporal punishment and Hebrew reading.[37]

Another *Voschod* correspondent wrote from Vitebsk:

Our Talmud Torahs are filthy rooms, crowded from nine in the morning until nine in the evening with pale, starved children. These remain in this contaminated atmosphere for twelve hours at a time and see only their bent, exhausted teachers. Most of them are clad in rags; some of them are almost naked. Their faces are pale and sickly, and their bodies are evidently not strong. In parties of twenty or thirty, and at times more, they all repeat some lesson aloud after their instructor. He who has not listened to the almost absurd commentaries of the ignorant melamed cannot even imagine how little the children gain from such instruction.[38]

Solomon Maimon, who later become a philosopher of note in Germany, discussed the *cheder* in his autobiography:

I must now say something of the condition of the Jewish schools in general. The school is commonly a small smoky hut, and the children are scattered, some on benches, some on the bare earth. The master, in a dirty blouse, sitting on the table, holds between his knees a bowl, in which he grinds tobacco into snuff with a huge pestle like the club of Hercules, while at the same time he wields his authority. The ushers give lessons, each in his own corner, and rule those under their charge quite as despotically as the master himself. Of the breakfast, lunch and other food sent to the cheder for the children, these gentlemen keep the largest share for themselves. Sometimes the poor youngsters get nothing at all; and yet they dare not make any complaint on the subject, if they will not expose themselves to the vengeance of these tyrants. Here the children are imprisoned from morning to night, and have not an hour to themselves, except on Friday and a half-holiday at the New Moon.[39]

Dr. Chaim Weizmann, a distinguished chemist and the first President of the State of Israel, who was by no means antagonistic to the masses of Russian Jewry, wrote in the same vein:

Like all Jewish boys I went to cheder, beginning at the age of four. Like nearly all cheders, mine was a squalid, one-room school, which also constituted the sole quarters of the teacher's family. If my cheder differed from others, it was perhaps in the possession of a family goat which took shelter with us in cold weather. And if my first Rabbi, or teacher, differed from others, it was in the degree of pedagogic incompetence. If our schoolroom was usually hung up with washing, if the teacher's numerous children rolled about on the floor, if the din was deafening and incessant, that was nothing out of the ordinary. Nor was it anything out of the ordinary that neither the tumult nor the overcrowding affected our peace of mind or our powers of concentration.

In the spring and autumn, when the cheder was a tiny island set in a sea of mud, and in the winter, when it was blotted out by snow, I had to be carried there by a servant, or by my older brother. Once there, I stayed immured within its walls, along with the other children, from early morning till evening. We took lunch with us and consumed it in a short pause in the proceedings, often with the books still opened in front of us. On dark winter afternoons our studies could only be pursued by artificial light, and as candles were something of a luxury, and oil lamps practically unobtainable each pupil was in turn assessed a pound of candles as a contribution to the education of the young generation.

In the course of my cheder years I had several teachers, and by the time I was eleven, or even before, considerable demands were made on my intellectual powers. I was expected to understand — I never did, properly — the intricacies of the law as laid down in the Babylonian Talmud and as expounded and knocked into me by a Rabbi who was both ferocious and exacting, and certainly far from lucid in his expositions. He was always at a loss to understand why things needed to be explained at all; he felt that every Jewish boy should be able to pick up such things, which were as easy as they were sacred, by natural instinct, or at least just by glancing down the pages. I did not share his view, but was too badly terrorized to join issue with him as to his methods — if, indeed, I was at all aware of their inadequacy.[40]

These strident denunciations of the *cheder* must be taken with a grain of salt, since they were written by people who wished to reform the *cheder* and therefore emphasized its unfavorable aspects. The *cheder* had its defenders, to be sure. Louis Ginzberg, a renowned professor of Talmud at the Jewish Theological Seminary in New York, who was of Lithuanian origin, wrote:

Life in the cheder was arranged with more than due

regard for individuality. Not only was the cheder as we have seen, a private institution in which the parents were given an opportunity of choosing the teacher with a view to their children's needs and gifts, but the teaching was also personal in character. Restricted in the number of pupils, they were nevertheless divided into groups. The teacher usually occupied himself with no more than four children at a time. In this way a close personal relationship could grow up between master and pupil. It was practically impossible to deceive a teacher by palming off work on him done by others at home.[41]

Ginzberg points out that the *melamed* was mild in meting out punishment:

The *melamed* was certainly more humane and gentle than most of the masters of the English schools, who till very recently ruled as tyrants. We may be quite sure that he was not the brute pictured by the morbid imagination of certain *maskilim* (enlighteners), whose animus against the *cheder* is probably to be sought in a hatred of the deeply Jewish atmosphere that prevailed there.[42]

One of the best-known defenders of the *cheder* was the famous German-Jewish philosopher Franz Rosenzweig, an almost completely assimilated intellectual who was once on the verge of converting to Christianity. In Warsaw, during World War I, he came into contact with *Ostjuden* (Eastern European Jews) for the first time and was greatly impressed. He was deeply moved by their prayers, their religious chanting, and their celebration of the "Third Meal" before nightfall on the Sabbath.[43] Their education made a great impression on him and it led him to study the *cheder*. Unlike the followers of the *Haskala* movement, he had only praise for it. He called it "closer to the ideal of an educational institution than the Western European school. The latter produces fragmentary people, totally lacking orientation, but from the *cheder* there springs the constant renewal of a whole people."[44] In the same letter there is an ironic remark aimed at his own grandfather: "I fully understand that S.M. Ehrenberg did not like the *cheder*. For people who wish to have baptized grandchildren, the *cheder* is a totally unsuitable institution."[45]

Nathan Morris, an Anglo-Jewish educator, also defended the *cheder:*

The old *cheder*, an institution which was much abused by ill-informed writers of the *Haskala*, but which would repay more serious study than has yet been given it by historians and educationalists, followed in most cases the readings of the Synagogue. It adopted a kind of grand universal syllabus and time-table, based on the synagogue and followed by the whole people wherever they were. The philosophy of this method, as indeed of historic Jewish education as a whole, can be expressed in entirely modern terms like this: the child is not only to be prepared for life, but from the beginning helped to live the life which is regarded as desirable.[46]

Notes

1. For broad coverage of Jewish education before the period under discussion in this chapter, see Nathan Drazin, *History of Jewish Education from 515 B.C.E. to 220 C.E.* Johns Hopkins University Studies in Education No. 29 (Baltimore: The Johns Hopkins Press, 1940) *et passim*; Salo W. Baron, *The Jewish Community* (Philadelphia: Jewish Publication Society of America, 1942), vol. II, Chap. 13; Isidore Fishman, *The History of Jewish Education in Central Europe; XVI to XVIII Centuries* (London: Edward Goldstein, 1944).
2. David Bencionas Teimanas, *L'autonomie des communautes juives en pologne aux XVI et XVII siecles* (Paris: Jouve et Cie, 1933), p. 43. In fact, Jewish autonomy with its organizational structure had existed in the first half of the sixteenth century.
3. Simon Dubnow, *Divrei Yimei Am Olam* (Tel Aviv: Dvir, 1939), vol. VI, p. 193.
4. Simon Dubnow, "Jewish Autonomy," *Encyclopedia of the Social Sciences* (New York: The Macmillan Co., 1933), vol. VIII, p. 392. See also Simon Dubnow, "Council of the Four Lands," *Jewish Encyclopedia*, vol. IV, pp. 304-305.
5. Dubnow, "Council of the Four Lands," p. 305.
6. Nathan Hannover, *Yeven Metzulah* (Venice, 1653). The quotation is from an English translation (New York: Bloch Publishing Co., 1950), pp. 119-120.
7. Dubnow, "Council of the Four Lands," p. 306.

8. *Ibid.*
9. Hannover, *op. cit.*p. 119.
10. Israel Friedlaender, *The Jews of Russia and Poland* (New York: G.P. Putnam's Sons, 1915), p. 163. See also Raphael Abramovitch, "Geshikhte fun yidn in poiln, lite, un russland," *Algemeine entsiklopedie*, Series "Yidn" (New York: World Jewish Culture Congress, 1950), vol. IV, columns 121-124.
11. Teimanas, *op. cit.*, pp. 151-152.
12. "Poland," *Cyclopedia of Education* (New York: The Macmillan Co., 1941), vol. IV, p. 732.
13. Emanuel Gamoran, *Changing Conceptions in Jewish Education* (New York: The Macmillan Co., 1924), p. 105.
14. Simon Bernfield, "Vospitanie," *Evreiskaia entsiklopediia*, vol. V, columns 806-809.
15. F. Wettstein, *Kadmoniot Mepinkasiot Yeshanim* (Cracow: Y. Fisher, 1892), quoted in Teimanas, pp. 152-153.
16. *Ibid.*
17. *Pinkas Hamedinah Shel Vaad Hakehilot Harashiot Bemedinat Lite* (St. Petersburg, 1909), articles 352 and 353.
18. Teimanas, *op. cit.*, p. 155.
19. Dubnow, *Divrei Yimei Am Olam*, vol. VI, p. 198.
20. Hannover, op. cit., pp. 110-112.
21. Philip Friedman, "Geshikhte fun yidn in ukraine biz suf 18tn yorhundert," *Yidn in ukraine* (New York: Ukrainian Jewish Memorial Society, 1961), pp. 51-54.
22. Abraham Menes, "The Yeshivot in Eastern Europe," *The Jewish People, Past and Present* (New York: Jewish Encyclopedic Handbooks, 1948), vol. II, p. 111.
23. For a history of the false Messiah Jacob Frank and his movement among Polish Jewry, see Meier Balaban, *Letoldot Hatenuah Hafrankit* (Tel Aviv: Dvir, 1934-1935), 2 vols.
24. The best-known work on the history of the Chassidic movement is Simon Dubnow, *Toldot Hahassidut* (Tel Aviv: Dvir, 1930-1932), 3 vols.
25. Menes, op. cit.

26. Louis Ginzberg, "The Gaon, Rabbi Elijah Vilna," *Students, Scholars, and Saints* (Philadelphia: Jewish Publication Society of America, 1928), pp. 125-145 et passim.
27. Menes, op. cit., pp. 113-114.
28. L.I. Mandelshtam, *Perezhitoe*, vol. I, pp. 24-25. Quoted in Louis Greenberg, *The Jews in Russia* (New Haven: Yale University Press, 1944), vol. I, p. 58.
29. Menes, op. cit., pp. 113-114.
30. Mark Zborowski and Elizabeth Herzog, *Life Is With People* (New York: International Universities Press, 1952), p. 100.
31. Chasidism began to develop sects shortly after its rise. One of the most interesting of the Chassidic groups was the Lubavitcher or chabad movement, which combines the cold rationalism of the Lithuanian Talmudist with the emotional ecstatic joy of the Ukranian and Polish Chassid. Chabad, which arose in the town of Lubavitch in White Russia, was the major Chassidic movement which made headway among Lithuanian Jewry. They were very active in the founding of yeshivot. See Koppel Pinson, "Chassidism," *Encyclopedia of the Social Sciences* (New York: The Macmillan Co., 1933), vol. III, pp. 354-357.
32. Gamoran, op. cit., p. 71.
33. Russia. Ministry of Public Instruction, *Izvlecheniia iz vse-podanieishago otcheta za 1899* (St. Petersburg, 1901), Supp. p. 100.
34. G. Voltke, "Kheder i melamed v rossii i tsarstve polshom," *Evreiskaia entsiklopediia* (Moscow, 1913), vol. XV, columns 591-592.
35. Jewish Colonization Society, *Sbornik materialov ob ekonomicheskom polozhenii evreev v rossii* (St. Petersburg, 1904), vol. II, Table 63.
36. *Ibid.*
37. *Voskhod*, 1893, Issue XIII, p. 100.
38. *Voskhod*, 1894, Issue IX, p. 1.

39. *The Autobiography of Solomon Maimon*, translated from the German by J. Clark Murray (London: East and West Library, 1954), pp. 31-32.

40. Chaim Weizmann, *Trial and Error* (Philadelphia: Jewish Publication Society of America, 1949), pp. 4-5. The genre of anti-*cheder* literature is endless. For other examples see *Max Lilienthal: American Rabbi, Life and Writings*, edited by David Philipson (New York: Block Publishing Co., 1915), p. 283. Especially vehement is: "The pity of it is that these centers of ignorance, in which disease is more successfully disseminated than knowledge, and from which Jewish children emerge sickly, stunted, and often deformed, are to be found throughout the ghettoes of the Russian Empire" (Beatrice Baskerville, *The Polish Jew* [London: The Macmillan Co., 1906], pp. 86-87).

41. Ginzberg, op. cit., p. 25.

42. *Ibid.*

43. Zvi Kurzweil, *Modern Trends in Jewish Education* (New York: Thomas Yoseloff, 1964), p. 202.

44. Franz Rosenzweig, *Briefe* (Berlin, 1935), pp. 326-327. Quoted in Kurzweil, p. 202.

45. *Ibid.*

46. Nathan Morris, *Curriculum and Method in the Hebrew Class* (London: Eyre and Spottiswood, 1946), p. 7.

Chapter 3

The Secular Yiddish School Movement
Before and After
the Russian Revolution

The Growth of the Jewish Socialist Movement

IN THE LATTER part of the nineteenth century, support for the socialist movement mushroomed among the Russian Jewish masses. Embodied in a number of educational ideas and institutions, the socialist movement became a significant force in directing the future of Jewish education.

Socialism, although it occurred relatively late among Jews in Russia, became a movement of great influence. It always was proportionately more widespread among Jews than among Russians, and in the early years of the Russian Social Democratic Labor Party the Jewish membership was even greater in absolute numbers. At the beginning of 1905, for example, on the eve of the Revolution, the entire Russian party (excluding the Poles and Letts) numbered only 8,400;

in the preceding summer the Bund, representing the Jewish workers alone, had a membership of 23,000,[1] not including the membership of the proletarian Zionist groups.

Socialism attracted many Jews for four reasons:

1. Industrialization was greater in the Pale of Settlement than in the rest of the empire. When industrialization began to occur in Russia at the time of the emancipation of the serfs in 1861, the occupations of many Jews became superfluous and they began to pour into the towns. In addition, the "temporary" May Laws of 1882 caused the cities to be overwhelmed by dispossessed village Jews. (See the data in Chapter One for the very high level of proletarianization among Russian Jews.)

2. The Jewish worker entered the modern era with a substantial store of experience and tradition. Jewish artisans had been organized for centuries in guilds (chevrahs) which provided for mutual aid, improvement, and protection.[2] In many cases the newly established proletarian organizations were the direct heir of the old *chevrahs*. Since they lived under internal autonomy, the Jews governed themselves according to Talmudic law, which made extensive provisions for regulating working conditions.[3] A writer on the subject commented:

> Because of these practices the Jewish workman suffered little, if at all, from a feeling of inferiority in his intercourse with the other members of the community. He received an elementary education in cheder. On the Sabbath and the holidays he was a free man. In the interval between *mincha* and *maariv*[4] he sat with his fellow townsmen in the House of Study. He felt himself an equal partner with all other Jews in the spiritual heritage of Israel. True, in the Jewish community, too, there were marked social cleavages between the rich and

poor, the scholar and the untutored. Even in the synagogue the prosperous member of the congregation occupied a more prominent position than the poor one. But there was absent that sharp gulf which divided the classes in the non-Jewish world.[5]

3. The Russian government's policy of racial discrimination helped to make the educated Russian Jews more conscious of their national individuality, and the idea began to gain currency that their best means of defense lay in an independent Jewish movement enjoying mass support.[6]

4. Secular education began to spread widely among Russian Jews after 1860. By the end of the decade there was a sizeable educated Russian Jewish intelligentsia, as witnessed by the rapid growth of the number of Jewish students in the Russian schools. In 1853, there were 159 Jewish students in all the gymnasiums and pregymnasiums of Russia, only 1.25 percent of the total student body. Ten years later their number had risen to 552, or 3.2 percent of the total.[7] In 1873, the number of Jewish students in all secondary schools for men rose to 2,362 or 13.2 percent of the total.[8] In the school region of Vilna, whose Jewish population had always strongly resisted secular education, the percentage of Jews in all the gymnasiums and pregymnasiums increased from 6.9 in 1865 to 26.7 in 1881. In 1865 Jewish students in all Russian universities constituted 3.2 percent of the total enrollment; in 1881 the percentage rose to 8.8 percent.[9] By 1887 the number of Jewish students in both the gymnasiums and the universities was so high that the government imposed a rigid *numerus clausus* on Jewish students.[10]

The first Jewish socialist groups were founded in 1875 and 1876 by students at the government-operated Vilna Rabbinical Seminary. Although the groups were broken up by the police, some of their members were heard from again. Aaron Lieberman, the most interesting figure among them, fled to Vienna where in 1877 he established a Hebrew language journal *Haemet* (The Truth), the first socialist Jewish periodical.[11]

Throughout the 1880s various circles and study groups of Jewish socialists arose in the Pale of Settlement. The activity was scattered, uncoordinated, and not too well-organized. Many of the leaders, working independently, arrived at similar goals. But there was no communication among the widely scattered towns. In 1880 there was a circle in Odessa; in 1882, in Minsk and in Radichev; in 1883, a circle in Poltava; in 1884, one in Kishinev; in 1887, one in Niazhim; in 1889, one in Riga and another in Mohilev.[12]

The first Jewish socialist groups considered themselves part of the Russian socialist movement and never dreamed of working for a specifically Jewish movement. They had no Jewish aims but appealed to Jews because they were the people they could reach. Aaron Lieberman, the first Marxist to write in Hebrew, made his position clear in *Haemet*'s first issue: "Not love of our people has prompted us to publish this periodical, but the love of men generally and the love of our co-nationals, because they are men — this alone induced us to address them in a language which they understand and to tell them the value of truth.[13]

The circles' early political activities were supposed to educate young people for further socialist leadership. Discussions and lectures were held on natural science, economics, socialist theory, and Russian language and literature. As early as 1887, however, a Vilna group of "Jewish Social Democrats" engaged in more organized activity. Their ideology is described in a report submitted by the subsequently organized Bund to the Internationalist Socialist Congress in 1900:

> The first Jewish intellectuals who started to carry on propaganda among Jewish workers had no idea of creating a specifically Jewish labor movement. Confined to the Pale and not having the possibilities to dedicate their energies to the Russian labor movement, they were forced willy-nilly to start working among the Jews, and thus at least quench to some degree their thirst for revolutionary activity. The Jewish labor movement occupies second place for them; they look chiefly to the Russian worker, upon whom they place all their hopes and from whom they expect also salvation for the Jewish proletariat. Their propaganda is carried on in the Russian language.[14]

From 1893 to 1895 the leaders of these groups began to be concerned about their lack of success. Many among them argued for an expansion of their activities from socialist discussion to mass agitation, a step that meant bringing the Jewish Social Democrats into closer contact with the Jewish masses, the Yiddish language, and the "Jewish problem." Julius Martov's famous speech, delivered on May 2, 1895 before a small group of agitators, marks a turning-point in this respect. Martov's speech contains in embryo the ideological basis for the later formation of the Bund. He proclaims the need for Jewish workers to act *as Jews* in the revolutionary struggle and to recognize specifically Jewish problems and situations. He admits that the Jewish Social Democrats had previously looked only to the Russian workers and had, therefore, merely "glanced" at specifically Jewish problems. They carried on their agitation in Russian and thus "forgot to maintain contact with the Jewish masses who understand no Russian." But life, Martov asserted, "forced us to change our tactics. The primary reason was that whilst all our hopes were tied up with the general Russian movement we, at the same time, although barely conscious of it, raised the Jewish movement to a level which the Russian movement had not attained." In changing their tactics to mass agitation, he declared, they were forced to adapt their propaganda to the masses, "and that meant making it more Jewish." Martov's next point was to become one of the most violent questions of dispute between the Bundists and the Polish Socialist Party, and even more so between the Bundists and Lenin and the Iskra group in the years 1902-1907. The Jewish proletariat, he contended, cannot rely solely on the Russian and Polish proletariat. It is always conceivable that, in order to gain their ends, non-Jewish proletarian leaders may be willing or obliged to make concessions at the expense of the Jews. Accordingly, the Jewish proletariat must be prepared to fight as an organized Jewish group, alongside of other groups, for "economic, civic, and political liberty. A working class that is content with the lot of an inferior nation will not rise up against the lot of an inferior class. The national passivity of the Jewish masses, therefore, is also a bar to the growth of its class consciousness. The growth of national and class consciousness must go hand in hand."[15]

Arkady Kremer's booklet *On Agitation*, written in Russian in 1893 and read before the group of Jewish Social Democrats in 1894, was a practical guide to mass agitation. It was distributed in written and hectographed copies and then published in Geneva in 1896 with a preface by Pavel Axelrod. Kremer's work marked a turning point in the nature of Russian revolutionary activity. His central idea was that political agitation should broaden its base by a greater appeal to the masses of the proletariat, that it should therefore cease being purely abstract and theoretical and, instead, attempt to integrate political and economic problems."[16]

In the winter of 1897 — the same year in which Herzl summoned the first Zionist Congress — a group of thirteen Jewish socialists assembled in the back room of a Vilna blacksmith's house to establish the Jewish socialist organization, the Bund. A number of cities sent accredited delegates, but the leading group, which had called the meeting, came from Vilna. By this time Vilna had become the center of the Jewish workingmen's movement and was responsible for distributing illegal literature to the provinces.

Arkady Kremer's writings illuminate the importance of Vilna for both the Jewish and the Russian revolutionary movement. He asserts that although the Bund officially began in 1897, it had actually existed since 1895; from that time or earlier the Jewish socialist circles of the northwest had acted as a group, with Vilna as their center. The 1897 conference simply ratified an existing situation. "It should be remembered," Kremer wrote, "that Vilna was then the center not only of the Jewish but of the entire Social Democratic movement in Russia. The Vilna method of mass propaganda formulated in my brochure *On Agitation* was then also adopted in St. Petersburg, Moscow, and Kiev."[17]

Although it was specifically a Jewish organization, the Bund always regarded itself as an integral part of the Russian Social Democratic Party. Prominent and active Bundists played a leading role in the formation of the party itself. Bund leaders organized the meeting held in Minsk in 1898 at which the Russian Social Democratic Workers Party was founded; and of the three delegates selected to serve on its central committee two were Jews, one of them being Kremer.[18]

Some sort of separate Jewish existence and program was implied when the Bund was founded, but it did not adopt a stand on the Jewish national question. The Bund was still little more than a party working among the Jewish masses. Neither the First nor the Second Congress of the Bund adopted a policy on the "national question" or such related issues as the battle for Polish Zionism.[19]

Historians have tended to attribute the adoption of a national program by the Bund to its decision to organize among the masses. In order to be closer to the masses of workers, to be responsive to their needs, the Bund had to become more Jewish. The more the Jewish working masses were drawn into the strike movement and the political struggles, the more "Jewish" the movement became. It proved essential to use Yiddish in order to reach masses. Thus the propagandists and agitators of the Bund had to concentrate on the kind of activity that may have seemed more appropriate for a cultural society than for a political party: while not neglecting practical revolutionary work, the Bund began to devote itself to the development, advancement, and propagation of Jewish culture in Yiddish.[20]

In addition to this motive, two others pressed the Bund into developing a national program for the Jews. First, the Bund developed simultaneously with the Zionist movement at a time of greatly heightened national awareness among Jews. The failure of assimilation as an answer to the Jewish problem was indisputable, given the fierce pogroms and the increasing amount of anti-Semitic legislation that restricted Jews more than ever before. Educated and assimilated Jewish youth were returning to their people. Russian Zionism was originally a middle class movement, but around the turn of the century it attracted the masses in great numbers. Proletarian Zionism, which in the long run came to be the dominant faction in the Zionist movement, began to develop. In response to this great pressure by the Zionists, the Bund had to develop and refine its own attitude on the national question.[21]

Secondly, vigorous nationalist movements had been waged by other groups inside the Russian Empire. The Polish Socialist Party (hereafter referred to as the PPS) wanted to cooperate with the Russian revolutionary movement, but insisted on a platform of national self-determination. They were, in fact, very bitter toward the Bund for its stand; moreover, the two competed for the allegiance of overlapping worker groups. The Bund's Warsaw committee was under constant attack by the PPS. There was a rivalry for Jewish membership in that city where the PPS had a Jewish division. The Bund had argued for a united social democratic movement to work for a free Russia, and that Russia should maintain the boundaries of the existing empire — a socialist government would make national borders unnecessary. It would even be an asset to have so large an area without borders; the links among workers would be strengthened. But the Poles argued for socialism within their own borders, and demanded that the Jews make a clear stand on the issue of national self-determination.[22]

John Mill, a member of the Central Committee of the Bund who strongly favored adoption of a national program, wrote:

Zionism in Jewish life had become a factor which we didn't dare dismiss out of hand .... The national movements in Poland and Lithuania, the political cultural needs of the Jewish masses, political Zionism — all drove the Bund to seek a clear answer to the Jewish question. It became impossible for us to remain in the same spot and be satisfied with the old formula of equal civil rights. This very formula by then pleased nobody.[23] The Bund, after years of stormy debate, adopted its national program at its Fourth Congress in 1901: The Congress recognizes, that, according to the Social Democratic program, no kind of oppression is admissible not only of one class over another, not only of government over citizens, but even of one nationality over another, the domination of one language over another. The Congress recognizes that the concept of "nationality" applies to the Jewish people.[24]

This declaration was weakened by inserting it as a demand to be satisfied in the future. The opposition within the Bund had not yet been completely won over; many of its members feared the reaction of the Russian Social Democratic Labor Party.

Two years before, the Foreign Committee of the Bund[25] had asked Chaim Zhitlowsky to write an article on Zionism for them. Zhitlowsky, though a radical, was not a Marxist, but his article was enthusiastically received by the committee. It appeared in March, 1899, in No. 6 of *Der Yiddisher arbeter*, the maiden issue of the paper as the official organ of the Foreign Committee. In his article, Zhitlowsky called the Zionist movement a reaction of the Jewish bourgeoisie to anti-Semitism. They looked to Palestine, he wrote, as a new home where they could exercise political control and thus better exploit the worker.[26]

The Bund Congress of 1901 also adopted for the first time an official position on Zionism, bitterly condemning it.[27]

The Bund removed all possible ambiguity in its national program at its Sixth Congress in 1905, when it demanded:

1. Full civil and political emancipation for the Jews.
2. The possibility for the Jewish population to use its own language in communications with the courts and with institutions of the state and of the local and territorial self-government.
3. National-cultural autonomy: to remove from the province of the state and from the local and territorial self-government the functions which are associated with matters of culture (education and others) and to transfer these to the nation proper in the form of separate institutions, central as well as local, elected by all members on the basis of general, equal, direct, and secret vote.
4. Note: national-cultural autonomy does not deprive the central legislative power of the right in instituting certain standards, which all are obliged to accept, in questions which have a general significance for all nations of Russia, as, for example, that all must secure elementary education, that the subjects of instruction must bear a purely secular character, etc., and of the right to exercise control so that all these standards should be observed.[28]

In fewer than ten years the Bund had been driven from almost assimilationist views to advocacy of national-cultural autonomy. This charge obligated the Bund to involve itself with larger matters entirely out of the field of emphasis of the ordinary revolutionary party. As a party of the masses it had to concern itself with the development of the language of the masses, Yiddish.[29] There were no schools in Yiddish; therefore, paradoxically enough, the Jewish socialist movement, which fifteen years before had conducted all its activities in the Russian language, scorning the "zhargon" of the masses, found itself the prime mover in establishing a system of secular schools in the Yiddish language.

An account of the rise of the socialist trend in Zionism may be properly said to belong in the section on Zionism, not to that on socialism. This is a matter of choice. Socialist Zionist parties gained great strength in the Zionism movement, but they did not achieve their present dominant hold until much later in the 1920s or even the 1930s. In the early period of their development, however, they had much in common with the rest of the Jewish socialist movement. In fact, in the early years they did not attend Zionist Congresses or cooperate with the Zionist movement because they did not want to be contaminated by the bourgeoisie.[30]

The first person to raise the banner of socialism within the Zionist movement was Dr. Nachman Syrkin, a Russian Jewish student in Berlin in 1898. In his *Die Judenfrage und der sozialistische Judenstaat* he wrote that socialism and Zionism were not incompatible; in fact, Zionism could only be realized in a socialist form.[31] Because Syrkin lived outside of Russia, his book did not have great influence on the Russian Jewish masses. He founded an organization of Zionist students in Germany, Cherut (Freedom) but this group is not usually considered a forerunner of the Russian proletarian Zionist movement.[32]

Proletarian Zionist[33] groups began to form in the Pale of Settlement about 1900-1901. The general Zionist movement with its middle class leadership and its emphasis on a long-range solution of the Jewish problem had little attraction for workers. The Bund was gaining great strength throughout the Pale because of its emphasis on an immediate solution of the Jewish problem and its tactics of struggle against autocratic oppression. Just as the Bund developed its national program because of the pressure of the Zionists and the attraction of the masses for some type of Jewish nationalism, so the Zionist movement developed a socialist wing because of the growing popularity of the Bund among the masses seeking a way out of their daily miseries.[34] The first Poale Zion (Workers of Zion) group was founded in Yekaterinoslav in 1900 by Ber Borochov.[35] A Poale Zion group which arose in Minsk at the same time opposed socialism and political activity in Russia.[36] This group was very much an exception; almost all proletarian Zionist groups were very interested in socialism and in political struggle — socialism was the means by which the proletariat of Russia would be liberated.[37] The following extract from a May Day 1905 leaflet by the Yekaterinoslav branch of the Poale Zion is a typical expression of their views:

> In the great family of the workers of all nations, we, the Jewish workers, are the most crushed, the most exploited, and the most plundered of rights of all the deprived of the world. More than any other nation the Czarist government oppresses us. It instigates pogroms. Capitalism also oppresses us more than others. While workers of other nations work in large factories we are humbled in miserable tiny workshops in dark cellars, cold and wet, where we bend our backs and spoil our eyes. Today, let us call out our protest to the world for our rights and demands.
> Let us proclaim the majesty of our flag, the flag of the Jewish workers, the flag of Poale Zion. Let us join the others and strengthen ourselves with our cry: Down with the rule of absolutism! Down with war! Long live the international social democratic workers party![38]

In the years 1903-1905 the various Poale Zion groups

thrashed out their ideologies. Some were greatly influenced by the proposal of the Zionist leader Dr. Herzl to accept Uganda from the British government as a place of settlement instead of Palestine. In 1904 these groups united to form the Zionist-Socialist Workers Party, usually known as S.S. (the Russian abbreviation for Sioniste Sotsialiti).[39]

Another faction of the Poale Zion saw their chief aim as the struggle for national-cultural autonomy for Russian Jews. They are usually called Seymists because of their belief that a Seym (Parliament) should rule all Russian Jews. They quickly gave up all effort to achieve the Jewish center in Palestine (as favored by the orthodox Poale Zionists under the leadership of Ber Borochov) or a Jewish center elsewhere (as favored by the S.S.). They called their party the Jewish Socialist Workers Party.[40]

The orthodox Borochov Poale Zionists officially founded their party in 1906 at a convention in Poltava. Its platform was based on two firm points: Marxist socialism and Palestinian proletarian Zionism. The official name was Jewish Social Democratic Workers Party — Poale Zion.[41]

Unlike the general Zionist movement, the proletarian Zionists generally supported the use of Yiddish rather than Hebrew, a choice which drew them into the Yiddishist cultural movement.[42]

The Yiddish Cultural Movement

The intensification of interest in Yiddish culture and schools stemmed from events entirely outside the Jewish community.

The Czar made considerable concessions to the Russian people after the 1905 revolt. A State Duma was established by popular vote, arousing great hopes among the Russian people. But when the Duma tried to assert greater powers than he was willing to grant, it was dissolved by the Czar. A second Duma, of a somewhat more conservative bent, was elected and met in March, 1907. It, too, was dissolved after only three months on the grounds that Social Democratic deputies were inciting the army to rebellion.[43]

The period of 1906 to June 1907 was one of struggle between revolutionary and counterrevolutionary forces within Russia. The reactionary forces won out; they used spies and provocateurs in the socialist and labor groups, arrested their leaders and deprived them of the opportunity to work, and instigated Great-Russian chauvinism against all minority groups. There was much unemployment, and hundreds of thousands of people emigrated from Russia to seek their economic and political fortunes elsewhere.[44] Among these were many members of the leftist Jewish groups.[45]

Elections were called in September 1907 for a third Duma to take office in November. This Duma was to be chosen under a new electoral law, which cut the representation of the Russian workers and peasants and of the non-Russian peoples of the Czarist Empire. Only the rightist Russian groups were allowed the right to continue to exist. This oppression helped increase the nationalist feelings of the minorities, and though they were too weak to struggle, they all became more culture-conscious and more determined to secure recognition of their linguistic and cultural rights.[46]

The Jewish masses, despairing of success, fell into political apathy. Until early in 1907, political organizations had been large and and active; but after the June crisis they all dropped in numbers and activity, and by 1908 they had all crumbled, their leaders in hibernation.

In 1906 there were many intellectuals and followers in the movements; they began slipping away in 1907; by 1908 they had all run out. The intellectuals had all become interested in their futures and their careers; then the active members, especially the younger ones who had joined during the good times, began to leave, then finally the old timers . . . some stealing away, others building up theories in their own defense.[47]

The former revolutionaries, who now had excess energy to use up, became interested in literature and the arts, and "more than one of the leaders of the Jewish socialist parties suddenly revealed that he was destined from birth to be a literary critic, the founder of a school of arts or esthetics."[48]

As literary and dramatic circles began to develop, people began to feel that art and culture were intrinsically good and did not require any connection with politics or economics. The literary circle served an important social function as the "only refuge where people can gather, meet their friends, and where the gendarme is not so frequent a caller."[49] In Vilna, the chief Jewish cultural center, for example, well-known writers arranged and attended these literary evenings, where folk songs were sung and once-inviolable party lines were crossed in the name of Jewish culture. Thus, in the Chanukah, 1907 literary collection edited by Nomberg, articles appeared by S. Niger, a member of the Zionist-Socialists (S.S.), B. Vladeck of the Bund, and Y. Zerubavel of the Poale Zion.[50]

At the same time, and as a culmination of the efforts of all the various forces in Jewish life to stimulate interest in Yiddish literature, the general Jewish public also developed an interest in Yiddish culture. Former revolutionaries who were leaders of the new cultural movement began to organize workers' evening schools and dramatic and literary groups in all the larger Jewish cities — Vilna, Riga, Lodz, Minsk, Warsaw, Odessa, Bialystok — seeing them as the last bastion of the revolution and hoping to prevent their becoming completely apolitical.[51] The weakened Poale Zion and Bund began to publish literary journals; they would smuggle in political ideas in the hope that "only because of it [the literature] will the readers also glance at the political-theoretical section."[52]

But the trend remained almost completely nonpolitical. In March, 1908 the first issue of the *Literarishe monatshriften* (Literary Monthly) which symbolized the new era, appeared. Edited by S. Gorelik, a Zionist, A. Vayter, a Bundist, and S. Niger, a member of the S.S, it declared that it would strive to be apolitical and would attempt to write in Yiddish on a high cultural level and on topics of cultural interest.

Forty years later, Yitzchak Greenbaum, a leading Zionist, wrote:

> After the Russian reaction the leftist Jewish groups discovered that there was no other central theme around which they could rally their former followers to Jewish nationalism but the one issue of Jewish language rights. Therefore the prestige of Yiddish began to increase as the sole tangible object for whose rights the national battle could be fought, and Yiddish language rights became the central national political demand of the leftist parties, including the Zionist left. Before the external battle with the governments of the countries in which they resided for the rights of Yiddish in education and literature could take place, an internal struggle was necessary for the recognition of Yiddish as the Jewish national tongue. This demand was aimed against Hebrew, at the Zionists who fought for revival of this language.[53]

The famous conference held in 1908 at Chernovitz, the capital of Bukovina, in Austria, convened to consider the recognition of Yiddish as the Jewish national language. The conference was called by Nathan Birnbaum, an assimilated Austrian Jew who had recently become renowned as a theorist on Jewish autonomy. It was supposed to be the founding conference of a great Yiddishist movement and at no other time have so many leaders of Yiddish culture come together.

The famous Yiddish writer Y.L. Peretz opened the conference, declaring, "we are a Jewish nation and Yiddish is our language. In our language will we survive and create our cultural values, and never give it up for the false interests of the 'State.' "[54]

Dr. Chaim Zhitlowsky, the father of Jewish cultural autonomy, declared that it was up to the conference to proclaim Yiddish the Jewish national language, for it was the best tool for Jewish national existence as a partner in European civilization. He likened Hebrew to a grandmother, too old to be useful any longer, who should willingly hand over the house keys to younger housewives, daughters or daughters-in-law. Hebrew's refusal to do so has provoked a battle between the two. Peretz called for continued cultural work in Yiddish in order to halt the drift of the best Jewish talents to foreign cultures, and Esther Frumkin of the Bund made the point that it was the proletariat which was the first to recognize Yiddish and work for it among the masses and intelligentsia.[55]

The precise wording of the final resolution of the conference was vehemently debated. At issue were whether Yiddish should be declared as *the* Jewish national language, as the Bund urged, or as *a* Jewish national language; and precisely what the role of Hebrew should be. The Bundists alone favored the complete exclusion of Hebrew. The final conference resolution, formulated by Dr. Zhitlowsky, was supported by all but the Bundists. It stated:

> The First Conference for the Yiddish language recognizes Yiddish as a national language of the Jewish people and demands its political, communal, and cultural equality. At the same time the Conference feels it necessary to declare that every participant in the Conference and also every member of the future organization retains the freedom to feel toward the Hebrew language as he personally sees fit.[56]

The conference also resolved to found and support model Yiddish schools and to publish model textbooks.[57] After the final conference resolution the famous Yiddish novelist Sholem Asch walked over to poet Abraham Reisin and bestowed a kiss upon him, symbolizing the final decision in favor of Yiddish.[58]

This step, the proclamation of Yiddish as a national language, immeasurably strengthened the Yiddishist movement in Russia and all over the world. A conference of Yiddishist teachers in Vilna in 1907, during Passover, also supported the school effort. Sixty delegates came from Kovno, Riga, Lodt, Warsaw, and several other cities. But the meeting, which was illegal, became known to the police and all the participants were arrested. The teachers, continuing their discussion in jail, passed resolutions that schools for Jewish youth should be primarily based on the Yiddish language.[59]

After these two events, the Yiddishists went to war against the *cheder*, the yeshiva, the national school, religion, the Hebrew language, and anything that savored of the old life. The stage for many of these battles between the Hebraists and the Yiddishists were the conventions of the *Chevrat Mefitzei Haskalah Be Yisrael Be Eretz Russia* (Society for the Dissemination of Enlightenment Among the Jews of Russia). Founded in the early 1860s by the wealthy Jewish bankers and railroad barons of St. Petersburg, this group proposed to train the Jews for "readiness for citizenship." Leon Rosenthal, one of the historians of the society and its first treasurer, said that the chief reason for the founding of the organization was that "whenever Jewish leaders broached the question of civic rights to government representatives, the latter countered by charging them with the task of educating the masses of Jewry."[60] The Society was to be a membership organization and was under the supervision of the Ministry of Education. With its central offices in St. Petersburg, it started to function on December 18, 1863, based on a three-point program of activity: to promote knowledge of the Russian language among Jews, to subsidize poor Jewish students in the general schools, and to publish books containing useful knowledge. The society encouraged Jewish writers by paying them honorariums and by publishing their works.[61]

In the succeeding years the work of the society expanded greatly. It began to support directly and to subsidize modern Jewish schools, and, by the early twentieth century, it was a major source of funds for most of the modern national Hebrew schools which were spreading throughout Russia. Of course, the Society had a role in determining the content of the schools' curricula. These schools, about which more will be said later, were inspired by the Zionist movement, and the Mefitzei Haskalah, which had started out as a society to assimilate Russian Jews into Russian culture, was now supporting a system of modern Hebrew schools, one of whose main functions was to cultivate Jewish nationalism. Of course, the society did not see it that way; they were utterly nonpartisan and would support all modern schools devoted to European culture.[62]

If the Yiddishists could get the Mefitzei Haskalah to support their schools it would be a great victory for them, a move "into the mainstream of Jewish schooling." Many fierce verbal battles were fought in the conventions of the Mefitzei Haskalah over the language question. The Hebraists were far from silent at these conventions; they vigorously debated the Yiddishists through their chief spokesmen, Achad Ha'am, Chaim Nachman Bialik, Vladimir Jabotinsky, and Dr. Y. Katznelson. In 1911 a group of Yiddishists took control of the Warsaw teachers association and began to demand the use of Yiddish in public schools. At the convention of the Mefitzei Haskalah that year in Petrograd a particularly acerbic debate took place. The Yiddishists declared: "Hebrew is as dead as Latin"; "The Bible is a religious book and modern pedagogy excludes religion from the school"; "The Bible and its source, the Hebrew language, should be sent from the school."[63]V

At the last prewar convention of the Mefitzei Haskalah, held in 1913, a positive resolution favoring Society support for the Yiddish school was approved for the first time.[64]

Secular Yiddish Schools under the Czarist Regime

There were few Yiddish schools under the Czarist regime because they were illegal. Instruction, with a few exceptions, had to be in Russian; the government did not permit schools in other languages.[65] Since regular schools in Yiddish were illegal, evening courses and Sabbath schools for workers assumed great importance in Yiddish education, and a number of such schools — for male and female workers — were set up at the turn of the century in the cities of the Pale. The Yiddish intelligentsia felt obliged to teach in these adult schools. The biography of the great writer Y.L. Peretz describes a school of this type in his home town of Zamosch in Poland. Together with several other young intellectuals he gave evening courses for these workers and artisans; his subject was Jewish history. Outside of reading, writing, and arithmetic, the *Pirkei Avot* (Ethics of the Fathers — a Talmudic tract emphasizing ethical behavior in daily life) was taught, and lectures were given on other great Jewish classics and scholars. In a small town like Zamosch, the authorities must have known that such a school existed; but apparently, they chose to look the other way in this instance.[66]

A report of the Mefitzei Haskalah lists Vilna, Grodno, Gomel, Ekaterinoslav, Kishinev, Kovno, Lodz, Tomsk, Kharkov, Kherson, Ackerman, Kertch, Mariopol, and Feodosia as sites of evening and Sabbath schools in 1901.[67] The first large and permanent Yiddish school of this kind was the Evening School for Adults in Vilna. According to the law, it was supposed to be teaching in Russian, but from 1906 to 1911 it gradually switched to Yiddish. The school, with separate sections for men and women, took pupils up to the age of 16. By 1916 the student body reached 1,000, it had an annual budget of 3,500 rubles, and served as a laboratory for Yiddishism because much terminology was established there.[68]

In 1911 a group of Bundist and Seymist teachers in Demyevka, a Kiev suburb with a large Jewish population, founded a Yiddish school which was legalized as a collective *cheder* of several *melamdim*. It was an extremely valuable school because, as a *cheder*, its program, textbooks and language were not subject to supervision. (Remember that the language of discourse in the *cheder* was Yiddish even though the language itself was not studied.) The Demyevka school was destined to be a model for the Yiddish secular school. Within a few years it had developed a five-year program with 150 pupils. The school continued to operate throughout the war; and after the 1917 revolution it was absorbed into the Yiddish school system that developed in the independent Republic of the Ukraine.[69]

In Warsaw the *Chevrat Chinuch Yeladim* (Children's Education Association) supported a Hebrew-Russian school. Yiddishists fought to capture the school and succeeded in having one of their number placed as principal in 1912. He instituted studies in vocational subjects, biology, and geography in Yiddish. This school was the first of its type in Poland.[70]

World War I, with its great dislocation of the Jewish population caused by expulsions and flight from the front lines, had far-reaching repercussions on Jewish education. Under the strain of the war, the Czarist government could not maintain its old supervision; moreover, Jewish nationalism was rapidly growing and took advantage of this weakness. The nurseries, kindergartens, and schools which were organized for the children of war-stricken and homeless Jews after 1915 were for the most part conducted openly in Yiddish. These institutions represented the first organized effort to establish a modern Yiddish secularist school system.[71]

In 1916 the first conference of teachers in Yiddish schools was held at Tombov. Immediately after the March

1917 Revolution a Yiddish teachers conference was held in Petrograd. The Yiddish language school grew more rapidly under the general breakdown of authority during the war.[72]

Yiddish Schools in the Ukraine after the Overthrow of Czarism

The first place in the world where Yiddish secular schools and cultural institutions were established on a mass scale with government support was in the independent Ukraine, a short-lived state which was born during the March Revolution of 1917 and died with the assumption of full Soviet power in 1920.

In May 1917 the Central Rada (Council) of the Ukrainian nationalists at Kiev demanded that the Provisional Government in Petrograd recognize it as the regional authority of the Ukraine. The Provisional Government agreed in principle, but felt it necessary to wait for the forthcoming Constituent Assembly to approve the policy. Disappointed, the Central Rada on June 10, 1917, issued its "First Universal," declaring itself the regional authority. The Provisional Government in July authorized it to act as the central government's agent, but in return required that 30 percent of the Rada's membership be composed of the Ukraine's minorities — the Great Russians, Jews, and Poles.[73]

The Ukrainians were willing to allot several portfolios in the General Secretariat (cabinet) to the national minorities, but the United Jewish Socialist Labor Party[78] and the Poale Zion insisted that this would not protect them; they demanded that specific posts be set up to supervise the affairs of each minority. On July 15, 1917, the Rada set up three Vice-Secretaryships in the General Secretariat for National Affairs to supervise Great Russian, Jewish, and Polish matters. Though nominally under the authority of the General Secretariat for National Affairs, they were, in practice, independent.[74]

The competence of these departments was uncertain, and, under the prodding of Moshe Zilberfarb, the first Vice-Secretary for Jewish Affairs, this authority was defined. The functions of the Vice-Secretaries for National Affairs were "to protect the rights of the national minorities of the Ukraine, and to safeguard the freedom of development of their national life." They were "to put in order the inner life of the national minority, to endow its institutions with the character of public agencies, to create for it new governmental institutions in order to satisfy the growing needs of national life and to regulate the activity of these institutions."[75] In the domain of school work the competency of each Vice-Secretariat included "the direction of the school education of each national minority." In practice this meant cultural autonomy, although this was not specifically stated.[76]

Each Vice-Secretary was to establish a national council to advise him; it would be composed of the members of his national minority in the Small Rada[77] and of representatives of various parties and groups. Since the Ukrainian government was controlled by moderate socialists, including the Bund, the Zionists were assigned only one-fifth of the seats. Outraged by this unfair representation, they boycotted the council.[78]

The Zionist complaint was a legitimate one, as is shown by the results of the elections to the All-Ukrainian Jewish National Assembly which met in November, 1918.

Table V

Results of the Election to the All-Ukrainian Jewish National Assembly (1918)[79]

Party	% of Votes	Deputies
Zionists	33.6	42
Achdut (Religious)	15.2	19
Folkspartei (People's Party)	3.2	4
Tzeirei Tzion (Young Zionists)	11.2	14
Bund	18.4	23
Fareinigte (United Jewish Socialist Workers Party)	9.6	12
Poale Zion	8.8	11
	100.0	125

Although its authority was not specifically spelled out, the Jewish Vice-Secretariat plunged immediately into work. It organized itself into three departments: Education, Kehilla (Community) Affairs, and a General Office. The director of the education department was A. Strashun, an active worker in the field of Yiddish culture.[80]

The Jewish Vice-Secretariat defined its educational role as follows:

In the sphere of people's education, the Vice-Secretariat must ensure that Jewish schools and out-of-school education stands in agreement with the demands of the new pedagogy and modern Jewish and world culture. The

Jewish school network must be sufficiently widespread
so that it will be able to realize the general obligatory
education. The great scarcity of teachers which gets
worse and worse causes us to put first priority on the
founding of a teachers institute with courses to prepare
teachers rapidly.[81]

The Jewish Vice-Secretariat requested that the state
treasury grant it a loan of 50,000 rubles for the newly created
Jewish Democratic Teachers Federation in order to prepare
desperately needed school texts in Yiddish. Later the Jewish
Vice-Secretariat received another 500,000 rubles, of which
370,000 was to be allotted for school texts in Yiddish, and
130,000 for setting up a state Yiddish language printshop. In
many local communities the newly created organs of self-
government also aided in an intensive Yiddish school effort.
For example, the provincial assembly of Volyn decided to
open its own Yiddish teachers seminary in Zhitomir.[82]

Throughout the country there were a small number of
Jewish gymnasiums — Jewish in nationality of the student
body, but not in curriculum content. The Jewish Vice-
Secretariat took over supervision of these gymnasiums and
directed that the language of instruction be changed from
Russian to Yiddish. The Czarist government's old Crown
Schools for Jewish children were also taken over and the
language of instruction became Yiddish.[83]

As an overall plan, the Jewish Vice-Secretariat planned
to enact a law requiring all government secondary schools
with a recognized number of Jewish pupils to include courses
in Jewish history, history of Yiddish literature, and Yiddish
(eventually also Hebrew) language in the school program.
However, before this reform could be put through, the "Central School Council," over the opposition of the representa-

tive of the Jewish Vice-Secretariat, adopted a resolution that private schools desiring the rights of government schools, and having a recognized number of Jewish pupils, must agree to offer a rather nebulous course in "Jewish Belief." This was not what the Jews wanted; they were striving for a full national curriculum in their native language. This was one of the rare instances when the government tried to preempt the role of the Jewish Vice-Secretariat.[84]

After the Bolshevik Revolution the relations between Petrograd and the Ukraine were severed. On November 1, 1917 (Old Style), a new Ukrainian government was formed. The Vice-Secretariats for National Affairs became fully recognized independent ministries. Shortly afterward the "Third Universal" was issued, proclaiming the Ukraine a "People's Republic." The national minorities were recognized in an additional statement:

> The Ukrainian people . . . will strongly guard the freedom of national development of all peoples who live in the Ukraine; we therefore declare, that we recognize for the Russian, Jewish, Polish, and other peoples of the Ukraine the right to national-personal autonomy, which will assure them freedom of self-government in their national life. We authorize our General Secretary for National Affairs to submit to us in the nearest future a law-project about national-personal autonomy.[85]

On January 9, 1918, in the "Fourth Universal," the Ukraine declared its political independence and passed the law of "national-personal autonomy" which for the first time established Jewish autonomy on a legal basis. However, a few weeks later Bolshevik troops occupied Kiev, abolished national-personal autonomy, and occupied the building of the Jewish ministry. Troops of the Ukrainian Rada counter-attacked and reoccupied Kiev in a few weeks. Jewish auto-nomy and the Jewish ministry were restored, and, on April 28, 1918, national-personal autonomy was included in the constitution of the Ukrainian People's Republic.[86]

The Ukrainian parliament was short-lived, however. The German occupation authorities dispersed the Rada, abolished the People's Republic, and brought to power a right-wing government with a Hetman, a former Czarist army officer named Skoropadski. Again national autonomy for minorities was abolished. That fall the Ukrainian socialist and democratic forces rebelled against the Hetman and his Ger-man masters, overthrew the reactionary regime and once again proclaimed the People's Republic, and restored national-personal autonomy. But the Bolshevist armies were soon to reoccupy Kiev and all agencies of minority autonomy were destroyed. The independent Ukraine with its Jewish ministry nominally existed until July of 1920 in Kamenetz-Podolsk, but it governed only a small part of the Ukraine.[87] The role of the Jewish ministry in education after the Hetman regime was insignificant. It probably reached its height in June, 1918, just before the Hetman's government repealed the national-personal autonomy law; in a lengthy memoran-dum written at that time it described the status of its work.

The education department of the Jewish ministry was divided into seven divisions:

1.   *Division of Administration.* This division managed the office work of the department, drew up the budget of the various divisions, and kept the records of the educational institutions and their personnel.

2.   *Division of Elementary Schools and Higher Schools.* This was the most important division. Its task was to create a

broad network of schools, give instructions to the local community councils on educational matters that were related to elementary schools, and also to create a network of Yiddish higher elementary schools. The division was also charged with changing the former Crown Schools for Jewish Children into higher elementary schools. With the Civil War, the German invasion, and a wave of pogroms erupting in the Ukraine, the ministry's task was impossible. It made desperate efforts to remedy the shortage of textbooks and teachers; it began to issue aids and proposed a bill to open a teacher's seminary in Kiev and teaching courses in other cities. On January 1, 1918 there were 270,000 Jewish children of school age in the Ukraine (ages 7-11), with 96,000 attending schools under the Jewish ministry. The other children probably attended *chedorim* or modern Hebrew schools of the Zionist organization. The department had plans in June to open 16 new schools in the coming year.

3. *Division of Secondary Schools.* This division was to work with the existing schools to make them suitable to the needs and interests of the Jewish people and the Ukrainian state. It would also create new schools that would operate according to the tenets of modern pedagogy.

4. *Division of Out-of-School and Preschool Education.* This division was to conduct courses itself and to help localities conduct their own. It sponsored 40 evening schools for young people, and more than 60 libraries. It also operated many dramatic groups and musical choirs and supervised a large number of preschool institutions: 14 playgrounds (all of which fed the children), 54 orphanages, four children's clubs, and five eating houses which served 9,000 children.

5. *Division of Vocational Education.* This division directed institutions for vocational education and trained

cadres who would become future teachers in new vocational schools. Many different types of schools came under its wing.

    6.   *Division of Publications.* This division was entrusted with the task of preparing suitable textbooks in Yiddish.

    7.   *Division of Art.* This division had not yet begun operations at the time of the memorandum.

    The ministry also intended to establish a division to supervise the training of teachers.[88]

    In mid-1918 the wave of pogroms was reaching its crest. In the history of the Jewish people only the Ukranian slaughter of 1648-1649 and the holocaust of World War II were more dreadful than the pogroms of 1917-1920 in the Ukraine. While civil war raged, each invading and defending army took its turn in attacking the Jews. The chairman of the Red-Cross-sponsored All-Ukrainian Committee for the Victims of Pogroms has written that 120,000 Jews were killed at this time.[89] This figure does not take into account the enormous number injured and left homeless and the wholesale property destruction.[90] One writer recorded the slaughter and expulsion:

> In 18 small towns where in 1897 22,380 Jews lived, only 34 remained in 1920; in another 15 small towns where in 1897 28,825 Jews resided, only 698 remained in 1920, only 2.4 percent; in a further five small towns where in 1897 12,227 Jews lived, only 2,699 remained in 1920, 22 percent; in a further five towns where in 1897 10,648 Jews lived, only a total of 4,155 remained in 1920, 39 percent; in a further five towns where in 1897 13,647 Jews lived, only 9,503 or 69.5 percent remained. In all 48 pogromized towns there lived 87,777 Jews in 1897. In 1920 only 17,089 or 19.5 percent remained. It should be taken into account that the Jewish population

increased considerably between 1897 and 1920 so the losses are greater than they appear.[91]

All the Jewish cultural energy generated by the Ministry of Jewish Affairs and its predecessors did not dissipate: when the Jewish ministry and its education department were closed, the activists sought new means of continuing their work. They formed the *Kultur Lige* (Culture League), which became the *de facto* Jewish ministry of education. It took over all the schools, kindergartens, libraries, people's universities, evening schools, and gymnasiums that the ministry had operated. Thus Jewish autonomy, no longer state-sponsored, continued under independent auspices.[92]

The Kultur Lige, created in Kiev in May, 1918, consisted of 25 local divisions at the outset. The organization encouraged individuals working alone in isolated areas during the Civil War and the pogroms. Its central committee was composed of 21 men from the following parties: United Jewish Socialist Workers Party, nine; Bund, seven; Poale Zion, two; and People's Party, three. Eighteen were from socialist parties. The Zionists, the Tzeirei Tzion, and the orthodox did not participate. The League had seven sections: literary, music, theatre, painting and sculpture, elementary schools, preschools, and out-of-school education. Every section was independent and responsible for its own work. Shortly after its establishment, publishing and book distribution were added. At the end of 1918 the Kultur Lige had 120 branches. The network of institutions it operated in Kiev illustrate the extent of its growth; there were 12 elementary schools, four kindergartens, a gymnasium, a people's university, a teachers seminary, a theatre, an art studio, and a musical studio.[93]

The Culture League became the pride and joy of all the

Yiddishist elements in the country. The Democratic Teachers Federation, the school section of the Culture League, published a pedagogical journal *Shul un Leben* (School and Life) which maintained a very high level of scholarship. The guiding spirit of the Culture League was Zelig Melamed; the soul of its school system was Simon Dobin. The finest Yiddishist intellectuals in the Ukraine belonged to the Central Committee of the Culture League; many of them had formerly worked in the Jewish ministry.[94]

Despite the terrible conditions described above, the Culture League persevered. Even in Kiev, which was devastated by pogroms, work continued. At its height the Culture League operated 283 institutions: 42 kindergartens, 11 orphanages, 63 elementary schools, three gymnasiums, nine playgrounds, 54 libraries, and numerous choirs, dramatic groups, evening schools, and people's universities.

As the Red Army approached Kiev, the League's demise seemed imminent. A number of its most important officials and workers went over to the Bolshevik side and in later years became prominent in the Soviet Yiddish school system, a very different operation. By the end of February 1919, the Soviet regime was strongly established in Kiev. The remaining anti-Communist members of the Central Committee of the Culture League tried to work out conditions which would make possible its survival under the new power. They were ready to accept a large number of Communists into the Central Committee if they could continue their work, but no compromise was possible. A decree of the Soviet authorities declared the League a Communist body and its assets "nationalized." The remaining anti-Communist members of the Central Committee refused to serve a Communist Culture League and fled to Poland, where they reestablished the

Culture League in Warsaw in a somewhat different form: The Warsaw League became one of the major Yiddish publishers in Poland.[95]

The Jewish ministry and the Culture League never had time to issue all the textbooks they had planned. Nevertheless, what they did publish and use gives us an indication of how the school system would have developed if they had been given the freedom to continue. Although the Yiddishists were anti-traditional in many ways, they revered the Jewish heritage and wanted to impart their secularist version of it to their pupils. The history books they did publish reveal their approach. One text was written by Ben Zion Dinaburg, a leading Poale Zionist and many years later the Minister of Education in the government of the State of Israel. It was primarily a book of readings of Jewish history.[96] Another volume began with the Biblical epoch and went up to the present time, but emphasized the Biblical period.[97] Other textbooks published were readers and courses in arithmetic.[98]

Notes

1. *Bolshaia Sovetskaia Entsiklopediia*, vol. VII (1932), column 98; vol. XI, column 531. The Bund also had numerous trade unions under its control, which conducted frequent successful strikes. See Sara Rabinowitsch, *Die Organisation fun judischen Proletariats in Russland* (Karlsruhe: G. Braun, 1903), pp. 152 ff.); also Ezra Mendelsohn, *Class Struggle in the Pale* (London: Cambridge University Press, 1970), Ch. 5, *passim.* The artisan element among the Jewish workers was very numerous, and this was one factor in the great success of the Bund. The Russian Social Democrats did not trust the Bund for this very reason, for in their view this element was not reliable (John L. H. Keep, *The Rise of Social Democracy in Russia* [Oxford: Oxford University Press, 1963], p. 45).

2. For an interesting description of the old Jewish artisan guilds, see S. Rombach, "Di yidishe balemeloches in russland in der ershter helft fun 19tn yorhundert," *Tzaitschrift*, vol. I (1928).

3. Abraham Menes, "The Jewish Socialist Movement in Russia and Poland (1870s-1897)," *The Jewish People, Past and Present* (New York: Jewish Encyclopedic Handbooks, 1948), vol. II, p. 357.

4. Afternoon and evening prayers. In Eastern Europe the cus-

tom grew up of saying the afternoon prayers late and the evening prayers at the earliest possible moment so people could be spared the necessity of coming to the synagogue a third time. The interval between the afternoon and evening prayers was a time for study.

5. Menes, op. cit., pp. 357-358.

6. Legal discrimination against the Jews is discussed in Chapter I.

7. S. Posner, *Evrei v obshchei shkole* (St. Petersburg, 1914), p. 38.

8. Ilya Tscherikower, "Obshchestvo dlia rasprostraneni mezhdu evreiami v rossii," *Evreiskaia entsiklopediia*, vol. XIII (1913), columns 61-62.

9. Pozner, op. cit., Supp. 58; Supp. 54.

10. *Evreiskaia entsiklopediia*, vol. I, column 835. It is interesting that in 1886, the year before the imposition of the *numerus clausus*, Jews made up 14.5 percent of university students, 10.2 percent of the student body in male gymnasiums, and 8.1 percent in female gymnasiums, but only 1 percent of the pupils in State elementary schools and most of these were in Warsaw and Odessa. The Kharkov educational district had more Jewish university students in 1886 than there were Jewish people in the State elementary schools. (G. Voltke, "Prosveshchenie evreev v rossii," *Evreiskaia entsiklopediia*, vol. XIII, pp. 57-58). Most of the Jewish university students went through traditional Jewish schooling and later prepared for the gymnasium on their own as "externs."

11. There have been several articles and monographs on Lieberman. Two of them are Y. Krol's *Chayei A. S. Lieberman* (Tel Aviv: Achdut Avoda, 1932), and Dov Weinryb's "Darko Harayonit Shel A. S. Lieberman," *Zion*, vol. IV (1939), pp. 317-348. It is interesting that Lieberman used the Hebrew language in his work since that language was always scorned by Jewish socialists — even some of the Zionist variety — in favor of Yiddish, the language of the masses. One historian

has written that Lieberman used Hebrew because of his desire to reach yeshiva students who were, in fact, many of the early revolutionaries (Shlomo Rechev, "Agudat Hasotsialistim Haivri," *Entsiklopedia Lemadeei Hachevra*, vol. I, 1963, column 21). This writer tends to the view that Yiddish had so little prestige as a literary language at the time that no one with any pretensions to being an intellectual would use it. The use of Hebrew did not have the Zionist connotations that it came to have later.

12. N. A. Buchbinder, *Di geshikhte fun der yiddisher arbeter bavegung in russland* (Vilna: Farlag Tamer, 1931), p. 56.

13. Quoted in Salo W. Baron, *A Social and Religious History of the Jews* (New York: Columbia University Press, 1937), vol. II, p. 312.

14. Quoted in K. Frumkin, "Der bund un seine gegner," *Zukunft*, vol. II (1903), 281.

15. *Arbeter luach*, vol. III (1922), pp. 71-90.

16. A Yiddish translation of this booklet is published in *Arkady: zamelbuch tzum ondenk fun grinder fun bund arkady kremer* (New York: Unzer Tzait, 1942), pp. 293-321.

17. Arkady Kremer, "Di grindung fun bund," *Arbeter luach*, vol. III (1922), pp. 95-96.

18. The Bund made the practical arrangements for the Congress which was held in its stronghold of Minsk March 1-3, 1898 (J. L. H. Keep, *The Rise of Social Democracy in Russia* [Oxford: Oxford University Press, 1963], p. 52).

19. John Mill, *Pionern un boier* (New York: Farlag Vekker, 1946), p. 251.

20. Raphael Abramovitch and Abraham Menes, "Di yiddishe sotzialistishe bavegung in russland un poiln," *Algemeine entziklopedie*, Series "Yidn" (New York: World Jewish Culture Congress, 1950), vol. III, column 565.

21. Oscar Janowsky, *The Jews and Minority Rights, 1898-1919* (New York: Columbia University Press, 1933), p. 1213.

22. Mill, pp. 251-256. See also P. Szwarc, "Di ershte yidishe

oisgabes fun der pps," *Historishe shriftn*, vol. I (1937), pp. 112-113.

23. Mill, op. cit., p. 283.

24. Contained in Abraham Menes (ed.), *Der yiddisher gedank in der naier tzait* (New York: World Jewish Culture Congress, 1957), vol. I, pp. 112-113.

25. The Bund was dealt a severe blow by police raids in 1898. See Raphael Abramovitch, "The Jewish Socialist Movement in Russia and Poland (1897-1919)," *The Jewish People, Past and Present* (New York: Jewish Encyclopedic Handbooks, 1948), vol, II, pp. 370-371). The Foreign Committee of the Bund consisted of party leaders living abroad. It served a very important role in directing the party in Russia from 1899 to 1905 (Janowsky, p. 80).

26. *Der yiddisher arbeter*, official organ of the Foreign Committee of the Bund, London, March 1899.

27. Menes, *Der yiddisher gedank in der naier tzait*, p. 114.

28. V. Shulman, *Bletlech fun der yidisher arbeter bavegung* (Warsaw: Kultur Lige, 1929), Part I, pp. 58-59. Quoted in Abraham Menes, *Der yiddisher gedank in der naier tzait*, pp. 114-115.

29. Almost all of the Jewish population of the Russian Empire used Yiddish. According to the census of 1897, 96.9 percent of the Jewish population of the Russian Empire listed Yiddish as their language. This included the Jews of the Caucasus, Georgia, and Central Asia whose mother tongue was not Yiddish. See Boris D. Brutzkus, *Statistika evreiskago naseleniia* (St. Petersburg: Jewish Colonization Association, 1909), vol. III, Appendix, Table V. After the Revolution of 1917 the use of Russian by the Jews became more widespread, but in the 1926 census, 70.4 percent still considered Yiddish their primary language. See L. Zinger, *Dos banaite folk* (Moscow: Emes Publishing House, 1941), p. 34.

30. Interesting information on the origins of proletarian Zionism is found in S. Kivin, "Bam vigele fun der partei," *Der yid-*

disher arbeter pinkas (Warsaw: Farlag Naie Kultur, 1928), pp. 31-46.

31. Part of Syrkin's brochure has been translated into English in Arthur Hertzberg (ed.), *The Zionist Idea: A Historical Analysis and Reader* (New York: Doubleday and Co., 1959), pp. 333-350.

32. Benjamin West, *Naftulei Dor* (Tel Aviv: Foreign Delegation of the Tzeirei Zion, 1946), p. 14. For an account of his life see the biography of Syrkin by his daughter, Marie Syrkin, *Nachman Syrkin, Socialist Zionist: A Biographical Memoir* (New York: Herzl Press, 1961).

33. "Proletarian Zionism," "Socialist Zionism," "Labor Zionism," and "Radical Zionism" are terms meaning the same thing and can be used interchangeably.

34. Raphael Abramovitch, "The Jewish Socialist Movement in Russia and Poland, 1897-1919," vol. II, pp. 388-389.

35. Ber Borochov, "Tsu der geshichte fun poale zion," *Der yiddisher arbeter pinkas* (Warsaw: Farlag Naie Kultur, 1928), p. 48.

36. Z. Abramovitz et al. (eds.), *Yalkutei Poale Zion* (Tel Aviv: M. Neumann, 1947), vol. I, p. 13.

37. Ben-Adir, "Modern Currents in Jewish Social and National Life," *The Jewish People, Past and Present* (New York: Jewish Encyclopedic Handbooks, 1948), vol. II, pp. 306-307.

38. Abramovitz, op. cit., vol. I, p. 15.

39. Ben-Adir, op. cit., vol. II, pp. 308-309.

40. Janowsky, op. cit., p. 127.

41. Abramovitz, vol. I, pp. 20-24.

42. Y. Zerubavel, "Fun poltava biz Krako," *Der yiddisher pinkas* (Warsaw: Farlag Naie Kultur, 1928), pp. 100-101.

43. Sidney Harcave, *Russia, A History* (New York: Lippincott, 1953), pp. 383-388.

44. The emigration from Russia of the Jews at this time reached the level of mass flight: 125,234 in 1906 and 114,932 in 1907

(Liebman Hirsch, "Yiddishe emigratzie," *Algemeine entzik-lopedie*, Series "Yidn" [New York: World Jewish Culture Congress, 1950], vol. I, column 360).

45. A. Kirzhnitz, *Der yiddisher arbeter chrestomatie tzu geshichte fun der yiddisher arbeter, revolutzioner, un sotzilisticher bavegung in russland* (4 vols.; Moscow: Central Publishing House, 1925-1928), vol. II, Pt. II, pp. 196-200.

46. Harcave, op. cit., p. 395.

47. Kirzhnitz, op. cit., vol. III, p. 70.

48. Yitzchak Greenbaum, *Hatnuah Hatzionit Behitpatchuteha* (Tel Aviv: Jewish Agency for Palestine, 1948), vol. III, p. 143.

49. Zerubavel, op. cit., p. 111.

50. Greenbaum, op. cit., vol. III, p. 145.

51. Kirzhnitz, op. cit., vol. III, p. 12.

52. Zerubavel, op. cit., p. 112.

53. Greenbaum, op. cit., vol. III, p. 144.

54. M. Weinreich (ed.), *Der ershte yiddishe shprach konferentz* (Vilna: Yiddish Scientific Institute, 1931), p. 76.

55. Ibid., pp. 78-80.

56. Ibid., p. 76.

57. Tzvi Scharfstein, *Toldot Hachinuch Beyisrael Bedorot Haacharonim* (New York: Ogen, 1949), vol. III, p. 24.

58. Z.E. Kurzweil, *Modern Trends in Jewish Education* (New York: Thomas Yoseloff, 1964), p. 136.

59. C. S. Kazdan, *Fun cheder un shkoles biz tzisho* (Mexico City: Kultur un Hilf, 1956), pp. 324-331.

60. L. Rosenthal, *Toldot Chevrat Marbe Haskalah Beyisrael Beeretz Russia* (St. Petersburg: Chevrat Mefitzei Haskalah, 1885), Preface, p. vii.

61. Louis Greenberg, *The Jews in Russia* (New Haven: Yale University Press, 1944), vol. I, p. 110.

62. The history of the Society has been written in two volumes. The period up to 1885 is covered in Rosenthal; from 1885 to 1913, by Ilya Tzcherikower. The Society was permitted to

exist in the Soviet period until 1929. However, its activities in the last years were restricted to the publication of several historical collections.

63. Scharfstein, op. cit., vol. III, p. 25.

64. Ibid.

65. Great Britain, Board of Education, *Special Reports on Educational Subjects*, vol. XXIII (Education in Russia) (London: His Majesty's Stationery Office, 1909), p. 194.

66. Kazdan, op. cit., pp. 324-331.

67. Ibid.

68. C. S. Kazdan, "Yiddishe shuln in mizrach europa," *Algemeine entsiklopedie*, Series "Yidn," (New York: World Jewish Culture Congress, 1950), vol. III, column 385.

69. Kazdan, *Fun cheder un shkoles*, p. 187.

70. Scharfstein, op. cit., vol. III, p. 25.

71. Kazdan, "Yiddishe shuln," column 386.

72. Ibid.

73. Janowsky, op. cit., pp. 230-231.

74. After the March Revolution the Zionist-Socialists (S.S.) accepted the Seymist emphasis on a territorial solution within the Russian Empire, and the two parties united to form the United Jewish Socialist Labor Party. (Kirzhnitz, vol. IV, pp. 73-74, 86, 126-127, 268-269.

75. Jamowsky, op. cit., pp. 232-233.

76. Scharfstein, op. cit., vol. III, p. 45.

77. The Small Rada, the executive committee of the larger body, was composed of members of the various parties in proportion to their membership in the larger body.

78. Avrahm Yarmolinsky, *The Jews and Other Minor Nationalities Under the Soviets* (New York: Vanguard Press, 1928).

79. N. Gergel, *Di lage fun yidn in russland* (Warsaw: Kultur Lige, 1929), p. 150.

80. Kazdan, *Fun Cheder un shkoles*, p. 433.

81. M. Zilberfarb, *Dos yidishe ministerium un di yidishe*

avtonomie in ukraine (Kiev: Yiddisher Folks Farlag, 1918), Supp., pp. 13-14.

82. Ibid., p. 37.

83. Ibid., Supp., pp. 37, 41.

84. Ibid., Supp., p. 37.

85. Ibid., p. 47.

86. Shalom Goldelman, "Di yiddishe natzionale oitonomie in ukraine," *Yidn in ukraine* (New York: Ukrainian Jewish Memorial Society, 1961), p. 119. Goldelman, who later went to Israel, was a Poale Zionist member of the Central Rada.

87. Ibid.

88. Zilberfarb, op. cit., Supp., pp. 36-38, 41-47.

89. Elias Heifetz, *The Slaughter of the Jews in the Ukraine in 1919* (New York: T. Seltzer, 1921), p. 180.

90. The subject of the pogroms in the Ukraine, while it has not been studied to anywhere near the same extent as the Holocaust of World War II, has been extensively investigated. The "Ostjuedisches Historisches Archiv" in Berlin planned a seven-volume survey, but only two were actually published at the time. A third came out after many years in New York. The three books are: E. Tscherikower, *Anti-semitism un pogromen in ukraine 1917-1918* (Berlin: Ostjuedisches Historisches Archiv, 1923); I. Schechtman, *Pogromi dobrovolcheskoi armii na ukraine* (Berlin: Ostjuedisches Historisches Archiv, 1932); and E. Tscherikower, *Di ukrainer pogromen in yor 1919* (New York: Yivo Institute of Jewish Research, 1961).

91. Y. Koralnik, "Di yidn in ukraine," *Bleter far yiddishe demografie, statistik un ekonomik* (Berlin, 1924), vol. I, p. 134.

92. Kazdan, *Fun cheder un shkoles*, pp. 435-436.

93. Ibid.

94. Ibid., p. 437.

95. Ibid.

96. Ben-Zion Dinaburg, *Yiddishe geshichte* (Kiev: Mefitzei Haskala, 1918).

97. C. Efrosi, *Yiddishe geshichte* (Kiev Vilna Publishing House Kletzkin, 1918).

98. Some examples: Ben-Zion Sidilkovsky, *Far yiddishe kinder: an alef beis far shuln un kinderheimer* (Odessa: Kultur Lige, 1920); Eliahu Spivak, *Yiddish: literarischchrestomatie far dritn shul yor* (Kiev: Kultur Lige, 1919); M. Levitan, *Arifmetishe oifgabn farn tzveitn un dritn lernyor* (Kiev: Vilna Publishing House Kletzkin, 1919).

Chapter 4

The Secular Hebrew School Movement
Before and After
the Russian Revolution

The Development of Jewish Nationalism

THE FIRST GENERATION of Russified Jewish intellectuals grew up in the 1860s. Although individual Jews had received a European education and had vigorously advocated modern culture and education for their people, their number was insignificant before 1860.[1]

The Jewish historian Simon Dubnow once observed that "liberty as a hope invariably arouses greater enthusiasm for self-rejuvenation than liberty as a fact, when the romanticism of the unknown has vanished."[2] The minor relaxation of anti-Jewish measures under Alexander II brought such great hope to the aspiring Russian-Jewish intelligentsia that they rushed headlong into Russian society, cutting off all ties with their own people. Under Alexander II, the most hated and feared of all anti-Jewish measures, juvenile conscription, was abolished, and residence outside the Pale was permitted to those Jews who possessed certain qualifications with regard to property, education, and profession.[3]

The most efficient tool of cultural regeneration was the secular school, both the general Russian and the Jewish Crown School.[4] A flood of young men, lured by the rosy prospects of a free human existence amidst a free Russian people, rushed from the farthermost corners of the Pale into the gymnasiums and universities. In 1865, 3.2 percent of University students were Jewish; by 1882, 9.9 percent were.[5] During the same period, the percentage of Jewish students in gymnasiums rose from 3.7 to 12.5 percent.[6]

The abrupt transition from rabbinic scholasticism and Chassidic mysticism to secular modernism was more liberating than unsettling for this first generation of Jewish students. They were captivated by the new world of ideas, by the opportunity for thought, by the demolition of all traditional fetters, and by the alleged elimination of all religious and national barriers.

The new generation of Jewish intellectuals did not recognize any tie or connection with their own people. Russification became the war cry of these Jewish circles just as it had been the watchword of the government. The one side was anxious to Russify, the other was equally anxious to be Russified; as a result, an *entente cordiale* was established between the government and the new Jewish intelligentsia.[7]

This alliance manifested itself in a number of ways. The Crown Rabbis from among the graduates of the rabbinical seminaries in Vilna and Zhitomir were government agents who even resorted to the use of police in their struggle against orthodoxy. They often went out of their way to offend the susceptibilities of the masses by their ostentatious disregard of Jewish ritual. When the communities objected to these rabbis, pressure on behalf of their appointment was brought by the central government or by provincial authorities.[8] So great was the attachment of the "enlightened" to the government that on a number of occasions they even persuaded the authorities to intervene in internal Jewish life. Thus, an 1864 regulation stipulated that all Chassidic books were to be subjected to a most rigorous censorship and Jewish printing presses were placed under even more rigid censorship than before. Chassidic leaders—tsadiks—were forbidden to visit areas where large numbers of their followers resided to receive their adoration and to perform the wondrous acts attributed to them. This made martyrs out of the tsadiks and had an unexpected effect: their followers came to them, in great waves of pilgrimages. All this only served to intensify the masses' distrust of the college-bred, officially approved intellectuals and in the long run retarded the cause of the modernization of the masses of Russian Jewry.[10]

Along with the great rush to assimilation and Russification there was also a small group of modernists who wanted to reform Judaism from within. Although they, too, were bitter opponents of religious obscurantism, they wanted to remain Jews and advocated a progressive Jewish program that would also bring Jews into European society. Known as the *Haskala* (the Enlightenment), this movement had originated in Prussia in the latter part of the eighteenth century under Moses Mendelsohn, the philosopher who translated the Bible into German and founded the first modern Jewish school in Berlin in 1778, where, in addition to the *cheder* subjects of Pentateuch and Talmud, French, German, and general subjects were taught.[11]

The originator of the Haskala in Russia was Isaac Ber Levinsohn. Along with the other *maskilim* (enlighteners),

Levinsohn believed that Jews could be modernized through the use of Hebrew as a language of culture and intellectual discourse. Levinsohn's most famous work was his *Bet Yehudah* (House of Judah), published in 1839, which advocated a five point program of reform for Russian Jewry:

1.   Modern schools should be established for children of both sexes, and theological seminaries set up in the cities of Warsaw, Vilna, Odessa, and Berdichev. In addition to Jewish subjects, students should receive instruction in secular subjects.

2.   A chief rabbi and council should be appointed to be in charge of the spiritual life of Russian Jewry.

3.   Competent preachers should be obtained to instruct the people.

4.   At least a third of the people should be encouraged to engage in agriculture.

5.   Jews should be discouraged from ostentatious display and luxurious living.[12]

Levinsohn's appeal fell on deaf ears. But the concept of Hebrew as a tool for modernizing Jewish life was to re-emerge in a modern school movement.

The man who actively sought to stem the rising tide of assimilation in the 1870s was Peretz Smolenskin. He worked on a number of Hebrew journals but was dissatisfied because he wanted to communicate his ideas without the hindrance of government censorship. He went to Vienna and founded *Hashachar* (The Dawn) in 1869. Smolenskin's journal—most of whose readers lived in Russia—was one of the leading factors in the Hebrew nationalist renaissance. Attacking the assimilationists in the first issue, he exclaimed:

Let us be like the nations. Yes, indeed, let us be like the

nations! Let us pursue knowledge and justice, let us be loyal citizens in the lands of our exile, but let us like them be unashamed of the rock from which we were hewn. And like them let us treasure and honor the language of our people! Just as other subjugated nations are not ashamed to hope for their national redemption, neither is it a disgrace for us to hope for an end of our exile.[13]

Smolenskin strongly criticized those Western Jews who said that Judaism was only a religion. Religion and nationalism, he maintained, go hand in hand and the Hebrew language is essential for both. Although Smolenskin did not actually propose a program of practical Zionist work, a leading critic of modern Hebrew literature considers him a direct forerunner of the Zionist movement.[14]

The trend toward nationalism found clearer expression in the writings of Eliezer Ben Yehudah. Ben Yehudah later became known for his work in reviving Hebrew as a spoken language and for compiling the first multivolume Hebrew dictionary. Although he received a comprehensive modern secular education in the 1870s and endorsed the program of the Narodniki and the nihilists, he nevertheless remained attached to Jewish culture and read Smolenskin's journal. His first writings were published there, and he corresponded at length with Smolenskin on the latter's theories of cultural nationalism. Ben Yehudah did not believe that a Jewish cultural revival could take place in Russia—its site must be Palestine. He said that the Jewish youths in Russia were abandoning Hebrew and efforts to persuade them of its importance would not succeed:

Let us therefore make the language really live again. Let

us teach our young to speak it, and then they will never betray it. However, we will be able to revive the Hebrew tongue only in a country in which the number of Hebrew inhabitants exceeds the number of Gentiles. Therefore, let us increase the number of Jews in our desolate land; let the remnants of our people return to the land of their fathers; let us revive the nation and its tongue will be revived, too.[15]

People like Smolenskin and Ben Yehudah, and others with similar views like Abraham Mapu and David Gordon, were read only by that small Hebrew-reading segment of the Jewish intelligentsia. Most of the educated Jewish youth had no connection with Jewish matters and did not believe that a special Jewish problem existed. They plunged wholeheartedly into the Russian revolutionary movement, certain that the liberation of the Russian people would mean the end of any discrimination against Jews.[16]

The series of pogroms that swept over the Ukraine in 1881 changed the views of these assimilationists and gave impetus to Jewish nationalism throughout Russia. The Hebrew writer Ben Ami has described how the pogroms affected Jewish students. In 1880 he had sought funds from them to establish a Jewish school and had been rejected. Some refused to contribute on principle, asserting they would give nothing to specifically Jewish causes; those who did give, gave reluctantly. However, when the pogrom occurred the students were the first to organize a self-defense group, and their sense of Jewish awareness grew steadily.[17]

Everywhere Jewish students who had turned their backs on Judaism were returning to their people. Abraham Cahan tells us in his memoirs of a Kiev student who addressed a congregation in Russian, saying, "We are your brothers, we are Jews just as you are. We repent the fact that we regarded ourselves as Russians and not Jews. The events of the last years have shown us that we were sadly mistaken. Yes, we are Jews."[18]

This situation of those young Jewish radicals who initially supported the pogroms as the first step in the revolution against the government was particularly pathetic. Moshe Ratner, a leading figure among the autonomist Jewish socialists, cites the case of a Jewish Narodnik who, wearing a red blouse to hide his Jewish identity, paraded among the pogromists in Kiev. But when he saw that the mob, having attacked and ruined the poorest quarters of the Jewish population, did not show the same hostility for the wealthier Russian classes or for the government, this misguided revolutionary suffered a nervous breakdown.[19]

The Rise of Zionism

One group which arose in the early 1880s as a direct result of the pogroms was the *Chibat Tzion* (Love of Zion) movement. The Choveve Tzion (Lovers of Zion), the members of the Chibat Tzion, collected money, conducted courses in the Hebrew language and Jewish history, and organized glee clubs. In the classic pattern of so many national groups, they pioneered gymnastic and self-defense organizations which they called Maccabee clubs. They had to conduct their meetings secretly, sometimes disguising themselves as wedding parties, for Zionism was illegal in Russia. When the Choveve Tzion held its national convention in 1884, they were obliged to meet in Kattowitcz in Upper Silesia, then a part of Germany, where they elected Dr. Leon Pinsker as president of the organization.[20]

Pinsker, a physician from Odessa, had in 1882 written the pamphlet *Auto-Emancipation,* generally considered the direct predecessor of the Zionist movement. In it he said that

> Nations live side by side in a state of relative peace, which is based chiefly on the fundamental equality between them.... But it is different with the people of Israel. This people is not counted among the nations, because since it was exiled from its land it has lacked the essential attributes of nationality, by which one nation is distinguished from another.... True, we have not ceased even in the lands of our exile to be spiritually a distinct nation; but this spiritual nationality, so far from giving us the status of a nation in the eyes of the other nations, is the very cause of their hatred for us as a people. Men are always terrified by a disembodied spirit, a soul wandering about with no physical covering; and terror breeds hatred.[21]

Zionism as an organized international force dates from the first Zionist Congress in Basel, Switzerland, in 1897. It was called by Theodor Herzl, the Austrian-Jewish journalist, who a year before had startled Europe by the publication of his *The Jewish State.* We do not intend to describe here the history of the Zionist movement in Russia[22] but a few words are in order. The Chibat Tzion movement came into the new Zionist organization which grew very rapidly. Within several years it had become the largest organization among Russian Jewry, and at its famous Helsingfors Conference of 1906 declared itself a political party of the Russian Empire.[23] Several distinct factions and groups became active in the movement. Asher Ginzberg (usually known under his pseudonym of Achad Haam) developed the theory of spiritual Zionism.

He opposed Herzl's emphasis on political activities, believing that it would be impossible to transfer most of the Jewish population to Palestine. Thus the Palestinian colonization could not put an end to the material Jewish misery, whereas a small Jewish center, gradually developing in Palestine, might, with the help of a proper organization, solve the national-spiritual problem of Judaism. He wrote:

> Chibat Tzion, no less than "Zionism," wants a Jewish state and believes in the possibility of the establishment of a Jewish state in the future. But while "Zionism" looks to the Jewish state to furnish a remedy for poverty and to provide complete tranquility and national glory, Chibat Tzion knows that our state will not give us all these things until universal righteousness is enthroned and holds sway over nations and states — it looks for Judaism and a cultural bond to unite our nation. Zionism, therefore, begins its work with political propaganda; Chibat Tzion begins with national culture, because only through the national culture and for its sake can a Jewish state be established in such a way as to correspond with the will and the needs of the Jewish people.[24]

In practice the Russian Zionist movement evolved as neither purely political nor purely cultural; both trends were important. After 1906 there was increasing emphasis on developing a national and cultural program for the Jews who were living in Russia, although this was frequently rationalized as a preparation for a future life in Palestine.[25]

Zionism quickly developed an orthodox wing, inspired by such men as Rabbi Samuel Mohilever, Rabbi Yechiel M. Pines, and Rabbi Abraham Isaac Kook.[26] The socialist idea also gained an early foothold within Zionism.

The Reformed Cheder *and* Zionist Cultural Work

The intensification of Jewish national feeling as expressed in the Zionist movement was quickly reflected in a new educational institution, the *cheder metukan* (reformed cheder). Although the *cheder metukan* was nationalistic rather than religious, it did not eliminate religion altogether. A primary place was given to the study of Hebrew; in this it differed from the old *cheder*. The old *cheder* students read exclusively religious works in Hebrew or Aramaic, but they were studied for their content only. Very rarely did a student learn anything about the Hebrew language as such.[27] In the *cheder metukan* an effort was made to use modern Hebrew for nationalist purposes.

In addition to Hebrew and a program of Jewish studies, the *cheder metukan* taught all the general subjects of the Russian primary school in the Russian language. By such a combination this movement hoped to create a new type of school which, while remaining purely Jewish in character and spirit, would in no way be inferior to any primary school in Russia with respect to equipment or general educational efficiency. The teachers were well paid by Russian standards and an efficient system of teacher training was set up. The number of these schools increased rapidly and the Chevrat Mefitzei Haskalah adopted the policy of refusing aid to any *cheder* which did not give instruction in general secular subjects.[28]

The contrast between the curriculum of the *cheder metukan* and the traditional *cheder* is shown by the following comparisons.[29]

Traditional Cheder

Elementary Cheder Age: 3-5, 4-6	*Chumosh (Pentateuch) Cheder* Age: 5-7, 6-8	*Talmud Cheder* Age: 7, 8, or 9-11
Subjects	*Subjects*	*Subjects*
Reading	Pentateuch	Talmud and Com-
Blessings	Rashi commentaries	mentaries on
Participation in	Former prophets	Talmud
daily prayer	Latter prophets (only	Midrash (Homi-
	in some cases)	letical book)
	Psalms	Pentateuch and
	Hagiographa (only in	Rashi (only a
	in some cases)	few hours
	Chanting the weekly	weekly)
	Torah readings	Jewish holidays
	Ethics of the Fathers	(laws of)
	Jewish holidays (Laws	Laws of phylac-
	and liturgy of)	teries (before
	(occasionally)	Bar Mitzvah)
	Beginning of the Talmud	
	(only in some cases)	

Cheder Metukan

Subjects

Reading	Jewish History
Prayers	Modern Hebrew
Pentateuch	literature
Prophets	Russian language
Grammar	General Subjects of
Hebrew as a spoken	Russian elementary
language	school taught in
Talmud	Russian

The rise of the *cheder metukan* created a legal dilemma. The *cheder* was regulated as a religious school; the introduction of secular subjects into the curriculum put it into an entirely different category with regard to language. The general rule in Russia was that instruction in all elementary schools had to be in Russian. The *cheder* was basically ignored as long as its curriculum was officially confined to religious studies. When secular subjects and modern Hebrew were integrated into the *cheder metukan,* governmental supervision began.[30]

The path to the achievement of a Jewish national school was a difficult one. The Mefitzei Haskalah, with its considerable store of funds for distribution, played a large part in shaping the curriculum of the modern Jewish schools. In Odessa, where this body was controlled by diehard assimilationists, thirteen elementary schools, four courses for adults, and eight schools for boys, had limited Jewish content and were conducted in a spirit of Russification.[31]

In 1901-1902, about forty Zionist and nationalist leaders of Odessa established a special Committee for Nationalization—headed by Achad Haam, Simon Dubnow, and Chaim Nachman Bialik—to work for the reform of the Jewish schools. They demanded that the Society increase the number of hours devoted to Jewish subjects and improve the quality of teaching of these subjects, but they met with limited success.[32]

Interest in Hebrew culture and educational work grew with the creation of the World Zionist organization in 1897. The first Zionist Congress in Basel decided to create a special body to deal with questions of Hebrew education, and the second Basel Congress decided to create an organization with headquarters in Vienna to stimulate and encourage the founding of Hebrew schools. Neither of these resolutions was realized.[33]

The Fourth and Fifth Zionist Congresses (London, 1900; Basel, 1901) also focused on the culture question. They were faced with the first instance of the "kulturkamf" in the Zionist movement, an issue which is still unresolved. The newly organized orthodox religious faction—the Mizrachi—under Rabbi Reines, was opposed to Zionist educational and cultural activity. They felt that Jewish education—entirely of a religious nature in the traditional Jewish school—was bound to become secularized if the nonreligious Zionist organization became active in it.[34]

"Kulturkamf" came to the fore again in 1902 at the Second Conference of Russian Zionists in Minsk, where a compromise settlement was reached. Two separate educational commissions were set up, one religious and the other representing the "democratic" faction, working independently of one another. At the conference, Achad Haam demanded that the Zionists become active in the school work of the community and shape it according to their ideas. He suggested the Zionists adopt the program of "Capture the school."[35]

The 1902 conference had a great influence on Zionist cultural work. The *cheder metukan* spread very rapidly until there were relatively few cities or towns in the Pale without one. There was no central organization to coordinate the activities for the *chaderei metukanim*; that is one reason why there are no reliable figures on the number of schools or students. Because there was no such organization, curricula were uncoordinated and the schools varied considerably. Some emphasized Russian more than others; some used Yiddish to a limited extent.[36]

A former student of a *cheder metukan* in the town of
Keidan in Kovno Province told the writer that he attended
that *cheder* in the morning and studied the Russian language
and general subjects taught in Russian. Hebrew grammar was
also part of the curriculum. The community was rather aghast
to find such modernism in its midst, and great pressure was
brought against his family to have him withdraw from the
school. They compromised by agreeing to send him to the old
cheder in the afternoon. As he entered the old *cheder*, the
melamed would greet him derisively: "Aha, kumt dy di klass-
nik." (Well, here comes the scholar).[37]

The *cheder metukan* movement grew to a greater extent
in the south than the north. The Jewish population in the
south was more sparsely settled, less tradition-bound and
usually better educated in general studies. Their economic
status was somewhat more favorable, and they were better
able to support the *cheder metukan.* In the south, the *chaderei
metukanim* served not only as schools for children but also as
meeting centers for the Zionist youth movements. Evening
courses for adults and public lectures were frequently held
there.[38]

The pupils of the *chaderei metukanim* came generally
from the well-to-do and middle-status homes. A survey of
pupils' family background in the *cheder metukan* at Bobruisk
in 1912, which had then existed for twelve years, showed the
following: 31 percent rich merchants; 22 percent middle
status storekeepers; 18 percent miscellaneous commerce and
white collar work; 12 percent artisans; 12 percent very rich
men; 3 percent teachers; 2 percent other free professions.
The rising Jewish middle class could not accept the old *cheder*
and did not want to send their children to the Russian public
school. The *cheder metukan*, with its modern and secular

outlook and ties to Zionism and the nationalist renaissance, appealed to them.[39] (As has been noted, the Russian Zionist movement was basically the movement of the Jewish middle classes.)[40]

Tuition covered most of the expenses of the *chaderei metukanim*. Deficits were made up by contributions from individuals and proceeds from public concerts and similar affairs. The teachers were well paid; their wages were three or four times higher than those of the old *melamed*.[41]

The founding and rapid growth of the *chaderei metukanim* created a great need for modern textbooks. Two publishing houses — Toshia in Warsaw and Moriah in Odessa — devoted themselves primarily to this task. These firms and others published numerous textbooks on Hebrew grammar, modern Hebrew literature, Jewish history, and the Agadah (the part of the Talmud which explains the Pentateuch homiletically through legends and stories).[42]

With the spread of the Hebrew school movement, a controversy arose over Hebrew teaching methods. Should Hebrew be taught by translation into another language, or by the system known as "ivrit beivrit" (Hebrew in Hebrew)? The latter method had been suggested as early as 1895 by Yehuda Grazovsky in the Jerusalem periodical *Hatzvi*. Yitzchak Epstein also advocated the nontranslation system in a book published in Warsaw in 1901. The question was debated from 1908 to 1911. Finally, despite the opposition of many prominent writers, the *ivrit beivrit* system was accepted for the modern Hebrew school.[43]

It was not until 1903 and 1905, at the time of the Zionist congresses, that Zionist commissions for the promotion of Hebrew schools began to be organized. The *chaderei metukanim* were spiritually Zionist but were not directly connected to either the Chibat Tzion or its successor, the Russian Zionist organization. A central committee consisting of Nachum Sokolov, Joseph Klauzner, and S.S. Gordon was set up to direct the establishment of a Hebrew culture organization, *Ivriah*. Because of the 1905 revolution, the committee could not start working immediately in Russia; it began in 1906 in Berne, Switzerland.[44]

In 1907 one of the great milestones in the history of the Hebrew culture movement occurred. At the time of the Zionist conference that year in The Hague, a meeting of Ivriah was held to define clearly its position in the ongoing language war between Hebrew and Yiddish among the Jewish communities in Russia and Austria.[45] Although the issue was not definitely decided two definite trends emerged. The moderate Hebrew nationalists, although they felt that only Hebrew could become the Jewish national language in their restored homeland, nevertheless adopted a very tolerant attitude toward Yiddish and believed it should continue to play an important role in the Diaspora. They favored bilingual schools where all Jewish subjects would be taught in Hebrew and where the general curriculum would be taught either in the language of the country or in Yiddish.[46] The leading spokesman for this point of view was the greatest poet of the Hebrew literary renaissance, Chaim Nachman Bialik. Bialik was emotionally tied to his mother tongue, Yiddish, and opposed excluding it from the modern cultural movement. In a national contest, he said, Hebrew would win out because Yiddish had no deep roots, no long tradition. Hebrew, which had hitherto been a literary language, was being revivified by close association with Yiddish, a homely, colloquial tongue. It was becoming impregnated by the "living"

Yiddish idiom, drawing life-blood from continuous warm and close contact with it.[47]

A second position at the 1907 conference was that of the radical Hebraists, led by the Russian Zionist leader Vladimir Jabotinsky, who fought for a completely Hebraized school, excluding any other language unless it was taught as a foreign tongue.[48]

Jabotinsky had changed his position on the role of Hebrew in the Jewish school. In 1905, in a published brochure, he vigorously denied the assimilationists' charge that proponents of a Jewish national school were demanding the immediate introduction of Hebrew as the language of instruction for all the subjects in the school curriculum. The important thing, Jabotinsky said, was not the language but the foundation on which the entire educational structure is based. It would be sufficient to infuse a new spirit into the Jewish school: to make national consciousness the very core of the educational system, to imbue the pupils with pride in Jewish history and culture, to instill the conviction that being a Jew is a privilege.[49]

Jabotinsky changed his views over the years and wrote frequently on the subject. From 1910 to 1913 he travelled and lectured all over Russia for the Zionist organization. At the 1907 conference and later, Jabotinsky reversed himself completely on the importance of the language itself. He now maintained that "...in national education the language is the essence and the content the shell"—exactly the opposite of what Achad Haam had been arguing. Jabotinsky bitterly attacked the existing system in some modern Jewish schools where 40 percent of the curriculum was devoted to Hebrew studies and the rest to general subjects in Russian:

A small child, especially a healthy one, is not interested in the national question. Altogether other things stir up his curiosity: why are there no horses harnessed to the railroad? What is the electricity that lights up the market lantern? Why is it warm in summer and cold in winter? Who is the Napoleon that so many people talked about last year? Note down for a month all the questions that your little son asks and you will find that only a small number relate to things Jewish and a large majority belongs to the general studies part of the curriculum. Therefore, the basic factor in influencing a child's mind and soul is the language in which the general subjects are taught. The dangerous thing would be to erect two separate sectors of knowledge in the pupil's mind: one that is purely national in content, Hebrew in its linguistic form, which has no bearing upon the realities of life; and the other, which embraces everything that is of general human interest and is being acquired through the medium of another language.[51]

The Hebrew school movement in Russia was strengthened in 1907 when the government legalized the Choveve Sfat Ever (Lovers of the Hebrew Tongue) society. The name was taken over from an organization which had served as the educational commission of the Mefitzei Haskalah. By 1910 the new society had 60 branches which maintained schools for boys and girls, kindergartens, evening classes, and similar institutions. In the same year that it was legalized, the Mefitzei Haskalah instituted training courses for teachers in Grodno, which developed many of the outstanding Hebrew pedagogues. These courses continued until 1915; during the war they were transferred to Bobruisk, then to Kiev, and finally to Kharkov. Despite the explicit government prohibition on Hebrew as a medium of instruction, even in religious studies, not only Jewish subjects, but physics and chemistry as well, continued to be taught in Hebrew at the teachers training courses.[52]

In 1909 and 1910 the first two Hebrew kindergartens were established in Warsaw. The pioneers in this field were Yechiel Halperin and Yitzchak Alterman. In Russia, kindergartens could be operated only in Russian, but the law in Poland permitted schools to use the children's mother tongue. It was difficult to persuade government officials that there were children in the city whose mother tongue was Hebrew. In 1910 Halperin introduced courses for kindergarten instructors in his school. Child attendance here increased from seven in 199 to 200 in 1914. That year some 70 young women attended Halperin's training courses. In 1911 similar courses were also started by Yitzchak Alterman.[53]

The dispute among Russian Zionists over which system of Jewish education it should favor was carried on in its press early in 1913. Jabotinsky bitterly accused the Zionist movement in Russian of a complete lack of clarity and action in the field of national culture. "Our most serious defect is that we Zionists, as a collective body, do not conduct any cultural work." He demanded that the Zionist organization itself undertake the task of full Hebraization of Russian Jewish education.[54]

Jabotinsky was opposed by Dr. Daniel Pasmanik, one of the leading intellectuals of the Russian Zionist movement, who wrote a series of five articles on Jewish creative power in the Diaspora. It would be sufficient, he insisted, to use Hebrew in Jewish schools for teaching Jewish subjects only. A Jewish youth must learn to read and write Hebrew, and an adult should study his national cultural tradition in the original language. "This can be implemented, but no more, since more than that Diaspora Jewry never achieved," Pasmanik asserted. For this purpose the existing Mefitzei Haskalah would be sufficient. "Cultural work in the national spirit must become an all-Jewish matter, and not a purely Zionist one.... It is impossible to introduce into this field a sectarian spirit."[55]

The question of Hebrew education had an important place at the conference of Russian Zionists held in Vienna in 1913 before the Eleventh Zionist Congress. Jabotinsky urged the establishment of all-Hebrew schools; Joseph Klauzner felt that such schools were not practical in the Diaspora. Chaim Nachman Bialik and Yitzchak Greenbaum argued that more time should be allotted to the study of Yiddish. Finally Jabotinsky's proposal was adopted with the amendment that if such schools were impossible to operate, Yiddish should be given preference over other languages for general studies.[56]

Hebrew Schools under the Provisional Government

The overthrow of the Czarist regime was greeted with joy by the Jewish population and the Zionist movement. *Haam* (The Nation), the Hebrew language organ of the Zionist organization, proclaimed:

> The war of generations has come to an end. The autocracy has yielded. . . . The Russian people have shattered the chains of submission in the midst of a quick revolutionary struggle. In the coming days when new

forms of life and peace among the peoples will be established, the Jewish people will also present its national demands. . . . We shall accomplish the tasks of our redemption in the conditions of freedom of the new Russia until a free national center is created in the Land of Israel.[57]

On March 6, 1917, the Provisional Government under Prince Lvov issued a decree annulling all religious and national restrictions. With a stroke of the pen the Pale of Settlement was abolished and the *numerus clausus* in schools and universities was eliminated, as were hundreds of restrictions against the Jews.[58]

Once these civil rights were granted, the Jews, along with other minorities, wantd national rights as well.[59] The Zionist movement, the Bund, and other Jewish parties began to expand their activities and to organize at a frenetic pace.[60]

The Jewish political parties and cultural groups made hurried plans to convene and plan their new work. In the past, their debates had been academic, since Czarist repression restricted their operation. The first group to meet was the Choveve Sfat Ever society, which assembled April 10-14, 1917. More than 200 delegates participated in the meeting, including 60 elementary and nursery school teachers. The convention was opened by chairman Hillel Zlatopolsky. An executive committee and a secretariat were chosen to establish and direct the work of the society.

The speakers addressed themselves to the fields in which the society proposed to work. Shoshana Persitz spoke on general cultural work; Yitzchak Alterman and Yechiel Halperin on kindergartens; Noah Pines on elementary schools; Chaim Greenberg on Hebrew secondary schools; Shoshana Persitz on future work programs and budget matters; and Shmuel Eisenstadt on out-of-school education.

The convention decided to change the name of the society to *Tarbut* (Culture) to reflect its new wider role. The old name connoted a passive approach; now was the time for practical, active work. Three chief goals were adopted:

1.   To make the Hebrew language the language of education, culture, and speech of the Jewish people.

2.   To make the creation of Hebrew culture the right of the entire Jewish people.

3.   To assist in the development of Hebrew creativity in all fields.

The means to achieve these goals were as follows:

1.   *Education.* Founding of kindergartens, elementary and vocational schools, secondary and higher schools, yeshivot, evening courses, training colleges for teachers and Froebelists, and people's universities.

2.   *Literature.* To publish books, newspapers, collections, textbooks, and teaching equipment, and to support existing facilities in these fields.

3.   *Art.* To found Hebrew theaters, art schools, exhibits, art associations of all types, and choirs and orchestras.

4.   *Public Cultural Institutions.* To establish pupil clubs, halls, meeting rooms, libraries, and associations for athletics and sport.

5.   *Organization.* To organize associations of teachers, Froebelists, writers, and artists.[61]

A month later the Seventh Congress of Russian Zionists met at Petrograd. Its membership was now at an all-time high of 150,000. In addition, there were 40,000 in the Tzeirei Tzion (Youth of Zion), a non-Marxist Zionist socialist party that operated separately from the general Zionist organization because of the latter's bourgeois leadership.[62] The Congress adopted a number of resolutions in the field of Hebrew culture, committing the Russian Zionist organization to support Hebrew education and culture as it never had done before. It reemphasized the resolutions of the preceding Tarbut conference concerning the status of Hebrew in an unequivocal manner:

> The Conference proclaims that the Hebrew language is the official language of all public institutions of the Jewish people; the Convention obliges all members of the Zionist organization to work for the use of Hebrew in communities, educational institutions, and other public agencies; the Conference asserts that Hebrew educational and cultural work is one of the chief missions of the Zionist organization. This work must be accomplished in a special body under the authority of the Zionist organization. The Congress establishes that this body will be the Tarbut organization.[63]

The Zionist organization agreed to take Tarbut under its wing and to underwrite a part of its budget.

Although the Zionists never questioned the primary role of Hebrew in Jewish education, a lively dispute occurred over what should be the second language if it temporarily proved impossible for a variety of reasons to have schools conducted exclusively in Hebrew. The suggestion to adopt Yiddish as a second language over Russian was adopted by a vote of 222 to 123.[65]

Before 1917, the efforts of the Zionist movement in the field of Hebrew education were essentially limited to proclamations of support and intent. After 1917, however, the movement plunged into this work, as Vladimir Jabotinsky had been advocating for years.

Another important milestone in the establishment of Hebrew as the language of Jewish education was the Petrograd conference of the Tzeirei Tzion in May, 1917. From the standpoint of membership, the Tzeirei Tzion was probably the largest Jewish socialist party and it was a major element in the Zionist structure. In the stormy debate on the language of Jewish education and culture, the "Socialist Faction" held out for Yiddish, while the "Workers Faction" and the "Democratic Faction" advocated Hebrew. The final decision to use Hebrew was adopted by a large margin.[66]

On November 2, 1917, the Balfour Declaration, which pledged the British government to work for the establishment of a Jewish National Home in Palestine, was made public. The Declaration encouraged the Zionist organization and the Hebrew culture movement tremendously. Previously they could be accused of secular messianism,[67] but now it seemed that the dreams of Zionism could be realized. The Zionist bloc showed great strength in the elections to the All-Russian Jewish Congress, securing more than half the vote in Petrograd, Moscow, and Kharkov and over one-third in Odessa. *The Zionist Review* (London) claimed that in the Ukraine the Zionists outpolled the opposing parties combined. However, owing to the chaotic wartime conditions, the Congress was unable to assemble, and in its place a National Council was organized in Petrograd in 1918. Various parties that had participated in the elections were invited to send representatives in proportion to their seats won. This served to strengthen further the political position of the Zionists, since the United Jewish Socialist Party and the People's Party refused to participate.[68]

Immediately after the Revolution the Mefitzei Haskalah had called a conference of the Jewish Teachers Union to plan a future course of action. Because the union was controlled by Yiddishist elements, the Hebraists seceded, and, in August, 1917, called a separate conference of Hebrew teachers. This group had 1,500 members and called itself Hamoreh (The Teacher). A. Kahanshtam, who had directed the courses for Hebrew teachers at Grodno, joined this organization and became the director of temporary courses for teachers at Kharkov. These courses aimed to prepare recruits for teaching and also to impart modern methods to experienced teachers who had never learned them. Similar courses were set up in Saratov and Ekaterinoslav. Hamoreh also began to publish a pedagogical journal.[69]

Tarbut was quite successful from its inception. In 1917 it sponsored 200 various institutions for Hebrew education and culture, including three Hebrew gymnasiums (in Kharkov, Baku, and Samarkand), a teachers seminary in Odessa, teachers courses in Kharkov, a Froebel institute in Moscow, schools for the children of indigenous Jews of the Caucasian mountain region, and evening classes in cities throughout the country.[70]

In the Ukraine the Ministry for Jewish affairs was in the hands of Yiddishists who bitterly opposed Hebrew schools. Moshe Zilberfarb, the first Minister of Jewish Affairs, especially tried to prevent the Hebrew schools from operating. Yiddish schools received immediate approval from the government and support from its treasury, but Hebrew schools found it very difficult to obtain official permission to open and never received government funds. Many local Jewish communites, however, sponsored and supported the schools. Only during the rule of the Hetman Skoropodsky were the

Hebrew schools not subjected to Yiddishist persecution; at that time the Ukrainian ministry did not concern itself with the language question and permitted Jewish schools of every type to open.[71]

In this period the headquarters of Tarbut was transferred to Kiev and it was shortly followed by Hamoreh. This was the time of the flowering of Tarbut schools in Russia. There were few Jewish communities of any size that did not have an elementary school and a kindergarten, and a number of gymnasiums were also started. Kiev had a seminary for Hebrew teachers, Froebelist courses, temporary courses for teachers, and miscellaneous Hebrew culture courses. In Odessa textbooks in Hebrew began to appear. In April, 1918, in the Ukraine, Tarbut sponsored 119 kindergartens, 188 elementary schools, five Hebrew gymnasiums, two peoples' universities, three training colleges for elementary teachers and two institutes for training nursery school teachers, one in Kiev and the second in Odessa.[72]

Tarbut was eager to publish and encourage the publication of Hebrew textbooks, which were needed in the expanding school network. Most were published in Odessa by the publishing house Moriah which had existed before the war. Moriah published new editions of some of their works, especially their fine editions of the parts of the Hebrew Bible, and brought out many new readers and chrestomathies. Hebrew language texts in arithmetic were issued by the Blatnitzky publishing house.[73]

Many teachers and educators began to bring out books on teaching methods and the program of studies in the Hebrew school. Noah Pines wrote a program of Hebrew studies. A. Kahanshtam, director of the Grodno teacher training courses that had since come to Kharkov, wrote on the teaching of history, while M. Tzuzmer wrote on the teaching of biology and geography. The Amanut publishing firm announced its intent to publish texts of general studies in Hebrew and affirmed its willingness to cooperate with Moriah in this project.[74]

Many outstanding Hebrew writers helped to prepare quality children's literature. Especially noteworthy were the beautifully colored set of readers for very young children.

The children's magazine *Shtilim* (Saplings) was put out by Amanut in Moscow in 1917 and 1918. Most of the leading Hebrew poets and novelists wrote for this journal, attempting to instill a love for Israel into the hearts of the children. Many Hebrew translations of classics of European literature—for example novels by Victor Hugo and tales by the Brothers Grimm—were also published.

Amanut transferred itself in 1918 from Moscow to Kiev and then to Odessa. But soon the Civil War, the pogroms and the seizure of power by the Bolsheviks made it impossible to oprrate. Thus Amanut moved to Berlin and several years later to Palestine.[75]

Hebrew Schools after the Bolshevik Revolution

The Bolshevik revolution did not immediately disturb the Hebrew schools, but those active in the promotion of Hebrew schools had reason to worry about the future. The uncompromising opposition of Lenin and other leading Bolsheviks to Jewish nationalism was well known. Since the Revolution a new negative factor had been added: the Yevsektzia, or

Jewish section of the Communist Party, whose opposition to Jewish nationalism and the Hebrew language even exceeded that of the party as a whole.[76]

Yet there was still a basis for hope that Hebrew schools would be permitted to survive. The Communist Party had emphasized time and again that while it vigorously opposed national autonomy and national schools, it did not oppose the existence of schools in the various national languages. Thus in its 1903 Program the Russian Social Democratic Labor Party promised support of "the right of the population to receive education in its own tongue."[77] In the new educational program proposed by Lenin in May 1917 and published by him at the instructions of the party's Central Committee, this wording was repeated without any change.[78] At the Eighth Congress of the Party, March 18-23, 1919, schools "with instruction in the native language"[79] were promised. In Lenin's writings there is an item, written on March 20, 1919, at the time of the Eighth Congress, favoring the inclusion of the proposal on teaching in the native language.[80]

The government's actions were fully in accord with these promises. On December 1, 1918, the People's Commissariat of Education published a decree in *Izvestia* legalizing schools for the national minorities while keeping them within the framework of Communist control. The decree stated that: (1) Every nationality of the RSFSR (Russian Socialist Federated Soviet Republic) has the right to set up in its own language both levels of the United Labor School. (2) Schools for the minorities would be opened in every area where there was a sufficient number of pupils to operate a school. The minimum number of pupils required was 25 in an age group.[81] The decree further stipulated:

1. For the purpose of directing the schools of the national minorities, the People's Commissariat of Education will found a special division, half of whose directing board will be appointed by the People's Commissariat of Education and half by the People's Commissariat of National Affairs.

2. In order to direct the affairs of the schools of the national minorities, the offices for popular education in the provinces and districts will set up divisions composed in the same way as the central office.[82]

Although this law certainly limited the right of the Tarbut central organization to operate the Hebrew school system, it in no way questioned the right of Hebrew schools to exist or to receive their budget from the government. Many Tarbut schools were absorbed smoothly into the government system.[83]

However, shortly afterward, the star of the Hebrew schools began to fall and by the middle of 1919 they were in effect deemed illegal. At the beginning of May 1919, the First All-Russian Convention on Education approved a resolution stating that "pre-school education cannot be conducted in a language other than the mother tongue, that is to say the language that the child actually speaks, without taking into consideration the nationality to which he belongs."[84] This resolution was a source of great bitterness in Jewish national circles. The children in the Hebrew school system came from homes where Yiddish or Russian was spoken; there were very few homes where Hebrew was the primary language. If applied literally, the resolution would mean the end of Hebrew schools.

The Second Conference of the Yevsektzia was held several weeks later, at the beginning of June 1919. It declared war on the Hebrew schools and petitioned the People's Commissariat of Education to close them.[85] The Narkompross (People's Commissariat of Education) responded on June 7, 1919, with a decree which in effect closed the Hebrew schools. The decree noted that "the mother language of the Jewish toiling masses in Russia is Yiddish and not the ancient Hebrew language."[86]

On the basis of this order many Hebrew schools were closed and support was withdrawn from others. Tarbut reacted with vigor to this decree, which in effect dissolved the organization. A memorandum was sent to the Narkompross and a large public protest meeting with held in Moscow.[87] The next day Rabbi Jacob Maze, one of the heads of Tarbut and the main speaker at the Moscow protest meeting, received a call from Commissar of Education Lunacharsky, who invited Maze to come and present the case for the Hebrew schools. Maze, the Rabbi of Moscow, was on good terms with the Soviet regime because the year before he had signed a petition, along with Patriarch Tikon, requesting President Woodrow Wilson to send food and medicines to Russian children.[88]

Lunacharsky seemed surprised to hear that the Hebrew schools had been closed and promised to "look into" the matter. The following exchange between Maze and Lunacharsky sheds light on the nature of the Soviet regime and its system of education:

Maze: Now that the new law explicitly states that any group consisting of no less than twenty-five people may found a school of their own, draw up their own curriculum, and will be aided by the government, why should Hebrew fare worse than other tongues? Even prior to the revolution our teachers were enunciating and disseminating the doctrines of liberty and freedom. If you shut down these schools, sir, you will be doing to death those very principles which we fought and died for.

Lunacharsky: I don't know of anyone who is disputing the value of Hebrew except your own brothers—the Jewish communists. They maintain that since Hebrew is the language of the bourgeois and not of the masses, it can have no rightful place in public schools. And am I not forced to agree with them?

Maze: I assure you sir that I am intimately acquainted with Jewish life, and I know that when a father speaks of sending his son to school he is referring to his learning Hebrew, and never Yiddish. As for Hebrew being the bourgeois tongue, it is precisely the bourgeois who makes certain that his children are taught every language under the sun except Hebrew. Our greatest authors, poets, and scholars have sprung from the poor and from the masses. And now what will be the end of it all? Yiddish is being forgotten, Hebrew is not being taught, and the Jewish people will be left without a language.

Lunacharsky: Such a contingency doesn't trouble me much. However, I am interested in your assertion that Hebrew is the language of the proletariat. That is new to me. You do have a poet, Bialik, I recall now — did he arise from poor stock?

Maze: From the very poorest, sir. And the same thing is true for almost every important Hebrew writer.[89]

Rabbi Maze and Menachem Rudnitzky, who accompanied him, were quite encouraged by the meeting and felt they had made a great deal of progress.[90]

The collegium of the Narkompross discussed the subject shortly afterward in the presence of a full delegation from Tarbut. The chief indicter of the Hebrew schools was Mikhail Pokrovsky, the Vice-Commissar of Education, whose bitter attack on Hebrew schools used all the arguments of the Yevsektzia. Before the meeting, Lunacharsky had said to David Mirenburg, one of the Tarbut delegation, "I am the only person here defending you."[91] But Lunacharsky's defense was evidently of little avail, for a month later, on August 30, 1919, the Narkonpross published in its official journal a decree which sounded the final death knell:

1. Hebrew is not the language of speech of the masses of the Jewish people and it cannot therefore be considered as the language of a national minority. It is a foreign language, not one of the languages of the masses of the RSFSR.

2. Instruction in Hebrew in schools of the first level is to cease immediately. The councils of the schools are to announce which language from among the recognized spoken languages of the RSFSR will be adopted in the coming school year.

3. Pupils of the second level who have already started their studies in Hebrew will be permitted to continue on condition that the new pupils who are accepted into the second level will start their studies in Yiddish or another language recognized in the RSFSR as a language of the masses.[92]

Hebrew cultural activities were liquidated in the Ukraine at about the same time as in the RSFSR. The Komfarband (Jewish Communist Party)[94] petitioned the Ukrainian Commissar of Internal Affairs in Kiev, asserting that it was "absolutely necessary to liquidate the activities of the Zionist party and all its factions and all cultural, professional, and economic institutions with which the Zionists and clericals conceal their activities.[95] Attached was a list of all institutions which the Komfarband recommended should be closed. Tarbut was included.[96]

The reply to this memorandum was made public on July 12 in a telegraphic order to the Kiev Commissariat for Internal Affairs. All local divisions were ordered "to stop at once the activities of the central and local committees of the Zionist party and its local affiliates . . . take a signed statement from every active worker that the activities of the aforesaid associations and institutions will be totally abandoned; to warn them that in the event of failure to heed this order the leaders will be turned over to the Revolutionary tribunal for trial."[97]

Bolshevik rule over the entire Ukraine was not secured until 1920. In the areas controlled by the White armies Hebrew schools managed to struggle on.[98] In the spring of 1920 the Soviet power seized Odessa, a stronghold of the Hebrew school movement. The government ordered Hebrew cultural institutions closed and ignored all protest.[99]

The status of Hebrew institutions was somewhat nebulous since they had never been actually outlawed. In January 1924 a group of Russian writers and scientists, including Professors Oldenberg and Marr of the Academy of Sciences, delivered a memorandum to Stalin asking that the government's anti-Hebrew policy be rescinded. No reply was received, but one of the petitioners, the writer David Hofstein, was rebuked in the Yiddish daily *Emes* for supporting the petition.[100]

In 1927 a group of Leningrad Jewish writers submitted a memorandum to Kalinin asking that the status of Hebrew be clearly defined. On April 28 they received a reply from the All-Russian Central Executive Committee of Soviets signed by its chairman Smidovich, which stated in part: "I know of no laboring masses who speak Hebrew. It is a dead language such as Greek or Latin, but if someone wishes to speak or write in it, there is nothing to impede him from doing so."[101]

In 1928 an illegal conference of Tarbut teachers addressed a memorandum to the renowned Russian author Maxim Gorki, pleading for the recognition of Hebrew schools in the Soviet Union. No reply was received.[102]

Despite the obvious suppression of all Hebrew publications, Lunacharsky, in an interview with the Polish Yiddish newspaper, *Haint*, in 1928, claimed that he knew of no persecution of Hebrew and Zionism in the Soviet Union; he supposed that any Jew who wished to could study Hebrew, but no one seemed to wish to.[103]

One place where the suppression of Hebrew did not occur was Turkestan. The local Jewish population were Bucharian Jews, 60,000[102] in all, and were of completely different origin than the overwhelming majority of Russian Jews who spoke Yiddish and had become Russian at the time of the three partitions of Poland. The Turkestan Jews spoke Tajik or Parsi as their native language; Yiddish was completely foreign to them. Also living in Turkestan was a very small group of Yiddish speaking Jews. After the Bolshevik Revolution, when local communists wanted to introduce Tajik or Parsi as the language of the Jewish schools, the Jews bitterly objected on the grounds that these were primitive and undeveloped languages with no written cultural traditions. The area Yevsektzie (Jewish Section of the Communist Party) favored Yiddish which was being used in the Western Soviet Union. The Turkestan Jews objected even more strongly to this, insisting on Hebrew which they considered their native language.[104] The people asking for Hebrew in Turkestan were the Jewish working population and their most vigorous representatives were the local Jewish workers' trade union. A short but bitter struggle ensued within the Communist Party, the main antagonists being the local Yevsektzie Jews who favored Yiddish and the Jewish trade union which was composed of Bucharian Jews who supported Hebrew. The issue was decided in favor of Hebrew by the Turkestan Communist Party (called the Fourth Section of the Russian Communist Party).[105] The following document is a verbatim extract of the minutes of the meeting where the resolution was adopted:

Protocol Extract

From the united meeting of the area Jewish Workers Trade Union with the Fourth Division of the Russian Communist Party (Bolsheviks) of September 14, 1919.

323 members were present.

Chairman — Comrade Menachem Achildiev

Secretary — Comrade S. Achildiev

Subject — The question of studying in Hebrew in local Jewish schools

Decision — The united sitting of the area Jewish Workers Trade Union and the Fourth Division of the Russian Communist Party (Bolsheviks) that has discussed and debated the question of the language in which the local Jewish schools are to be conducted . . . has decided to protest against forcing upon the proletarian Jewish masses the Parsi language which they do not want, and demands the decree to this effect to be abolished before the beginning of the new school year and the teaching in Hebrew be introduced. If this is not done not one pupil will be sent to school. We also find it necessary to warn that no efforts can suppress our efforts to educate our children in the Hebrew language.

(Signed)
Chairman of the Jewish Workers Trade Union — M. Achildiev; Representative of the Chairman of the Russian Communist Party — Y. Tzechanov.[106]

Pursuant to this resolution the language of the schools was changed to Hebrew, but the Yevsektzie did not give up the struggle against Hebrew. When a Hebrew language geography text was proposed, the Yevsektzie brought enough pressure to bear so that the national minorities division of the state publishing house declined to print it. It was finally issued by the Turkestan Peoples Commissariat of Education. The national pressure against Hebrew was so great, however, that this anomaly could not endure. Hebrew was replaced in Turkestan by Tajik and Parsi by 1921.[107]

Notes

1. Simon Dubnow, *History of the Jews in Russia and Poland,* translated from the Russian by Israel Friedlaender (Philadelphia: Jewish Publication Society, 1918), vol. II, pp. 206-214 et passim.
2. Ibid., p. 206.
3. Louis Greenberg, *The Jews in Russia* (New Haven: Yale University Press, 1944), vol. I, p.75.
4. Dubnow, op. cit. p. 209.
5. S. Pozner, *Evrei v obshchei shkole* (St. Petersburg, 1914, Supp. 2.
6. Ibid., Supp. 4.
7. Dubnow, op. cit. pp. 210-211.
8. M. Morguilis, *Voprosy evreiskoi zhizni* (St. Petersburg, 1889), pp. 149-195. This work describes very well the Crown Rabbis and teachers of the 1860s.
9. Chassidism had deteriorated from a great popular and democratic religious movement into superstition. Hereditary dynasties of tsadiks (virtuous ones) developed. Ordinary Chassidism believed their tsadik was a miracle worker, and the rabbis' courts became centers of pilgrimage. For an

account of the deterioration of Chassidism, see Simon Dubnow, *Toldot Hachassidut* (Tel Aviv: Dvir, 1930), vol. II. A very thorough and documented study of Chassidism in this period is Raphael Mahler's *Chassidut Yehahaskalah* (Merhavia: Sifriat Poalim, 1961).

10. Dubnow, *History*, vol. II, p. 212.

11. Much has been written on Moses Mendelssohn. Some well-known works are Walter Rothman, "Mendelssohn's Character and Philosophy of Religion," *Yearbook of the Central Conference of American Rabbis*, vol. XXXIX (1929); Hermann Walter, *Moses Mendelssohn* (New York: Block Publishing Co., 1930); Felix A. Levy, "Moses Mendelssohn's Ideals of Religion and Their Relation to Reform Judaism," *Yearbook of the Central Conference of American Rabbis*, vol. XXXIX (1929).

12. Isaac Ber Levinsohn, *Bet Yehudah* (Warsaw: M. Romm, 1878), Part II, pp. 130-134.

13. *Hashachar*, vol. I (1869), 6.

14. Joseph Klauzner, *Kitzur Toldot Hasifrut Haivrit Hachadashah* (Tel Aviv: Joseph Sreberk Publishing House, 1954), p. 89.

15. *Hashachar*, vol. X (1880), p. 244. Quoted in Arthur Hertzberg (ed.), *The Zionist Idea: A Historical Analysis and Reader* (New York: Doubleday and Co., 1959), pp. 163-164.

16. Greenberg, op. cit. vol. II, p. 160.

17. Ibid.

18. Abraham Cahan, *Bleter fun mein leben* (New York, 1926), vol. I, p. 500.

19. M. B. Ratner, "Evolutzia natzionalno-politicheskoi mysli v russkom evreistve," *Sbornik Serp* (St. Petersburg, 1908), 24-26.

20. For a description of the Kattowicz Conference and a general description of Choveve Tzion in Russia, see Israel Klauzner, *Behitorer Am* (Jerusalem:Hasifriah Hatzionit, 1962).

21. Leon Pinsker, *Self-Emancipation* (London, 1891), p. 76.

22. The standard works on the history of the Zionist movement are Adolf Boehm, *Die Zionistische Bewegung* (Vienna: Juddischer Verlager, 1935); Nahum Sokolow, *History of Zionism* (London: Longman's Green and Co., 1919). A volume specifically on the Russian Zionist movement is *Katzir: Kovetz Lekorot Hatenuah Hatsionit Berussia* (Tel Aviv: Massadah, 1964). A new history of the Zionist movement is Walter Z. Laqueur, *A History of Zionism* (London: Macmillan, 1972).

23. Arnold Margolin, *The Jews in Eastern Europe* (New York: T. Selzer, 1926), p. 38.

24. Achad Haam, "Medinat Hayehudim Vetsarat Hayehudim," *Al Prashat Drachim* (Berlin: Verlag "Achiasaf," 1903), vol. II, pp. 29-30.

25. Oscar Janowsky, *The Jews and Minority Rights (1898-1919)* (New York: Columbia University Press, 1933), p. 113.

26. Aryeh Tzentziper, *Esser Shnot Redifot* (Tel Aviv: Vadd Historit Shel Brit Kibbutz Galuyot, 1930), pp. 155-164. For some selections from the writings of Mohilever, Pines, and Kook, see Arthur Hertzberg (ed.), *The Zionist Idea: A Historical Analysis and Reader* (New York: Doubleday and Co., 1959), pp. 401-405, 409-415, 419-431.

27. A current student of an old-style yeshiva in New York has told the writer that although he has studied the Talmud and Pentateuch for many years and can translate with the greatest fluency, he has so little knowledge of grammar that he cannot form a simple plural.

28. M. Upansky, "Cheder Metukan," *Russkaia shkola* (1904), May-June.

29. Emanuel Gamoran, *Changing Conceptions in Jewish Education* (New York: The Macmillan Co., 1924), vol. I, pp. 206-207.

30. Uspensky, op. cit. The experience and difficulties of obtaining approval for a modern Hebrew school are recounted in

Yaakov Aharoni, "Bet Sefer Haivri Besaratov," *Heavar*, IX (1962), 157-158.

31.   Joseph B. Schechtman, *Rebel and Statesman: The Vladimir Jabotinsky Story* (New York: Thomas Yoseloff, 1956), p. 172.

32.   Simon Dubnow, *Kniga zhizni* (Riga: Autora Izdevume, 1934), vol. I, pp. 384-385.

33.   L. Spizman, "Di hebraishe shulvezn in mizrakh europa," *Algemeine entsiklopedie*, Series "Yidn" (New York: World Jewish Culture Congress, 1950), vol. III, column 427. For a general history of the Hebrew school movement see Avraham Levinson, *Hatenuah Haivrit Bagolah* (Warsaw: Haeksekutiva shel Habrit Haivrit Haolamit Belondon, 1934).

34.   Ibid.

35.   Ibid., column 428.

36.   Zevi Scharfstein, *Toldot Hachinukh Beyisrael Bedorot Haacharanot* (New York: Ogen, 1945), vol. I, p.377.

37.   The modern school in Keidan is described in Bernard Cassel, *Di shtat keidan* (New York: Keidan Association, 1930), p. 40.

38.   Scharfstein, vol. I, p. 378.

39.   C.S. Kazdan, *Fun cheder un shkoles biz tsisho* (Mexico City: Kultur un Hilf, 1956), p. 307.

40.   Raphael Abramovitch, "The Jewish Socialist Movement in Russia and Poland," *The Jewish People, Past and Present* (New York: Jewish Encyclopedic Handbooks, 1948), II, 387.

41.   Scharfstein, op. cit.

42.   Ibid.

43.   Spizman, op. cit., column 428.

44.   Ibid.

45.   The Jews of Austria had formerly lived together with the Russian Jews in a united Poland. When Poland was partitioned, Polish Jewry was divided into three nations: Russia,

Austria, and Prussia. The Jews of Russia and Austria retained their Yiddish language and customs; those of Prussia, the smallest of the three groups, became Europeanized and blended into the Prussian Jewish community.

46. Zvi Kurzweil, *Modern Trends in Jewish Education* (New York: Thomas Yoseloff, 1964), p. 130.

47. Ibid., pp. 130-132.

48. Ibid., p. 132.

49. V. Jabotinsky, *Evreiskoe vospitanie* (Odessa, 1903), pp. 5, 8, 19. Also published in a Hebrew translation in Z. Jabotinsky, *Ketavim* (Jerusalem, 1919), vol. VIII.

50. V. Jabotinsky, *Gola Vehitbollelot* (Tel Aviv, 1936), p. 300.

51. Ibid., pp. 302-303.

52. Spizman, op. cit.

53. Spizman, op. cit., column 428-429.

54. *Rassviet* (organ of the Russian Zionists), April 19, 1913. Quoted in Schechtman, p. 178.

55. Ibid., April 26, May 3, 10, 17, and 24, 1913. Quoted in Schechtman, pp. 178-179.

56. Spizman, op. cit., column 429.

57. *Haam* (Moscow), March 10, 1917. The Central Zionist headquarters published a Yiddish language daily newspaper, *Togblat*; a Russian language weekly, *Rassviet*; and a Hebrew language weekly, *Haam*, which became a daily in July 1917. *Haam* was the only newspaper in Hebrew letters which was permitted to appear in Russia during the war because the entire Yiddish press had been banned in 1914. For a description of the entire Zionist press in Russia in Hebrew, Yiddish, and Russian, see Aryeh Rafaeli, *Bemaavak Legeulah* (Tel Aviv: Davar, 1956), pp. 111-119.

58. F.A. Golder, *Documents of Russian History: 1914-1917*, trans. Emanuel Aronsberg (New York: The Century Co., 1927), p. 309.

59. National-cultural autonomy was supported by all major political parties except the Bolsheviks. The principle of

national-cultural autonomy would certainly have been upheld by the Constituent Assembly had it had the opportunity to write a constitution. (Solomon Schwarz, *The Jews in the Soviet Union* [Syracuse: Syracuse University Press, 1951], p. 92). For a discussion of the fate of the national minorities during the revolution and the Civil War, see E.H. Carr, *The Bolshevik Revolution* (London: Macmillan, 1951), vol. I.

60. Tzentziper, op. cit., pp. 16-17.
61. Rafaeli, op. cit., pp. 72-73.
62. Dan Pines, *Hechalutz Bechor Hamapeicha* (Tel Aviv: Davar, 1938), p. 5. "Membership" had a different meaning in various groups. In the Zionist organization membership was conferred on anyone who bought the shekel, the annual Zionist tax. The Poale Zion was a revolutionary socialist organization where membership involved a much stronger level of commitment. The Poale Zion took part in the joint meetings of the various socialist parties in Russia just after the overthrow of the Provisional Government, the so-called Vikhzel negotiations (Raphael Abramovitch, *The Soviet Revolution, 1917-1939*[New York: International Universities Press, 1962], p. 118).
63. Rafaeli, op. cit., p. 24.
64. Ibid., p. 76.
65. Spizman, op. cit., column 428.
66. Ibid.
67. Simon Dubnow, the great philosopher of Jewish national rebirth in the Diaspora, accused Zionism of being "secular messianism." A student of Dubnow has written in this connection: "The Zionist dreamers, at least for part of this 'dream fantasy,' proved to be wiser than Dubnow and to Dubnow's credit it must be said that he admitted it later in life" (Simon Dubnow, *Nationalism and History: Essays on Old and New Judaism,* edited with an introduction by Koppel Pinson [Cleveland: World Publishing Co., 1958], p. 54).

68. Guido Goldman, *Zionism Under Soviet Rule, 1917-1928* (New York: Herzl Press, 1960), pp. 15-16.
69. Scharfstein, op. cit., vol. III, pp. 42-43.
70. Spizman, op. cit., column 430.
71. Scharfstein, op. cit., vol. III, p. 47.
72. Ibid.
73. C. Shmeruk (ed.), *Pirsumim Hayehudiim Bebrit Hamoetzot, 1917-1960* (Jerusalem: Historical Society of Israel, 1961), pp. xxx-xxxii.
74. Ibid.
75. Ibid.
76. For a picture of the early years of the Yevsektzia, see Mordecai Altschuler, *Reishit Hayevsektzia, 1918-1921* (Jerusalem: Aguda Lekheker Tefutzot Yisrael, 1966).
77. *Programmy politicheskikh partii*, ed. S.S. Zack (Odessa, 1917), p. 22.
78. Ibid., p. 27.
79. William E. Rappard et al., *Source Book in Foreign Governments* (New York, 1937), p. 31.
80. *V.I. Lenin on Youth* (Moscow: Progress Publishers, 1967), p. 211.
81. Tzentziper, op. cit., p. 31.
82. Ibid., p. 32.
83. Ibid., p. 31.
84. Ibid., p. 32.
85. Zvi Y. Gitelman, *Jewish Nationality and Soviet Politics* (Princeton: Princeton University Press, 1972), p. 277.
86. Tzentziper, op. cit.
87. Ibid., p. 33.
88. Leo W. Schwartz (ed.), *Memoirs of My People* (New York, 1943), p. 523.
89. Jacob Maze, *Zichronot* (Tel Aviv, 1936), vol. IV, 12-14. The English translation of Maze's interview with Lunacharsky included in Schwartz (p. 253) is highly inaccurate. For example, where in the original Lunacharsky says that only

"Jewish Communists" oppose Hebrew, the English translation says "Yiddishists."

90. Tzentziper, op. cit., p. 33.

91. Ibid.

92. Ibid., p. 34.

93. H. Freier, "Nit kain shprakh kamf," *Kommunistishe Fon* (Yiddish daily of the Ukrainian Komfarband published in Kiev), July 31, 1919.

94. The Komfarband was the new party formed by the left-wing factions of the Bund and the United Jewish Socialist Party (Guido Goldman, p. 45).

95. *Kommunistishe Fon*, May 29, 1919.

96. Guido Goldman, op. cit., p. 46.

97. *Kommunistishe Fon Yedies* (supplement to daily *Kommunistishe Fon*), July 1919.

98. "Paradoxically, the one factor that prevented the total liquidation of the Zionist movement was the temporary victory of Deniken's forces in the fall of 1919, which forced the Soviets to relinquish most of the Ukraine. Although this meant new anti-Semitic pogroms, it did not adversely affect the functioning of the Zionist movement as differentiated from other Jewish groups. All Jews were subject to random barbaric persecution as Jews, but not specifically for being Zionists" (Goldman, p. 48).

99. Benjamin West, *Naftulei Dor* (Tel Aviv, 1945), vol. I, pp. 145-146. The English translation of West's book, *Struggles of a Generation* (Tel Aviv: Massadah, 1959), is a different book.

100. Goldman, op. cit., p. 122.

101. All-Russian Central Executive Committee of Soviets document M-13645 (April 28, 1927) in Russian, in Yitzkhak Rabinovitch, *Mimoskva Vead Yerushalayim* (Jerusalem: Rubin Mass, 1957), pp. 180 ff.

102. Spizman, column 431.

103. Tzentziper, op. cit., p. 247.

104. Eliahu Tscherikower, "Kommunistishe kemfer far hebraish in Turkestan," *In der tekufe fun revolutzie* (Berlin: Ost-juedischer Historisches Arkhiv, 1924), vol. I, pp. 356, 157-158.
105. Tscherikower, op. cit., p. 359.
106. Ibid.
107. **Ibid.**, pp. 360, 364.

Chapter 5

The Rise and Development of the Soviet Communist School in Yiddish

Marxist Theorists and "the Jewish Question"

THE HOSTILE ATTITUDE of the classic theorists of Marxism towards the Jews and Jewish nationalism and culture presaged what would occur when a Marxist regime came to power in the Soviet Union. This question must be considered in the context of the general Marxist theory on nationalism and religion. However, although both classic and Soviet Marxism opposed all nationalism and religion, it attacked the Jewish manifestations far more ferociously than it did all others. In the Soviet Union today, Jewish culture and religion are subject to greater restrictions than are any others.[1]

Many of Karl Marx's pronouncements on the Jewish

question could have been written by Joseph Goebbels or Adolph Hitler.

"Money is the zealous one God of Israel, beside which no other God may stand."

"The God of the Jews has become secularized and is now a worldly God. The bill of exchange is the Jew's real God. His God is the illusory bill of exchange.[2]

"The law of the Jew, lacking all solid foundation, is only a religious caricature of morality and of law in general, but it provides the formal rites in which the world of property clothes its transactions.[3]

"The social emancipation of Jewry is the emancipation of society from Jewry."[4]

"It is the circumstance of law that makes the religious Jew a religious Jew."

"The Jews of Poland are the smeariest of all races."

"Ramsgate is full of Jews and fleas."[5]

"We see therefore in Judaism today a general antisocial element which has been carried to its present height — a height where it must necessarily break up — by historical development, the Jews themselves having zealously cooperated in this bad relation."[6]

Marx's attacks on Ferdinand Lassalle abounded in such terms as "Jewish nigger" and "Baron Itzig."[7]

Marx never really knew very much about Russian-Polish Jewry. In 1877 he made the acquaintance of Heinrich Graetz, the great Jewish historian and professor at the University of Breslau and the Judisch Theologisch Seminar. A letter of his to Marx does not concern itself with Jewish questions and remarks that the subject matter of his eleven volume *Geschichte der Juden* is "far, far outside your horizon."[8] Marx's attitude to the Jews was summarized by Dr. Chaim Zhitlowsky in the following way: in the first place, the Jews are not a nation but a religious sect; secondly, every religion, including Christianity, is an expression of "dirty-Jewish practice"; and finally, the Christians have no right to deny civic equality to the Jews since they are not a whit better themselves.[9]

Karl Kautsky, the man who completed *Das Kapital* from Marx's notes, and a great socialist theoretician in his own right, was implacably opposed to any Jewish nationalism or cultural perpetuation:

> . . . for the friends of human progress there is even less reason than for conservative Jews to shed tears over the death of Jewry. . . . The Jews are an appreciable revolutionary factor, whereas Jewry is a reactionary one. Jewry is a leaden weight which hampers the stride of those Jews who want to push on towards progress; it is one of the last remnants of the feudal Middle Ages, a social ghetto which still has a hold on the mind after the tangible ghetto has disappeared. We are not entirely free of the ghetto so long as Jewry still exists in our midst. The sooner it disappears, the better for society and for the Jews themselves.[10]

To nineteenth-century socialists, nationalism was an anachronism. The growth of capitalism was putting an end to national barriers. Marx and Engels said in *The Communist Manifesto* that "national differences and antagonisms between the peoples are vanishing, owing to the development of the bourgeoisie, to freedom of commerce, to the world market, to uniformity in the mode of production and in the conditions of life corresponding thereto. The supremacy of the proletariat will cause them to vanish still faster."[11] Of course the nineteenth-century socialists had to make some compromises with nationalism; nevertheless, they regarded it as an evil force that was retarding the march of history. To preserve or to cultivate nationalistic feeling was to be backward and reactionary, as can readily be seen in the writings of Marx and Kautsky.

The Austrian socialist movement at the end of the nineteenth century developed a somewhat different attitude on the minority question. Austria was an empire composed of many different nationalities all clamoring for freedom. To avoid subdividing the country, some thinkers, notably Social Democrats, favored a complete reorganization of the state. The 1899 conference of the Social Democrats held at Brunn proposed that Austria be remodeled into a federation of territorial units delimited along ethnic lines. All units belonging to one nationality would form a national league which would enjoy complete autonomy in its national affairs. All nationalities were to be absolutely equal, and would be assured full rights of self-development and self-expression. A special law was to guarantee the rights of national minorities in the mixed districts.[12]

The idea of abandoning the historic provinces and grouping the national units together meant the reorganization of Austria into a country formed not of multinational territorial units but of "nations" to which every citizen belonged personally. Two brilliant socialist thinkers, Otto Bauer and Karl Renner, developed this concept of the personal principle in their works. All members of each nationality, whatever their residence, were to form a single public body, or association, endowed with legal personality and competent to deal with all its national-cultural affairs. This body would organize the educational system of its members, in the broadest sense of the word, and help them in the courts and other public bodies, where their ignorance of the language made help necessary. It would be empowered to levy the necessary taxes upon its members. Through this system, competition between nationalities in those questions which were genuinely national in character would be entirely eliminated, since no nationality would have any concern with the national affairs of another, nor any means of interfering with them.[13]

The Jews were a nationality that was everywhere in the minority and did not live within a clearly defined territory; thus this theory seemed to justify their demand for national and cultural rights, and several theorists of Jewish national autonomy and minority rights based their writings on it.[14] However, Bauer was unwilling to concede that the Jews were a nationality and he excluded them from having the right to their own educational and cultural institutions. In his famous work on this subject, *Die Nationalitatenfrage und die Sozialdemokratie* (first published in 1907), he wrote:

> The Jews were historically made into a nation because they existed under the general condition which made one. However, capitalist society does not give them the possibility of realizing the conditions necessary for a nation . . . . The new society is putting all peoples into the money economy . . . . Just as it is certain that capitalism will not be delayed and the son of the peasant will become a worker, there is also no doubt that the end of the course of events will result in the assimilation of the Jews of Eastern Europe. Here and there, there may be temporary postponements but economic conditions always triumph over sentiment . . . . We are of the opinion that the Jewish workers of Galicia and Bukovina will immediately recognize their self-interest and will not establish separate Jewish schools.[15]

Thus, according to Bauer, Jewish cultural rights were contrary to the march of history. Capitalism was destroying all national barriers; for the Jews to struggle against assimilation was only to delay the inevitable.

For the Bolsheviks Lenin spoke on the Jewish national question. He labelled Bauer inconsistent and insincere because he excluded the only truly extraterritorial nation from his plan of national cultural rights. Lenin developed his general national theories during his protracted polemical debate with the Jewish socialist Bund. We have discussed the Bund's struggle for recognition by the Russian Social Democrats of cultural autonomy for national minorities. Lenin bitterly opposed this because he conceived of the party as a monolithic centralized unit. Any kind of autonomy for individual units would interfere with the power of the center. His collected works contain many passages where he denounces the national theories of the Bund.[16]

Lenin's first detailed statement of his views on the Jewish question appeared in an article in *Iskra* on October 22, 1903, after the conference of the Russian Social Democratic Labor Party where the Bund had walked out when its demand for autonomy had been rejected:

> Hence, neither the "local analysis" of authority nor the appeals to history can provide even the shadow of a "principle" justifying the isolation of the Bund. But the Bund's third argument, which invokes the idea of a Jewish nation, is undoubtedly of the nature of a principle. Unfortunately, however, this Zionist idea is absolutely false and essentially reactionary . . . .
>
> Absolutely untenable scientifically, the idea that the Jews form a separate nation is reactionary politically.

Irrefutable practical proof of that is furnished by generally known facts of recent history and of present-day
political realities . . . .

That is precisely what the Jewish problem amounts to:
assimilation or isolation? — and the idea of a Jewish
"nationality" is definitely reactionary not only when
expounded by its consistent advocates (the Zionists),
but likewise on the lips of those who try to combine it
with the ideas of Social-Democracy (the Bundists). The
idea of a Jewish nationality runs counter to the interests
of the Jewish proletariat, for it fosters among them,
directly or indirectly, a spirit hostile to assimilation, the
spirit of the "ghetto."[17]

Lenin never deviated from his early views on the Jewish
question. In 1913 he wrote:

What conclusion is to be drawn from this? The conclusion is that *all* liberal-bourgeois nationalism causes the
greatest corruption among the workers and does
immense harm to the cause of freedom and proletarian
class struggle. It is all the more dangerous because the
bourgeois (and the bourgeois-serf-owning) tendency is
hidden by the "national culture" slogan. In the name of
national culture — Great Russian, Polish, Jewish,
Ukrainian, and others — the Black Hundred reactionaries and clericals, and also the bourgeoisie of all
nations, do their dirty work.

Such are the facts of the present-day national life, if it
is examined from the Marxist standpoint, i.e., from the
standpoint of the class struggle, and if the slogans are
tested according to the interests and policies of classes
and not from the viewpoint of vapid "general principles," declarations and phrases.

The slogan of national culture is bourgeois (and often also a Black Hundred and clerical) deception. Our slogan is the international culture of democracy and of the world working class movement . . . .

The significance of the slogan of "national culture" is not determined by the promise, or good intention, of some petty intellectual to "interpret" this slogan "in the sense of introducing international culture by means of it . . . ."

The same applies to the most oppressed and persecuted nation, the Jews. Jewish national culture is a slogan of the rabbis and the bourgeoisie, a slogan of our enemies . . . .

Whoever, directly or indirectly, puts forward the slogan of a Jewish "national culture" is (whatever his good intentions may be) an enemy of the proletariat, a supporter of the old and of the caste position of the Jews, an accomplice of the rabbis and the bourgeoisie.[18]

Joseph Stalin also addressed himself to the Jewish question. His major work on the subject was *Marxism and the National and Colonial Question*, a collection of articles and speeches dating back to 1913, published in 1937 in the Russian original. Stalin's work resembled Lenin's writings on the same subject. One writer commented: "the almost literal following of Lenin's reasoning was striking. Indeed, Stalin's article contained scarcely a single original idea. But it dotted the *i*'s and crossed the *t*'s in places where Lenin had chosen to be less explicit."[19] Stalin, like Lenin, expressed his national theory in general and his Jewish theory in particular as part of a polemical controversey with the Bund. He thought little of the movement for Jewish cultural autonomy: "The Jewish nation is coming to an end, and therefore there is nobody to demand national autonomy for. The Jews are being assimilated." The Jews were not a nation, according to Stalin:

> Bauer explains the impossibility of preserving the existence of the Jews as a nation by the fact that "the Jews have no closed territory of settlement." This explanation, in the main a correct one, does not however express the whole truth. The fact of the matter is primarily that among the Jews there is no large and stable stratum associated with the soil, which would naturally rivet the nation, serving not only as its framework but also as a "national" market. Of the five or six million Russian Jews only three to four percent are connected with agriculture in any way. The remaining 96 percent are employed in trade, industry, in town institutions, and in general live in towns; moreover, they are spread all over Russia and do not constitute a majority in a single gubernia.
>
> Thus, interspersed as national minorities in areas inhabited by other nationalities, the Jews as a rule serve "foreign" nations as manufacturers and traders and as members of the free professions, naturally adapting themselves to the "foreign nations" in respect to language and so forth. All this, taken together with the increasing reshuffling of nationalities characteristic of developed forms of capitalism leads to the assimilation of the Jews. The abolition of the Pale would only serve to hasten this process.
>
> The question of national autonomy for the Russian Jews consequently assumes a somewhat curious character; autonomy is being proposed for a nation whose future is denied and whose existence has still to be proved.[20]

In any case, Stalin said, institutions of autonomy are no guarantee that cultural freedom will be maintained. "Obviously, the point lies not in 'institutions,' but in the general regime prevailing in the country. If there is no democracy prevailing in the country there can be no guarantee of 'the complete freedom of cultural development' of nationalities."[21] Stalin does not mention it, but all of the Jewish political parties had long realized this and worked with the Cadets, Mensheviks, and Social Revolutionaries to bring democracy to Russia.

Thus the ideologists of the new Soviet state all denied the existence of the Jewish nation and assailed efforts to preserve Jewish culture as reactionary and anti-socialist. Their views boded ill for the future of the language and culture of Soviet Russian Jews.

The Jewish Cultural Policy of the Early Bolshevik Regime

The Bolsheviks had no influence at all among the Jewish masses before the Revolution. The Jewish community was highly organized politically, but the Bolshevik party was the only nonreactionary Russian party that did not have some equivalent among the Jews.[22] When the Commissariat of Jewish Affairs was organized in 1918, there were no Bolsheviks active in Jewish affairs available to staff it.[23] There were not enough Bolsheviks to put out a Yiddish newspaper; two returned exiles from London were put on the staff.[24] The first Commissar of Jewish Affairs has written that " . . . our situation at that time was such that we had to place a comrade who did not understand a bit of Yiddish in the post of executive secretary of the Commissariat for Jewish National Affairs."[25]

The official historian of the Jewish workers' movement, Samuil Agurskii, has commented on the effort to create a Bolshevik press in Yiddish:

> The fulfillment of this task was beset with the greatest difficulties. Bolshevik literature in Yiddish that could have been reprinted immediately, did not exist. . . . Among the few Jewish Communists who had gathered around the Jewish Commissariat, there was none who could have written in Yiddish a pamphlet for publication. Consequently, translations had to be made from the Russian. But even translations were hard to come by. Everybody had so much work to do that you did not know where to start. We had to look for Jewish writers willing to do the job for a substantial fee. But no money on earth could produce a Jewish writer willing to translate Bolshevik literature.[26]

The agency responsible for Jewish national affairs was staffed by people so unfamiliar with Jewish issues that they could not speak the Jewish language. Such a group could hardly be expected to be a vigorous representative or defender of Jewish rights.[27]

Given the bitter Marxist opposition to any kind of Jewish nationalist activity and the unfamiliarity of the Jewish Commissariat and the Jewish Section of the Communist Party — the Yevsektzia — with Jewish culture, we may ask why the Soviet regime sponsored such an extensive program of schools and other cultural activities in Yiddish. The answer is quite clear. When the Bolshevik Party came to power it found itself with two and a half million Jews on its hands.[28] The Smolensk papers edited by Merle Fainsod at Harvard give us great insight into this question. The Jews in Smolensk were bitterly antagonistic to the Soviet regime. There were hardly any Jewish party members and only a handful who belonged to the Komsomol (Communist League of Youth). Most of the children still used Yiddish and spoke Russian poorly. A report observed, "In the Pioneer detachment the work suffers in view of the fact that among the Jewish children work is also done in Russian which they cannot master. Completely different results may be expected if the educational work, both among the Komsomols and the Jewish Pioneers, were to be conducted in Yiddish."[29] If this were merely a single statement it would not be sufficiently reliable, but taken in the context of other evidence it reveals why the Soviets undertook Yiddish cultural activity — to bring the Jewish youth and masses to embrace Bolshevism. Another report in the Smolensk papers tells us that seven Komsomol and an unspecified number of Pioneer detachments had been authorized to use Yiddish in order to attract the Jewish youth who had difficulty speaking Russian. Elsewhere we are told that the primary mission of the Yevsektzia was not to carry out a specific Jewish program in the context of an analysis and outlook on Jewish life but to destroy the power of orthodoxy and to attract the Jewish masses into the Communist fold. In the words of a 1926 resolution of Smolensk Yevsektzia workers, "Komsomols, Pioneers, teachers, reading-room and library personnel, leading organs of associations of Jewish artisans — all of these are called upon to wage a struggle against the rabbi, the cheder, the cantor, the ritual slaughterer, Hechalutz, Zionism, etc."[30]

To Commissar Dimanshtein, Communists had only two tasks: the "technical" one of assuring a flow of party propaganda in Yiddish; and the political one of making "the dictatorship of the proletariat prevail in the Jewish street." "Special national tasks" simply did not exist for Jewish Communist "internationalists."[31]

When the Jewish socialist parties split under Communist pressure and a number of former Bundists, Poale Zionists, and United Jewish Socialist Party members came into the Jewish Commissariat and Yevsektzia, they acquired for the first time a number of experienced workers in the Jewish community. Most repudiated their previous beliefs and became dedicated Communists.[32] However, in some instances Zionist socialists joined the Yevsektzia and Jewish Commissariat in order to carry on their program *sub rosa*. In Smolensk, for instance, "the Poale Zionists, instead of conducting matters in such a way as to make the first and foremost task of the Jewish Commissariat the rallying of the Jewish workers to the Soviet regime, had turned the Commissariat into a nationalist outfit which the Smolensk Soviet was forced to close."[33]

No provision was made for representing the Jewish minority in public life and institutions outside the Communist Party; even inside the Party the Jewish Sections were not to represent minority Jewish interests as distinguished from general party interests. Nor were the Sections to elect their own officers; Section officials were appointed by the party and were answerable solely to the general party persons of the local party officials (the city committee). The Commissar for

Jewish Affairs deemed it necessary to point out that even the party's membership cards for the Jewish Sections were to be issued by the general party organization, rather than by the Sections.[34]

Shortly after its founding in 1918, the Jewish Commissariat set up a "Culture and Education Section" which issued an impressive plan of organization and a program of activities. It declared that "the reorganization of the Jewish school on new foundations, the transformation of the Jewish elementary school into a true people's school, the working out of programs of studies that will agree with the above-mentioned basic principles, the creation of a real people's school in the Yiddish language, a school which aspires to develop the physical and moral attitudes of poor children — is the basic goal of the activities of the "Culture and Education Section."[35]

Toward this end several divisions were established in the Section: the School Division was the largest and took on the following tasks: 1) developing a system of Yiddish language elementary schools throughout Russia; 2) working out teacher plans and programs; 3) reorganizing the Jewish Crown Schools on new foundations; 4) establishing secondary school institutions; 5) preparing pedagogical personnel through teachers seminaries and temporary courses; 6) setting up a pedagogical museum and other educational exhibits; 7) formulating the budget; 8) considering and working out a program for student health; 10) publishing school texts in the Yiddish language; 11) issuing a professional journal dedicated to the problems of education; 12) representing the activities of the Jewish Section in the local educational councils.[36]

The Jewish Commissariat announced that a school wishing to receive its support must conform to the following conditions:

1) the language of instruction is the mother tongue, Yiddish; 2) Hebrew may not be taught in the first grade; 3) in the second grade Hebrew may be taught six hours a week; 4) in schools which open from now on, Hebrew may only be taught beginning with the fourth grade; 5) religious elements must be completely excluded from the Yiddish language elementary school.[37]

This apparently tolerant attitude toward Hebrew existed because this was the period of greatest growth of the Tarbut schools and any schools of the Jewish Commissariat would have to compete with them. Given the favorable attitude of the Jewish people toward Hebrew, a complete exclusion of it would have given the Tarbut schools a great advantage. However, the tolerance was short-lived; the teaching of Hebrew was soon banned along with Jewish history and anything reminiscent of the traditional life of the Jewish community.[38]

On occasion Soviet authorities boasted of great progress in the educational work of the Jewish Commissariat. A report of the "First Conference of Jewish Workers in the Sphere of Socialist Culture and Education" claimed that 62 Yiddish schools were opened in White Russia in 1920.[39] This is actually a very modest figure considering the total Jewish population in White Russia.[40] Usually it was admitted that the results were meager but the "White-Polish bandit occupation" was blamed.[41]

Agurskii, the Communist historian of the Jewish workers' movement concedes that "the plans which the Culture and Education Section made were, in the beginning, completely unfulfilled." The reason, he states, was that the Jewish intelligentsia "conducted a fanatical campaign against the Soviet power and especially the Jewish Commissariat. Every effort by the Jewish Commissariat was met by bitter opposition and sabotage by the Jewish intelligentsia . . . . It was extremely difficult to find loyal education and culture workers."[42]

The first important Jewish culture figure to join the staff of the Jewish Commissariat was S. Niger, an important literary critic, who agreed to edit a weekly journal *Kultur un bildung* (Culture and Education), the first number of which came out on August 19,1918. Niger did not last long in this position,[43] and the first issue was assailed by the Jewish Commissariat. Agurskii said, "With such 'loyal' culture workers as Niger we could never create a revolutionary proletarian culture. The first number of the journal was impossible. It reflected the culture ideas of the Vilna *Yidishe velt* and smacked of religious obscurantism."[44]

Beginning with the 1921-1922 school year, the Communist Yiddish school system began to develop. In that year in White Russia 22 percent of Yiddish-speaking children were in State Yiddish schools. In 1924-1925 the figure rose to 41.6 percent, in 1925-1926, 44.5 percent, and in 1926-1927, 47.9 percent. These are actually quite modest figures and it is surprising that such a perceptive and sophisticated observer of the Soviet scene as Raphael Abramovich, the Menshevik leader, could say that "the results achieved in the first years were imposing."[45]

Although the October Revolution and the coming to power of the Bolsheviks were responsible for a great advance in the cultural level of the other peoples of the Soviet Union, they spelled disaster for the Jews. The Jews had had their own system of universal education, the *cheder*, as well as the yeshivot for higher level studies. The anti-religious campaign of the Bolsheviks destroyed them. The Jewish *kehilot* (communities) were officially disbanded in 1919 by an order countersigned by Joseph Stalin, then the Commissar of National Affairs. An order issued in 1921 transferred all synagogues, yeshivot, churches, and mosques to the jurisdiction of the state. This move gave the Yevsektzia a weapon to accelerate the closing of synagogues and the arrest of rabbis and teachers. Jewish workers were persuaded or compelled to sign petitions requesting the closing of synagogues or their transformation into clubs. Religious functionaries were arrested on various pretexts, and religious education was made virtually impossible by a law which prohibited group religious instruction to persons under eighteen years of age.[46]

The Suppression of the Cheder

Although technically illegal, the *cheder* managed to survive under intermittent harassment until 1921, when a major campaign was directed against it. The attack started in Vitebsk with a public "trial" of the city's 49 *melamdim* who operated 34 *cheders*; the accused were convicted.[47] All over the Soviet Union ruthless suppression of *chedorim* and the *melamdim* ensued. The *melamdim* struggled hard but, as one Jewish Communist activist put it, "the iron hand of revolutionary law caught up with them and the *melamdim* and rabbis are handed over to trial and punished by forced labor."[48] In 1922 and 1923 several thousand *chedorim* were forcibly closed. The Zhitomir correspondent of the Moscow Yiddish daily *Emes* wrote:

> On the orders of the *Guboisfirkom* (Regional Executive Committee) of cheders and yeshivot, both in the smaller towns and throughout the provinces, have now been closed. Exceptions may exist here and there in some forgotten hamlet, but even these will in time be shut.[49]

When the State closed the *chedorim* and yeshivot, the believers reopened many of them clandestinely, causing the arrest of *melamdim* and rabbis. Throughout the 1920s the Soviet press reported many trials of *melamdim* maintaining secret *chedorim* and even old Jewish women were sentenced to prison for teaching prayers to small groups of children. A close watch was kept on all former *melamdim*. On several occasions they were forced to sign formal pledges that they would not maintain illegal schools.[50]

Local authorities devised other ways of fighting religious schooling. In the town of Kamenetz-Podolsk, for instance, brigades of school boys were organized to "discover illegal Hebrew schools which cripple the children's minds" and to denounce Hebrew teachers to the state.[51]

American Jewish sources reported that by the end of 1929 about 12,000 Jewish children were still receiving illegal religious instruction and 800 students in 22 localities were attending yeshivot. The network of illegal Jewish educational establishments persisted until about 1936.[52] Soviet sources give, if anything, a much more impressive picture of the illegal Jewish educational system. They assert, for instance, that in 1930 yeshivot were attached to virtually every synagogue in the White Russian Republic. Each of these yeshivot were said to have about 50 students. Religious schools of a lower order existed even in quite small towns. This picture of the extensiveness of the underground network was probably exaggerated by the Soviet regime in order to justify stern repression of this "menace". A few illegal *chedorim* and yeshivot must have survived until the beginning of 1938, for in April of that year a Soviet newspaper published the disclosures of a Jewish boy who had just run away from an underground yeshiva.[53]

The closing of the *chedorim* threw many Jewish children out into the streets. The same dispatch of the *Emes* Zhitomir correspondent in 1922 said that "unfortunately, however, it has not yet been found possible to extend the network of ordinary schools to cover the children from the former institutions."[54] The expansion of the Soviet Yiddish system was a slow process. It was not until the late 1920s that the State Yiddish schools were able to accept all who wanted to enter. In general, in the first decade of Soviet rule, the number of public schools was utterly insufficient, and compulsory primary education was not introduced until 1930-1931. By 1927, 70.9 percent of school-age children were in school, but the percentage varied in different areas: thus 97 percent of children in the RSFSR attended school, while only 60 percent of children in the Ukraine attended.[55]

The imposition of Communist rule and the suppression of the Jewish school system meant that for the first time in the history of Eastern European Jewish life a large group of illiterate Jews were emerging. The Soviets launched a great campaign in the 1920s and 1930s to abolish illiteracy and the Jews themselves worked to combat the trend. The government took great pride in the successful results; but the Communist regime was responsible for Jewish illiteracy in the first place.

The Soviet Yiddish School in the 1920s

In 1920 the People's Commissariat for National Affairs was reorganized, and its Jewish Commissariat lost status, becoming a Jewish Department in the People's Commissariat. In 1923 the staff of the Department was reduced to five. (It shrank to one by the end of the year.)[56] The People's Commissariat for National Affairs itself was abolished in April 1924; its duties were. assigned to the Department of Nationalities under the Presidium of the Central Executive Committee of the RSFSR. No Jewish department was included.[57] This means that Jewish national affairs were deprived of organized government representation and guidance; they were to be entrusted to the Jewish Sections of the Communist Party. However, the Jewish sections (Yevsektzia) were in no sense independent agents. At the First Conference of the Jewish Sections in October, 1918, S. Dimanshtein said:

> Our main task is to carry out everything the Communist Party undertakes to do. We are not a separate party existing by itself; we are merely a part of the Communist Party, the part made up of Jewish workers.
> Since we are internationalists, we do not set ourselves any special national tasks, but only class tasks as proletarians. Since we speak our own language, we have to see to it that the Jewish masses have a chance to satisfy all their intellectual needs in that language.[58]

The Jewish Sections, since they were unable to take any action independent of Communist Party policy, could hardly represent Jewish interests. They were just an agency for representing the Communist Party in the Jewish street. However, even this miniscule recognition of Jewish individuality was too great and the Yevsektzia was abolished in 1930. Describing the dissolution, the *Bolshaia Sovetskaia Entsiklopediia* said, "In order to overcome once and for all the nationalist tendencies still observable in the activity of the Jewish Sections, the latter had been reorganized into a Jewish Bureau according to a decision of the Central Committee of the Communist Party of the Soviet Union. In January, 1930, the Jewish Sections were liquidated at the center as well as locally."[59]

After 1924, supervision of Yiddish education devolved upon Central Bureaus of Jewish Education under the Commissariats of Education of the RSFSR, the Ukraine, and White Russia. Unlike the former Jewish Commissariat, these bureaus had local organizations in the provinces. For instance, there was a Central Bureau of Jewish Education in the Commissariat of Education of Kiev and Odessa. The Bureau was responsible for the control and direction of Yiddish education and for seeing that the Yiddish schools were properly provided for in the provincial education budgets.[60]

The Yiddish school and other cultural institutions in Yiddish grew steadily after 1923. At the First All-Union Conference of Jewish Cultural Workers in 1924 the following educational institutions in Yiddish were reported to exist: Ukraine: 268 first-level schools with 42,000 pupils; 1,562 teachers; 18 kindergartens; 9 children's clubs. White Russia: 98 first-level schools and 46 second-level schools with 18,000 schildren. RSFSR: 73 first-level schools and 10 second-level; 13 kindergartens, 12 orphanages. The total enrollment in all institutions was 12,884.[61]

The development was not restricted to school work but also included extensive activity in the field of general culture. In 1924, in all of the USSR, there were 20 evening courses, 33 reading rooms, 74 clubs, and 405 libraries. Twenty-one newspapers and journals in Yiddish were issued and the Soviet Yiddish publishing houses in 1924 put out 83 books with a general printing of 320,650.[62]

The 1924 Conference declared that

> The great achievements in all spheres of Jewish cultural work speak clearly that only under the dictatorship of the proletariat in the Soviet lands which are free from nationalist oppression can the culture of the Jewish masses further develop . . . . The Jewish culture workers know thoroughly that the development of the culture is dependent on the development of the socialist economy of our land. Therefore all of our effort is dedicated to the strengthening of the cultural, political, and economic activities of our union.[63]

One of the leading students of Soviet Jewry, Jacob Lestchinsky, has written that one reason for the decline of the Yiddish schools was the insufficient number of secondary schools. "It is clear," Lestchinsky wrote, "that upon an inadequate foundation, a healthy building of Jewish education cannot be made." Lestchinsky continued, "We do not know exactly how widespread the network of Yiddish middle [secondary] schools is, but there is no doubt whatsoever that it is much smaller than the network of elementary schools."[64]

The facts do not seem to bear Lestchinsky out. In reality, statistics for one year in the Ukraine (the center of both the Jewish population and of Yiddish schools) show that the number of children in grades 5-7 in the Yiddish schools was approximately 13 percent of the total number of students, compared to slightly over 8 percent in the general schools.

Table VI

Education in the Ukraine, 1925[65]

Total Ukraine	Schools	Teachers	Pupils	Pupils in Grades 5-7
Four-year schools	13,367	24,191	1,168,730	143,555
Seven-year schools	1,573	19,589	568,248	143,555
	14,940	43,780	1,736,978	143,555

Yiddish Schools	Schools	Teachers	Pupils	Pupils in Grades 5-7
Four-year schools	163	488	16,473	
Seven-year schools	86	884	23,001	5,441
	249	1,372	39,474	5,441

In 1925 the percentage of Jewish children studying in Yiddish schools was 41.6 in White Russia, 36.7 in the Ukraine, and 7.2 in the RSFSR. In 1926 there was a total of 800 schools with 110,000 pupils in all of the U.S.S.R. There were seven technicums and 12 trade schools conducted in Yiddish.[66]

In 1928 when the Second All-Union Conference of Jewish Culture Workers assembled, the network of Yiddish educational and cultural institutions had doubled from the figure of four years before. There were 129 kindergartens with 7,215 children; 513 first-level schools with 40,492 pupils; 275 second-level schools with 80,423 pupils; 66 children's homes; 53 trade and factory schools with 5,123 pupils; 8 pedagogical technicums with 2,313 students; and 9 Yiddish divisions of higher schools. The entire educational network consisted of 1,053 institutions which, outside of the children's homes and institutions of higher learning, enrolled 136,670 pupils.

General cultural development also increased at a rapid pace. In 1928 there were 276 schools for the eradication of illiteracy, 54 evening courses, 226 clubs, 182 reading rooms, and 356 libraries. There were 42 Yiddish newspapers and journals (double the 1924 figure) and 238 Yiddish books published with a printing of 875,000 copies, a threefold increase from 1924. There were Republic State theatres in Yiddish in Moscow, Minsk, and Kharkov, and a variety of regional Yiddish theatres.

The development continued for the next few years. In 1932 the total number of preschool institutions had almost doubled, rising from 129 to 226. However, this does not include the many hundreds of seasonal kindergartens and playgrounds that were opened every summer in the Jewish national districts and villages. The number of first-level schools had grown from 523 to 887; second-level schools, from 275 to 316. The entire network had increased from 927 to 1,469, with 160,000 pupils on all levels.[67]

The Development of Higher Education in Yiddish

The system of technicums and professional schools in Yiddish was extensive. One writer gives the following list for the Ukraine alone:

Table VII

Yiddish Technicums and Professional Schools in the Ukraine[68]

Type of Institution	Total Institutions	Total Students
Yid. Sectors, by the Inst. of Social Education	3	595
Yid. Sectors, by the Inst. of Vocational Education	2	246
Yid. Sectors, by Physical and Chemical Inst.	1	292
Yid. Sector of Communist Univ. of Artiam	1	70
Yid. Sector, by Communist Inst. of Journalism	1	20
Transportation schools	2	230
Stalin Agricultural Inst.	1	400
Yid. Pedagogical Inst.	3	805
Yid. Industrial Technicums	16	7,970
Yid. Sector of General Industrial Technicums	8	900
Yid. Agricultural Technicums	4	967
Yid. General Agricultural Technicums	5	502
	47	12,997

In White Russia there were nine trade schools, two industrial technicums, one agricultural technicum, one agricultural school, four Yiddish sections of evening rabfaks (workers' faculties), six Yiddish sections of day-session rab-faks, a Yiddish section of the pedagogical institute in Vitebsk, a Yiddish section of the Minsk Higher Pedagogical Institute, a Yiddish section of the preschool technicum, two pedagogical technicums, and the Yiddish section of the pedagogical faculty of the White Russian State University at Minsk.[69]

In the RSFSR there were a theater technicum in Moscow, a Yiddish medical technicum, an art technicum, a political enlightenment technicum, and a Yiddish section of a book and newspaper printing technicum.[70]

There were two Jewish state museums: the All-Ukrainian Jewish Museum (in Odessa) named for Mendele Mocher Sforim, and the White Russian Jewish Museum (in Minsk). Jewish sections also existed in a number of city museums at Poltava, Zhitomir, Uman, and several other places.[71]

One of the most important institutions in the Yiddish educational system was the Jewish Section of the Pedagogical Faculty of the White Russian State University at Minsk.[72] Established at the same time as the rest of the university on December 30, 1921, it consisted of four divisions — social-historical, literary-linguistic, physics-mathematics, and natural science — which prepared specialists to teach in second-level schools. Its importance derived from its being the highest level of school in Yiddish in the Soviet Union and the training center for secondary school teachers.

Subjects taught in the Jewish Section included dialectical materialism; Leninism; political economy; history of the Jews in Poland, Lithuania, the Ukraine, and White Russia; economic history of the Jews in Russia; history of pedagogy; history of social movements among Jews; Jewish folklore; pedagogy; modern Yiddish literature; history of the Yiddish language; Yiddish dialectology; introduction to German linguistic science; introduction to Semitic linguistic science; methods of teaching language and literature; economic politics of the USSR; history of Russia in the epoch of imperialist war and proletarian revolution; physics; methods of teaching mathematics; analytical geometry; methods of teaching natural science; inorganic chemistry; differential calculus; and practice teaching. Entrance examinations to the Jewish Section were conducted in Yiddish.

The Section's 201 students were divided as follows: literary-linguistic, 58; social historical, 43; natural science, 62; physics-mathematics, 38. Two assisting institutions operated along with the Jewish Section — a seven year model school where the students did their practice teaching, and a special library on Jewish affairs possessing 1,650 books on Jewish history and literature; Yiddish, German, and Semitic linguistic science; and art.[73]

The Smolensk Yiddish Pedagogical Technicum was one of the oldest Yiddish technicums in the Soviet Union. Situated in Homel, from 1921 to 1929 it was transferred to the center of the Western district — Smolensk — in 1929 and occupied a large three-story building. Of the 200 students in the technicum, 64 percent were women. Most of the students were children of farmers and workers who had been prepared for entrance by a special course. The staff consisted of 16 lecturers, 14 of whom had higher education. A model school was attached to the technicum. By 1934 the technicum had 500 graduates who were teaching in Yiddish schools all over the Soviet Union.[74]

The Kharkov Yiddish machine-building technicum twice won prizes in an All-Union competition for the best technicum. By 1934 it had graduated 200 technicians who held responsible posts in various Soviet machine-building factories. The pedagogical staff numbered 32, mostly engineers working in Kharkov factories.[75]

Although there is much indirect evidence in Soviet and other sources regarding the decline of the school system, no statistics were ever published in the Soviet Union. In 1941 Zelik Akselrod, a Yiddish poet from Minsk, visited Vilna and Kovno, the leading Lithuanian cities and traditional centers of Jewish culture, which had just been incorporated into the Soviet Union. At a meeting with writers and local Jewish public figures he revealed that the Yiddish schools within the former borders of the USSR had been closed down. Akselrod claimed that within the new territories attempts would be made to close down the Yiddish schools; only categorical demands by parents for the continuation of Jewish education for their children could prevent the shutdowns. Shortly after his return to Minsk, Akselrod was imprisoned and then shot in June, 1941 because of propaganda on behalf of Jewish nationalism.[76]

Among the most important institutions of scholarship for Soviet Jews were the Jewish divisions of the White Russian and Ukrainian Academies of Sciences. In White Russia the Jewish division, a part of the Academy[77] from its founding on November 4, 1924, published a number of journals and research projects that represent the high water mark of Soviet Jewish scholarship.[78]

The Jewish Division of the Ukrainian Academy of Sciences at Kiev was not organized until 1926, and did not begin its formal work until 1928.[79] By the early 1930s, it had a staff of 100 and a budget of 650,000 rubles furnished by the Ukrainian government.[80] Its work was divided into eight sections: historical, social-economic, pedagogical, literary, linguistic, ethnographic, bibliographic, and Birobidjan knowledge. The historical section was devoted to the history of Ukrainian Jewry, which is, in a sense, a somewhat narrow topic, because it is questionable if the history of the Jews in the Ukraine is independent of the history of the Jews in Russia or the rest of Eastern Europe.[81] An unpublished manuscript written in the late 1920s lists the four main projects of the historical section as economic life and activities of the Jews in the context of the economic history of the Ukraine; social-political history of Ukrainian Jewry; history of the revolutionary movement among the Jewish proletariat, and the cultural history of Ukrainian Jewry.[82]

The pedagogical section turned out such works in Yiddish as Gorochov and Reznik's *The Polytechnical School According to Marx-Engels-Lenin; Struggle on Two Fronts in Pedagogy: A Collection; The Work of Study in School: A Collection; Knowledge of Society in School*, and various other books on methods of teaching and organizations of school work.[83]

Another important aspect of the work of the Institute was its aspirant program, a graduate school. Usually, when higher education in Yiddish in the Soviet Union is described, this program is omitted, but its importance was considerable: it was the highest level institution in the Soviet Union conducting its work in Yiddish which offered degrees.[84]

The graduate program began slowly in the late 1920s; there were few applicants since there were few graduates of higher schools in Yiddish. (In 1928, only 30 percent of the aspirants had completed higher education at the time of their admission; but by 1933 100 percent had.[85]) Until 1931 the work was poorly organized — there was no systematic direction of the students according to regular programs and most of them studied on their own. In 1931 things improved: the pedagogical section adopted an organized plan of study, as did the literary section in 1932 and the rest in 1933. A special section to supervise the aspirant program in all sections was set up. Many of the aspirant program graduates became leaders in educational and scholarly work in Yiddish language institutions in the Soviet Union.

A source of embarrassment and regret in the Soviet literature on the Kiev Institute was that, initially, few incoming aspirants were from working class backgrounds or were members of the Communist Party or Komsomol. Only 18 percent were workers' children; 40 percent were party members. Of the students admitted in the latter part of the program's existence, however, 30 percent were from working-class homes and 50 percent were party members.[86]

An issue of the Yiddish language journal of the Ukrainian Academy of Sciences gives a detailed description of a dissertation defense of a student who was finishing the aspirant program in the literature section of the Institute for Jewish Proletarian Culture. The aspirant, Alexander Pomerantz, had written a thesis entitled "Proletarian Pen: Studies and Material on the History of the Struggle for Proletarian Literature in America." The defense was on July 25, 1935.[87] After a vigorous examination the examining committee accepted the dissertation and conferred the degree of Candidate of Sciences upon Pomerantz in the following resolution:

Comrade Pomerantz has made known through his dissertation "Proletarian Pen" that he possesses the Marxist-Leninist method of literary investigation and that he has himself mastered the great amount of factual material of his theme. He has written his dissertation in good literary language and with lively form. The examining committee recognizes that Comrade Pomerantz has earned the title of Candidate of Sciences in Yiddish literature and will recommend to the presidium of the Academy that it should ratify this decision.[88]

Shortly afterwards the Yiddish divisions at Kiev and Minsk were both closed down and the scholars imprisoned and shot.

Yiddish Schools in the 1930s

Because regular and systematic statistics were not published on the number of students in the Yiddish schools in the various republics, tables must be pieced together from various sources. Table VIII lists the schools and students for White Russia.

Table VIII

Yiddish Schools in White Russia[89]

Year (Ending in August)	Number of Schools	Number of Pupils	% of Yiddish Speaking Children in Yiddish Schools
1922	106	10,475	22.0
1923	98	12,241	—
1924	—	—	—
1925	140	19,085	41.6
1926	175	22,535	44.5
1927	184	24,073	47.9
1928	190	26,020	54.6
1929	—	—	56.0

1930	209	28,310	—
1931	262	31,340	62.3
1932	334	33,398	64.0
1933	339	36,501	—

No official statistics were published after 1933. In 1937, *Emes*, the central Yiddish daily in Moscow, mentioned that there were 30,000 pupils in the Yiddish schools in White Russia.[90]

Statistics for the Ukraine are even scarcer and less complete. Table IX is put together from many different sources, some contradictory.

Table IX

Yiddish Schools in the Ukraine[91]

Year	Schools	Pupils
1924	268	42,000
1925	—	—
1926	—	58,384
1927	—	69, 69
1928	668	79,000
1929	—	—
190	996	83,414
1931	1,096	94,872
1932	—	—
1933	—	—
1934	—	85,489
1935	—	73,412

The RSFSR had relatively few Yiddish schools; most were located in the traditional areas of Jewish settlement. In Czarist times most of the territory that later became the

RSFSR was outside the Pale of Settlement. The Jews who lived outside the Pale were generally more Russified and did not send their children to Yiddish schools. Table X gives the statistics, to the extent they are available, for attendance in Yiddish schools.

Table X

Yiddish Schools in the RSFSR[92]

Year	Schools	Pupils
1923	83	10,000
1924	83	12,884
1925	—	—
1926	118	12,193
1927	—	6,315
1928	129	—
1929	—	—
1930	—	—
1931	110	11,000

Regional school figures for the RSFSR show the relationship between attendance in the Yiddish schools and the traditional pattern of Jewish settlement. In the western provinces of the RSFSR where there were many towns of the former Pale with compact Jewish settlements, 18.4 percent of the Jewish children attended Yiddish schools in 1926. In the central part of the Republic, only four percent of Jewish children attended Yiddish schools; in the Asian part, 5.3 percent did, and in the Crimea 4.8 percent.[93] The latter three were areas of more recent settlement. After 1926 an intensive effort at Jewish agricultural settlement in the Crimea took place and the number of Yiddish schools increased.[94] The large drop in the total number of pupils from 1926 to 1927 is probably attributable to the fact that the city and district of Gomel, a center of traditional Jewish life, was transferred to White Russia in 1926.[95]

Soviet writers on the subject of Yiddish schools in the USSR took pains to point out the supposedly great achievements of the Communist regime's Yiddish schools, both in comparison with what had existed previously, and what existed during the interwar period in Poland, the twin center of Eastern Jewry. Thus S. Klitenik wrote that "the rapid growth of the Yiddish schools continues. . . . It is quite superfluous to point out that not one highly developed capitalist land could point out such a thing to us . . . . We are creating a Soviet revolutionary proletarian Jewish culture which is rapidly expanding."[96]

At the First Conference of Jewish Culture Workers in 1924, a resolution was adopted declaring that "the great achievements in all spheres of Jewish cultural work speak convincingly, therefore, that only with the dictatorship of the proletariat in the Soviet lands which are free from the yoke of national persecution can the culture of the Jewish masses develop."[97]

P. Rosenfeld, a writer on Jewish cultural problems, said:

> The kind of land we should not have is told in the persecution and discrimination that exists with the Jewish national minority in Poland. The total of schools for the Jewish working population is insignificant and these schools are supported by collected money since the budget of the capitalist ministry of education does not include funds for the support of national minority

schools. The Jewish school is particularly persecuted by the fascist school inspectors of the patriotic intelligentsia. . . . Polish fascism builds cheders and disperses schools. In Poland more than 300,000 children are packed into cheders. 300,000 in cheders and only 24,000 in schools. This is the kind of culture that Polish fascism gives the Jewish working class.[98]

In the impressive collection of articles on socio-economic results of the October Revolution in White Russia in 1932, I. Dardak compared the Soviet Yiddish schools and the Jewish schools of Poland:

Ours: The national minority schools are state schools, fully recognized, and have the same rights and resources as the general schools.

Theirs: The national minority schools are private schools and are supported by charitable societies and philanthropists and are not included in the national school network. They have no rights.

Ours: Equality of languages. All levels of study are conducted in the mother tongue (Yiddish) beginning with the preschool and ending in the higher school.

Theirs: Compulsory Polonization. General studies must be conducted in Polish, the only language recognized by the State.

Ours: A growth in culture.

Theirs: A crisis, a collapse of culture.[99]

The above writers boasted of great achievements; yet, in comparison with the schools of other national minorities in the Soviet Union, the number of Yiddish language schools is surprisingly small. Table XI gives the percentages of the children of nine national minorities who are attending schools in their own native languages.

Table XI

Children of Nine Soviet National Minorities Attending Schools in Their Native Languages on December 15, 1927[100]

Nationality	In Nat'l Lang. (%)	In Two Lang., Nat'l & Other (%)	Russian (%)	Other (%)
Germans				
In Volga Republic	98.2	0.5	1.3	0.0
In Russian Federation	84.2	5.0	10.5	0.3
In Ukraine	84.6	4.7	3.6	7.1
Georgians				
In Transcaucasus	98.1	1.1	0.6	0.2
Ukrainians				
In Ukraine	93.9	3.5	2.4	0.2
Belorussians				
In Belorussia	90.2	7.3	2.2	0.3
Armenians				
In Transcaucasus	88.3	1.9	5.0	4.8
Kazakhs				
In Kazakh Republic	89.1	6.0	4.0	0.9
In Russian Federation	88.6	5.9	4.4	1.1
Kirgizians				
In Kirgiz Republic	94.9	—	1.3	3.8
In Russian Federation	90.5	0.2	4.6	4.7
Poles				
In Ukraine	45.7	6.6	3.9	43.8
In Belorussia	47.4	0.8	2.4	49.4
In Russian Federation	4.5	1.4	92.5	1.6
Jews				
In Ukraine	49.6	3.4	19.6	27.4
In Belorussia	55.5	1.6	11.5	31.4
In Russian Federation	8.0	3.1	86.6	2.3
In Crimean Auton. Rep.	10.0	9.7	78.4	1.9

In the areas of traditional Jewish settlement only about half of the Jewish children attended the Yiddish language school. In the RSFSR there were only eight percent in Yiddish schools and, as we have shown above, most of these were in the western provinces. In the other republics of the USSR there were few Jews and almost no Yiddish schools. Other minority nationalities, in contrast, attended schools in their native language to a very great extent. Volga Germans attended German language schools, not only in their own republic, but also in areas where they were a much smaller proportion of the population.

A word is in order here about the invidious comparison made between Yiddish schools in the Soviet Union and Jewish education in Poland to the disadvantage of the latter. The Polish government did in truth discriminate against minorities and singled out the Jews for special persecution. According to the Minorities Treaty, The Little Treaty of Versailles, between Poland and the Principal Allied and Associated Powers, signed at Versailles on June 28, 1919, Poland pledged to open schools where instruction was carried on in the language of the minority nationality. Although schools were opened for other minorities not one government Yiddish or Hebrew school was ever opened, nor was government support given to the privately operated Jewish schools. Some municipalities, especially those whose governing bodies were under socialist control, did furnish limited support, but this was entirely eliminated by the mid-1930s.[101] Many other difficulties were placed in the way of the Jewish schools: they were often denied permission to open, their graduates were not recognized, there was interference with the curriculum.[102] Nevertheless, the total enrollment in the various types of Jewish schools in the 1930s was approximately 227,000, 42 percent higher than the highest total of the Yiddish schools in the Soviet Union, 160,000.[103] The Jewish population of Poland was 15 percent larger than the Jewish population of the USSR. However, the 160,000 total was only reached in the Soviet Union in the early 1930s. In the 1920s it was considerably smaller and, as we shall see later, it fell drastically in the late 1930s. In Poland the number of pupils in Jewish schools was much more constant.

It is curious that the Soviet description of the poor status of Jewish education elsewhere does not include the Baltic republics of Lithuania, Latvia and Estonia. The Jewish population there was no different from the Jewish population of Vilna, Grodno, Bialystok, Minsk, Vitebsk, Mohilev, Pinsk, Gomel, or any other Eastern European Jewish city or town. The reason for the omission is that the educational situation of the Jews there was excellent. Most of the Jews went to Hebrew or Yiddish schools. The schools were government-supported and there was relatively little interference with their internal operation.[104]

The achievements of the Yiddish schools were much less impressive than some avid publicists claimed, but they did expand considerably in the 1920s and early 1930s. One reason for this expansion was a policy of compulsory attendance in Yiddish schools for Yiddish-speaking children in many areas. Compulsory Yiddishization existed for two reasons: Stalin was anxious to win the allegiance of nationalist intellectuals; to accomplish his goal, he pushed policies of Ukrainization and White Russification, making vigorous efforts to propagate the study of Ukrainian and White Russian language, literature and history.[105] So great was the desire to avoid the use of things Russian that William Henry Chamberlin reports that on a visit to the Ukraine in 1927, officials of the Ukrainian Commissariat of Education at Kharkov spoke to him in German, even though they probably knew Russian much better. Chamberlin relates:

> The new nationalism in Ukraine has its intolerant
> sides. There is a commission of Ukrainization which is
> ruthless in weeding out state employees who are in-
> dolent or too wedded to the Russian language to learn
> Ukrainian. One day the Kiev newspapers printed a
> warning list of thirty-six persons who had been dismissed
> for this reason. The old Russian population of Ukraine is
> inclined to feel that it has suddenly transferred to a
> strange and not very hospitable country.[106]

Since Ukrainians and White Russians did not want
Jewish children to be the carriers of Russification, their governments encouraged Yiddish education. But this emphasis
on Ukrainization and White Russification made things very
difficult for the Yiddish school, as four languages now had to
be learned: Yiddish, Russian, the local language, and a
foreign language. Many believed that the Russian and Ukrainian or White Russian languages were not being taught ade-
quately.[107]

A second reason for the expansion that did occur was the
hope that the "reactionary" influence of Jewish nationalism,
Zionism, Hebraism, clericalism, and Yiddishism would be
avoided if all children were forced to attend the pro-Soviet
and anti-traditional government Yiddish school. One
authoritative writer on Jewish national problems wrote that
"in 1924-1928 no consideration was given in many places to
the wishes of the children and their parents. It was enough to
establish that the child's mother tongue was Yiddish to force
him — in many instances — to attend a Yiddish language
school against his wishes."[128] Another said, "In order to force
Jewish children to attend the Yiddish school, they were
denied admission to general schools; a situation arose in

which non-Jewish schools were closed to Jewish children." [109]

Compulsory Yiddishization was dropped at the end of the 1920s because, Jewish nationalist and religious movements no longer being a threat, it was unnecessary to force Jewish children into Yiddish schools to Communize them; moreover, the policy of Ukrainization and White Russification was abandoned. [110] Stalin regarded the Ukrainian "national Communists" as a threat to his totalitarian state and brutally suppressed them. [111]

As we have mentioned, there were no systematic statistics on the Yiddish schools after 1933 — only a note or scrap of information appears here or there. Actually the school situation was disintegrating but this never became evident abroad. Jacob Lestchinsky, an extremely knowledgeable writer about Soviet Jewry, wrote that in 1940 there were 85,000-90,000 Jewish children studying in Yiddish schools throughout the Soviet Union — approximately 20 percent of Jewish children of school age. Of these there were 50,000 in the Ukraine, about 25,000 in White Russia, some 3,000 in Birobidjan, 3,000 in the Crimea, approximately 5,000 in the western parts of the RSFSR, and 2,000 in other parts of the Soviet Union. [112] Most of the few writers on the subject of the Yiddish schools in the Soviet Union have picked up Lestchinsky's statistics, [113] but in fact they are incorrect. From what we know today there were few, if any, Yiddish schools in the entire Soviet Union in 1940. According to the *Bolshaia Sovetskaia Entsiklopediia* there were in 1939 only 19 Yiddish schools in the Ukraine and these probably contained only upper grades. [114]

Although systematic descriptions of the Yiddish schools were not published after 1933, a careful examination of the Soviet Yiddish press for that period gives ample evidence that the Yiddish school system was in a state of disarray and collapse. The collapse did not begin to accelerate until after 1937, but the beginnings can be traced to 1934. Most of the information about this appeared in *Emes*, the central Yiddish daily published in Moscow. In 1938 *Emes* was suppressed,[115] and no more information of that type appeared.

On June 30, 1934 a leading article in *Emes* bemoaned the fact that they had received information from many towns and villages about the weakening of national minority (Yiddish) cultural and educational work.

> They are liquidating national clubs and the cultural divisions of cooperatives. Libraries and circles are being closed and all in the name of a "higher" level of work. In Malev Yiddish and White Russian schools are being "combined," i.e., the Yiddish schools are being liquidated. The number of places where the "mixing" is taking place is difficult to determine but it is deplorably large.[116]

On August 17, 1935, *Emes* wrote that in the coming school year there would be only three Yiddish pedagogical technicums instead of five. "This has been done in order not to waste resources." If there were sufficient teaching positions available in the Yiddish schools, there would have been no prospect of a wastage in resources. The same article says later that the director of the Yiddish pedagogical technicum in Zhitomir has requested that the number of students in his incoming first year class be cut since he has no prospect of being able to place them when they become graduates.[117]

Several days later *Emes* sounded the bitter alarm that it will be necessary to make great efforts to seek out children for the first grades in the Yiddish schools.

> Up to the present Odessa Yiddish School No. 52 has repaired all classrooms but the school stands in danger of

remaining without a first grade because the director criminally forgot to register one . . . . Such a dastardly attitude to registration also exists in other places. Registration in various Kiev Yiddish schools is by no means certain. Yiddish School No. 17 has insufficient enrollees in the first and eighth grades. An example of the bureaucratic attitude to enrollment is revealed by Yiddish School No. 25 in Kiev. The location of the office is not even marked by a Yiddish sign.

The newspaper feels very strongly that if it had not been for the unexplainable forgetfulness on the part of the school directors, there would have been enough pupils.[118]

Absence of a first grade in Yiddish schools was frequently mentioned in the press. Ten days after the above article, *Emes* printed a despatch from Zhitomir reporting that two Yiddish schools had been combined because the schools did not have enough pupils for the first grade.[119]

Two months later an article appeared in *Emes* on the Jewish situation in Berdichev, a medium-sized city in the Ukraine where a majority of the population was Jewish. In the early and middle nineteenth century Berdichev had been the Jewish book publishing center in Russia. The article said that the Berchev city council had ceased to use Yiddish in municipal affairs and liquidated the positions of Yiddish cultural workers. Jewish police circles had begun to write reports only in Russian or Ukrainian. "The Yiddish schools of the city education division had become a forgotten thing. Teachers and learning equipment were wanting."[120] If this was occurring in Berdichev, where the Jewish population was concentrated and where there was a long tradition of Jewish cultural activity, one can imagine the decline in Yiddish educational activity elsewhere.

A consistent theme of the 1930s Yiddish press was that some institutions were Yiddish in name only. Thus early in 1936 *Emes* printed a report on a Yiddish machine-building technicum. "In the second year course of the technicum eight of the subjects taught are in Russian; in the third year course, seven out of ten subjects are taught in Russian, and in the fourth year course all courses are entirely Russified."[121]

In many areas of the Ukraine, White Russia, the Crimea, and the western parts of the RSFSR where there were compact masses of Jews, administrative autonomy was granted to the Jews This reached its height in 1932; in the Ukraine alone there were 113 Jewish village Soviets and 55 Jewish market-town Sovets. In the same year there were eleven Jewish village Soviets in the Westen RSFSR[122]; White Russia had 23 Jewish small-town Soviets and four Jewish village Soviets.[123] Most of these were Jewish in name only, and in the early 1930s frequent complaints began to appear in the Yiddish press about the dropping of the use of Yiddish in these districts. In August a dispatch appeared in *Emes* from Larindorf in the Ukraine which was legally a Jewish national district. "In what kind of a Jewish national district is the cultural work carried on systematically in languages other than Yiddish? . . . An eighth grade is opened not in the Yiddish school but in the Russian."[124]

Toward the end of the 1937 school year an article appeared in *Emes* blaming "nefarious Trotskyites and nationalists" for rumors that the Yiddish school was useless and had no basis for existence.

Over the blindness of the national minority (Yiddish) workers in the ministry of education, this "theory" developed and became accepted. People are found that have begun to agitate that eight-year-old children should be sent to Russian or Ukrainian language schools even if their mother language is Yiddish. This has come to such a state that many Yiddish schools remained without a first grade at the beginning of the school year.[125]

Elsewhere in the same article there is a protest that Yiddish schools were being weakened because many of their best teachers were being lured to the general schools. In order to keep the Yiddish teachers, *Emes* complains that the *melamdim* were reemerging; if the Yiddish schools did not remain open, religion would reestablish its hold.

Reports continued to appear with great frequency about schools being closed or about the absence of a first grade, which meant the school would close in a few years. On May 27, 1937, *Emes* printed a report from Bobruisk stating hat the Yiddish kindergartens were conducted in White Russian and Russian.[126] Several weeks later an article stated that in Dniepropetrovsk, one of the largest Jewish centers in Russia, the Yiddish schools were being "merged" with the general schools,[127] and a week later an *Emes* editorial spoke of the widespread closing of the first grade in the Yiddish schools. There were no first grades in the Odessa Yiddish schools; in Kiev, it was said that "on the first of June registration was begun but the Kiev Yiddish schools have not been able to organize first grades. It is deplorable that this cannot be done. Kiev had an important network of Yiddish kindergartens but they were Yiddish only according to their description. In reality the educational work carried on inside them is done in Ukrainian or in Russian."[128]

In July a report on the Yiddish section of the Bubnov

Institute in Moscow stated that "in the twelfth year of its existence the Yiddish section shows signs of growth. However, the growth is now shown more in quality than in quantity. We have too few students. Not only are we missing a full complement in the first class but also in the second."[129]

The complaint about the absence of first grade appeared with the beginning of the new school year in August, 1937. *Shtern*, the Yiddish daily in the Ukraine, carried far fewer items about the decline of the Yiddish schools; at this time, however, a dispatch noted that the Yiddish schools in Berdichev had no books for the coming year.[130]

One of the worst aspects of the decline in the Yiddish school system was the decay of the Malachovka children's colony in Moscow. This colony, the prize of the Yiddish schools, was a model school which undertook many educational experiments. Foreign guests were always taken there; and teachers from all over the Soviet Union came to observe.[131] In September, 1937 *Emes* wrote:

> The colony has done much in the field of educational practice. This is what has been. The colony is now passing through a very critical period. What have we met on the first day of the new school year? The school is not ready. The houses where the children live have not been repaired. The children sleep on the ground on dirty linen without matresses. How can it be that an educational institution existing for 18 years should come to the beginning of the new school year without books or any plan of educational work? The reason is a simpl one . . . . The Moscow district educational department to which the colony belongs is as interested in the colony as last year's snow.[132]

In 1938 there were many articles of this nature. On

August 30 an article appeared refuting the idea that the Yiddish schools taught Russian and Ukrainian poorly and that, therefore, parents ambitious for their children should transfer them to a Russian or Ukrainian school. On the contrary, the article said, every pupil who finished the tenth grade in the Yiddish school passed the entrance examinations for higher schools and was accepted into them.[133] But after this information about the Yiddish schools ceased to appear: from 1938 to 1940 there were no pieces on the subject in the Yiddish press.[134]

When the Yiddish schools began to open, they lacked suitable textbooks, but shortly after the revolution the necessary textbooks began to be issued. Table XII gives an indication of the rapid growth in textbook publishing, a rate which generally follows the growth rate of schools.

Table XII

Yiddish Textbook Publishing in the Soviet Union[135]

Year	Texts	Printer's Sheets
1918	14	86
1919	27	121.5
1920	9	53.5
1921	10	32.5
1922	8	46
1923	15	125.5
1924	23	281.5
1925	45	423.5
1926	49	493
1927	49	517.5
	249	2,180.5

Apparently publishers of textbooks and children's literature cooperated. The Jewish department of the National Minorities Publishing House in the Ukraine provided most, if not all, of the textbooks and literature; the other two large Yiddish publishing houses in Minsk and Moscow concentrated on other categories.[136]

The educational books published in Yiddish covered the fields of geography, mathematics, natural sciences, physics and chemistry, biology and physiology, language and literature, and methods of teaching. In the first five areas, the books were translations of standard texts used in the general Soviet schools. In language and literature and "methods" — which meant how to teach Yiddish — the books were specifically written for the Yiddish schools and had Jewish content. Methods books intended for teachers were published in editions of 1,000-2,185 copies. Texts for grades 1-7 came out in editions of 2,000-40,000; for grades 8-10 2,000-2,500 were usually printed.[137]

Analyzing the Decline of the Yiddish Schools

The question of why the Yiddish school system declined and disintegrated is a crucial and controversial one. The best-known explanation has been given by Solomon Schwarz in *The Jews in the Soviet Union*. Schwarz's is the only scholarly study exclusively devoted to the subject of Soviet Jews that has attempted to analyze education and culture. It is read by most advanced students and scholars in the field, and its evaluation thus merits detailed examination. Schwarz sees assimilation as bringing about the decline of Yiddish schools. We feel that he overstates his case, as can be shown using

Schwarz's own data. We therefore take the liberty of quoting him at length:

The Jewish masses were moving away from the old ghetto locales. The Soviet government had no reason to oppose the dispersal of the Jewish population in industrial districts, a development that accelerated assimilation and made the Jewish school seem a hindrance rather than a help to progress . . . .

Not only were school facilities more abundant in larger cities; the Jewish population was smaller relative to the general population, Yiddish was less frequently in use, and there was a more widespread desire on the part of Jewish parents to send their children to non-Jewish schools. The larger the city, the less the importance of the Yiddish language school; in large urban centers in the Ukraine it virtually did not exist. At the height of the development of the Jewish school system, the school census of December 15, 1927 showed that of all students in the six largest cities of the Ukraine, only 5.5 percent had Yiddish as their language of instruction in the school year 1927-1928. Yet Jews accounted for 26.2 percent of the population of these cities. Assuming that the percentage of Jews in the student body was about the same as that in the total population this would mean that only 21 percent of all Jewish students attended schools taught in Yiddish. Table A gives a breakdown by cities in percentages.

In smaller Ukrainian cities, Jews accounted for 29.4 percent of the total population and students in schools using Yiddish as the language of instruction, for 10.4 percent of the total student body. Assuming that the percentage of Jewish students approximated the percentage of Jews within the total population, this would mean

Table A

Jewish Students Attending Yiddish Schools

City	% Jews Within Total Population	Students Attending Classes in Yiddish as % of Total Enrollment, Jewish and non-Jewish
Odessa	36.4	9.0
Kiev	27.3	8.0
Dnepropetrovsk	26.6	2.9
Nikolayev	20.8	2.3
Kharkov	19.4	2.9
Stalino	10.7	None

some 35 percent of the Jewish students in the smaller cities attended Jewish schools, or Jewish sections of mixed schools. In all communities classified as urban in the school census (but apparently not including the semirural *shtetl*), the Jewish population amounted to 27.4 percent of the total population, and the number of students in Jewish schools and Jewish sections of mixed schools, to 7.6 percent of the total enrollment — or, on the same assumption, about 28 percent of the total number of Jewish students.

The situation in the *shtetl* was obviously much different. This may be seen, not only in individual cases, where the number of students in Jewish schools accounted for over 90 percent of all Jewish students, but also in the percentage statistics for all schools in the Ukrainian SSR. On December 15, 1927 some 49.6 percent of all Jewish students attended Yiddish language schools, and on July 1, 1932, it was 53 percent (probably the highest point ever reached). The proportion of Jewish children attending schools with Yiddish as the language of instruction must have been considerably larger in communities not classed as urban in the school census. The decline of the *shtetl*, clearly discernible in the late 1920s, reduced the demand for schools in Yiddish and radically changed the climate in which they had thrived.[138]

Mr. Schwarz's argument is unconvincing for several reasons. First of all, assimilation does not occur in a very short period of time. A strongly rooted culture does not give in quickly; it has the strength to resist the blandishments of the dominant society. Certainly nowhere has a well-established, literate culture disappeared naturally in the space of four years as the Yiddish schools did in the Ukraine from 1935 to 1939. Moreover, Schwarz says that in the large urban centers to which many of the Jews were moving, Yiddish was less frequent and "there was a more widespread desire on the part of Jewish parents to send their children to non-Jewish schools." In the large cities of the Ukraine, according to Schwarz, Yiddish schools "virtually did not exist." There is no reason why parental "lack of desire" to send their children to Yiddish schools should result from moving to larger cities. Odessa's Jewish population had come from small towns in the last half of the nineteenth century; in that sense it was very similar to the "new" Jewish populations in the cities of the Soviet period. Yet prerevolutionary Odessa was a center of Jewish culture, Hebrew and Yiddish literature, and Jewish nationalism. In any case, according to Schwarz's own statistics, Yiddish schools did exist in the larger cities. He says that 21 percent of urban Jewish children attended Jewish schools, a sizeable figure. And that describes a time before the Yiddish school enrollment had reached its height.

Schwarz also says that "the larger the city the less the importance of the Yiddish language school." According to the figures he cites, the percentage of Jewish children attending Yiddish language schools was greatest in the cities like Kiev and Odessa where the Jews formed the largest proportion of the population. If one follows his logic, the percentage of Jews attending Yiddish language schools should have gone up as the percentage of Jews among the general population rose. That is, in fact, what happened in Eastern Poland where the Jews were a very high proportion of the urban population. In this area, where the proportion of Jews in the urban population was the highest in all Poland, the center of the various school movements was to be found.[139]

It is true that the Soviet authorities saw fit not to establish Yiddish schools in such large cities of the RSFSR as Moscow and Leningrad. Schwarz gives the impression that most of the Jews left their traditional areas of residence for these cities. This is not true. According to the census of 1939, only 31.4 percent of the Jewish population lived in the RSFSR; 50.8 percent still lived in the Ukraine and 12.4 percent in White Russia.[140]

Thus Schwarz reasons erroneously in the following manner: (a) Jews in large cities do not go to Yiddish schools. (b) Jews in small towns do attend Yiddish schools. (c) Therefore, as the Jewish population moves to the large cities they will adopt the characteristics of the Jews who preceded them there. It did not happen that way in Poland, Lithuania, Latvia, and Estonia, where increased urbanization did not lead to assimilation.

Why then did the Yiddish schools decline? Clearly, not because of a natural process of assimilation, but because of an official policy of suppression.

The overall Soviet minorities policy supports this thesis. Of course, Jews were always treated more harshly than other national minorities. When nationalism was encouraged among the national minorities, Jews benefitted the least; when nationalism was suppressed, Jewish culture was almost obliterated. In the 1920s the Soviet regime, in order to establish itself, had to make concessions in the field of national culture. We have spoken earlier of the Ukrainization and White Russification policy, designed to gain the allegiance of the minority intelligentsia.

Evidence from the Smolensk papers cited above indicates that in the field of Jewish culture too the policy was motivated by a desire to attract the minorities. That this emphasis on national cultures was not in contradiction to the traditional Bolshevik opposition to nationalism was clearly emphasized by Joseph Stalin in a famous address in 1925:

> How are we to make the building of a national culture, the development of schools and courses in the native tongue, and the training of personnel from among the ranks of local people, compatible with the building of a proletarian culture? Is this not an unresolvable contradiction? Of course not! We are building a proletarian culture. That is absolutely true. But it is also true that proletarian culture, which is socialist in content, assumes different modes forms of expression among the various peoples that have been drawn into the work of socialist construction, depending on differences of language, way of life, and so forth. Proletarian in content and national in form — such is the universal human culture towards which socialism is moving. Proletarian culture does not eliminate national culture, but lends it content. Conversely, national culture does not eliminate proletarian

culture, but lends it form. "National culture" was a bourgeois slogan so long as the bourgeoisie held power and the consolidation of nations took place under a proletarian slogan with the assumption of power by the proletariat and the carrying forward of national consolidation under the aegis of the Soviet government. Whoever has not grasped the difference in principle between these two different situations will never understand either Leninism or the essence of the national question from the standpoint of Leninism.[141]

The end of the 1920s and the beginning of the 1930s was marked by a change in the Soviet government's attitude toward national cultures. Much more emphasis was now put on "socialist in content" than "national in form." During the same period, Stalin took total power, crushed the opposition, and began the first five-year plan for the reconstruction of Russia. With Stalin in complete control, it was no longer necessary to placate the minorities, and a policy of cultural assimilation was established, concentrating particularly on national languages, literature, art, and culture in general, and waging struggle against manifestations of "bourgeois nationalism" in these domains. The Communists found such manifestations in all areas of cultural, intellectual, and scientific work. They were especially diligent in searching out originality of linguistic, verbal, and phraseological resources, orthographic peculiarities, and the formation of "artificial barriers" against the Russian language.[142]

Thus, in the Ukraine, the Ukrainian language orthography, which had been standardized in 1928 by a conference of distinguished Ukrainian scholars, was changed in 1933 when a number of the laws of Ukrainian phonetics and etymology were violated in order to remove the "artificial barriers," between the Ukrainian and the Russian languages.[143]

In White Russia the campaign against national features in the White Russian language began in 1931 when a writer said, "The hegemony of the proletariat in linguistics must be achieved in accordance with the demands of the working class for hegemony over the whole field of culture and ideology." The reform of the White Russian language in 1933 was, as in the Ukraine, carried out by the government without the agreement of White Russian scientific institutes and in direct contravention of the opinion of the Academic Orthographic Conference held in Minsk in 1926.[144]

The same policy was directed towards other groups in the USSR — Moldavians, Armenians, Turko-Tatar peoples, Finno-Ugric peoples and others. An interesting exception to the general policy was made with respect to the Poles. One writer advances an explanation for this exception:

> Soviet Moscow temporarily granted them some concessions in order that the Polish language of the Communist Polish papers, printed in the Soviet Union and smuggled into Poland, might be understood in Poland, and that the Polish linguists and writers in Poland might not begin a protest action against the Russification of the Polish language in the Soviet Union.[145]

This policy affected the Jews almost immediately. In October 1929 the Ukrainian Commissariat for Education ordered an orthographical change, which in effect denationalized Yiddish.[146] In 1929 the Historical-Ethnographical Society and the Mefitzei Haskalah, the two prerevolutionary scholarly societies which had been allowed to carry on their research and publication work, were closed and their libraries confiscated.[147] The nature of the work done by the Jewish divisions of the White Russian and Ukrainian academies of sciences was changed. In the 1920s their publications, albeit Communist-oriented, were serious journals containing many outstanding articles. They were replaced by new journals more "internationalist" in their outlook and propagandist in flavor.[148] The Jewish Section of the Communist Party (Yevsektzie) was disbanded; it was "no longer needed."[149]

Jewish cultural institutions were not officially abandoned and the campaign against them developed slowly and uneventfully. The knowledgeable Yiddish journalist B. Z. Goldberg has written about this period that "those who were sensitive to political currents began to sniff the cooling of the air, but in the absence of a new party decision, even they abided by the official line and ascribed the cooling to the inefficiency or personal resistance of minor officials, who were failing in their duty."[150]

We cannot here deal at length with the purges after the assassination of Sergei Kirov in 1934. The purges fell with particular ferocity among the Jews and marked the end of Yiddish schools and most other Jewish cultural institutions. Virtually every single important figure in Jewish educational and cultural work was liquidated. No important and authoritative figures remained.[151] Most of them had been members of other parties before the Revolution: the Poale Zion, and the United Jewish Socialist Party. They were accused of being "spies," "diversionists," "fascists," "Trotskyites," "Zinovievites," "counter-revolutionaries," or "enemies of the people."[152] Among those liquidated were Moishe Litvakoff, former socialist-Zionist who had been editor of *Emes* for sixteen years; Esther Frumkin, ex-Bundist and dean of the Western University in Moscow; Alexander Chashin, former leader of the Poale Zion in the United States and later editor of *Emes*; S. Dimanshtein, the first Jewish Commissar and long considered Stalin's agent in Jewish affairs; Professor David Liberberg, first president of the Jewish Division of the Ukrainian Academy of Sciences, and first president of the Soviet of the Jewish autonomous district of Birobidjan; Max Brik, outstanding Marxist critic of Yiddish literature; Samuil Agurskii, Jewish historian; Rachmiel Weinstein, Yevsektzia leader; and many, many others. Not only were former Bundists and Poale Zionists purged but also the few Jews in Jewish work who had been active Bolsheviks before the revolution such as Dimanshtein.[153]

Since many of those purged were not replaced in their jobs, many institutions were closed; if they reopened, they operated on a very restricted basis. The Russian people, and especially the Jews, are sensitive as to which individuals, policies, or institutions fall out of favor. They began leaving the Jewish schools in droves, as can be seen by the many excerpts we have included from Soviet Yiddish papers. In some places when the principal was arrested, no one would risk his future in a career that was so out of favor and would probably soon be liquidated. Therefore no one replaced him. Lacking leadership or direction, the school system fell apart.

After Krushchev's famous speech to the 20th Congress of the Communist Party, much more information was released about the demise of Yiddish schools and culture in the 1930s. Michael Mirsky's article in the Warsaw Yiddish paper *Folksshtimme* early in 1957 was extremely revealing. According to Mirsky, the Yiddish school network began to be liquidated in the 1930s, not through assimilation as Solomon Schwarz had suggested, but through "administrative pressure" brought by the authorities together with the execution of educational and cultural workers. Even in the newly acquired Polish districts in 1939, where Yiddish schools were started, great pressure was put on the Jewish population to switch over to Russian schools. The liquidation of Jewish schools and cultural institutions began, Mirsky said, in 1936 when the scientific institute in Kiev was closed and its leaders arrested and shot.[154]

I. B. Saltzberg, the Canadian Jewish Communist leader, wrote a series of articles late in 1956 in the Yiddish-language New York *Morgen Freiheit* which essentially confirm what Mirsky said. Saltzberg adds that he himself in 1938 tried to persuade the Soviet leaders in Moscow to halt the liquidation of Yiddish schools and cultural institutions but to no avail.[155]

An American Jewish writer, in a recent undocumented pamphlet, has said that in 1938 all the Yiddish schools were closed down by an administrative order stemming from Stalin.[156]

Notes

1. The literature on discrimation against the Jews of the Soviet Union is voluminous. For a summary article see Zvi Gitelman, "The Jews," *Problems of Communism*, XVI (1967), Sept.-Oct., 92-101. For a book-length collection see Ronald Rubin (ed.), *The Unredeemed: Anti-Semitism in the Soviet Union* (Chicago: Quadrangle Books, 1968). The latter is also useful for its bibliography.
2. Karl Marx, *A World Without Jews*, introduction by Dagobert D. Runes (New York: Philosophical Library, 1959), p. 41. Marx wrote the material in this book under the title "On the Jewish Question."
3. Ibid.; p. 42.
4. Ibid., p. 45.
5. Ibid., p. vii.
6. Quoted in Solomon F. Bloom, "Karl Marx and the Jews," *Jewish Social Studies*, vol. IV (1942), 8.
7. Ibid., p. 11.
8. A. Cherikowsky and B. Nikolaevsky, "A Briv fun Heinrich Graetz tzum Karl Marx," *Historishe Shriftn*, vol. II (1937), 658.
9. Chaim Zhitlowsky, *Der sotzializm un di natsionale frage* (Warsaw, 1935), p. 236.
10. Karl Kautsky, "Rasse und Judentum," *Die Neue Zeit Ergangzungshefts*, No. 20 (October 1914), 93 ff. Quoted in Solomon Schwarz, *The Jews in the Soviet Union* (Syracuse: Syracuse University Press, 1951), p. 57.

11. Karl Marx and Friedrich Engels, "Manifesto of the Communist Party," *Great Books of the Western World* (Chicago: Encyclopedia Britannica, 1952), Vol. 50, p. 420.

12. C. A. Macartney, *National States and National Minorities* (Oxford: Oxford University Press, 1934), p. 148.

13. Ibid., p. 149.

14. The theorist of Jewish autonomous rights in Russia was Simon Dubnow, who developed his theory in a series of articles in the Russian-Jewish journal *Voskhod* between 1897 and 1903. They were later collected and published in book form as *Pisma o starom i novom evreistve* (St. Petersburg, 1907). An English translation, together with some of his other writings, was published in 1958 under the title *Nationalism and History*. The socialist theorist Chaim Zhitlovsky developed similar theories at the same time, or possibly earlier, but his were published abroad and had to be smuggled into Russia. See Chaim Zhitlovsky, *Gezamelte shriftn* (10 vols.; New York: Zhitlovsky Jubilee Committee, 1912-1919), especially vols. IV-VIII.

15. Quoted in the appendix of Yekhiel Halpern, *Yisrael Vehakommunizm* (Tel Aviv: Israel Labor Party, 1951), pp. 260-261. The Jewish population of Galicia and Bukovina was different in its cultural character from that of the city of Vienna. The latter were "German" Jews; those of Galicia and Bukovina were Ostjuden.

16. The following volumes of Lenin's collected works contain selections dealing with his controversy with the Bund: Vol. 6 (1961), eight selections; Vol. 7 (1961), three selections; Vol. 8 (1962), one selection; Vol. 11 (1962), two selections; Vol. 19 (1963), two selections; and Vol. 20 (1964), seven selections.

17. V. I. Lenin, *Collected Works* (Moscow: Foreign Languages Publishing House, 1961), vol. VI, pp. 99-101.

18. V. I. Lenin, *Questions of National Policy and Proletarian Internationalism* (Moscow, n.d.), pp. 28-31.

19. Kautsky, op. cit.

20. Joseph Stalin, *Marxism and the National and Colonial Question* (London, n.d.), p. 35-36.

21. Ibid., p. 39.

22. The Jews were highly organized politically. The largest Jewish party, the Zionists, was closely allied to the middle class liberal Constitutional Democrats (Kadets). Several small middle class groups were also associated with that party. The Bund was very friendly to the Mensheviks, and the United Jewish Socialist Party was close to the Social Revolutionaries. The Poale Zion favored a moderate socialist program (Schwarz, p. 92, and Guido Goldman, *Zionism Under Soviet Rule, 1917-1928* [New York: Herzl Press, 1960], p. 79).

23. It is true that there were a number of Jews who were prominent Bolsheviks — Trotsky, Kamenev, Zinoviev, and Sverdlov — but they were culturally far from their own people and did not speak its language. They took no part whatsoever in Jewish communal affairs. Jews were actually much more prominent in the Menshevik party. The most eminent spokesmen of Menshevism, such as Julius Martov, Raphael Abramovitch, and Feodor Dan, were Jewish (Isaac Deutscher, *Stalin* [New York: Vintage Books, 1960], p. 346). Ivan Steinberg, the Left Social Revolutionary Minister of Justice in Lenin's first cabinet, was active in Jewish internal affairs.

24. Samuil Augrskii, *Der yidisher arbeter in der kommunistisher bavegung, 1917-1921* (Minsk: State Publishing House, 1925), pp. 5 ff.

25. Ibid., p. v.

26. Ibid., p. 9.

27. Zvi Gitelman, *Jewish Nationality and Soviet Politics* (Princeton: Princeton University Press, 1972), Chap. IV *et passim*.

28. L. Zinger, *Dos banaite folk* (Moscow: Emes Publishing House, 1941), p. 36.

29. Merle Fainsod, *Smolensk Under Soviet Rule* (Cambridge, Mass.: Harvard University Press, 1958), p. 442.

30. Ibid., p. 443.

31. Samuïl Agurskii, *Di yiddishe kommasariatn un di yiddishe kommunistishe sektsies (protokoln, rezolutsies, un dokumentn, 1918-1921* (Minsk: State Publishing House, 1928), pp. 21 ff.

32. A former Russian Zionist has written that the struggle to keep Hebrew legal in the early years of the Soviet regime "was not actually being fought between the Hebrew public and the authorities but between conflicting groups of Jews with some of our worst antagonists having only recently been with us in the Zionist camp" (Benjamin West, *Struggles of a Generation* [Tel Aviv: Massadah Publishing Co., 1959], p. 148.

33. Samuil Agurskii, *Di oktiaber revolutsie in veisrussland* (Minsk: State Publishing House, 1927), p. 294.

34. Agurskii, *Der yiddisher arbeter*, p. 45.

35. Ibid., p. 137.

36. Ibid., pp. 137-138.

37. Ibid., p. 29.

38. Schwarz, op. cit., p. 131.

39. I. Dardak, "Unzere dergreikhungen in 15 yor oktiaber afn gebit fun folk bildung," *Tsum 15 yortog fun der oktiaber revolutsie, sotsial ekonomisher zamelbukh* (Minsk: White Russian Academy of Sciences, Jewish Sector, 1932), p. 148.

40. The Jewish population of Russia had a great attachment to the Yiddish language. In the census of 1897, 96.9 percent were recorded as speaking Yiddish as their primary language. In 1926, 70.4 percent were still speaking Yiddish. The 1897 figures are from Boris Brutskus, *Statistika evreiskago naselenie* (St. Petersburg: Jewish Colonization Association, 1909), vol. III, Appendix, Table 5. The 1926 figures are from L. Zinger, *Dos banaite folk*, op. cit., p. 40.

41. *Der vekker* (Minsk), August 8, 1921, in a report of the

Central Jewish Bureau of the People's Commissariat of Education of White Russia.

42. Agurskii, *Der yiddisher arbeter*, p. 28.

43. He left Russia, eventually came to the United States, and was a leading Yiddish literary critic who published several volumes and many journal articles. Unfortunately he has not been translated into English.

44. Agurskii, *Der yiddisher arbeter*, p. 29.

45. Raphael Abramovitch, "Geshikhte fun yidn in poiln, lite, un russland," *Algemeine Entsiklopedie*, Series "Yidn" (New York: World Jewish Culture Congress, 1950), vol. IV, volumn 188.

46. Jacob Lestchinsky, "Jews in the USSR — II," *Contemporary Jewish Record*, vol. III (November-December, 1940), 608.

47. The "trial" is described in *Der mishpet ibern cheder* (Vitebsk, 1922). A general survey of the history and vicissitudes of the Jewish religion in the Soviet Union is given in A. A. Gershuni, *Yahdut Berussiah Hasovietit* (Jerusalem: Mosad Harav Kook, 1961).

48. Esther Frumkin, *Doloi ravinov* (Moscow, 1923), p. 4.

49. *Emes*, November 4, 1922.

50. Walter Kolarz, *Religion in the Soviet Union* (London: St. Martin's Press, 1961), pp. 379-380.

51. *The American Jewish Yearbook 5671* (Philadelphia: Jewish Publication Society of America, 1930), p. 120.

52. Lucy Dawidowicz, "What Future for Judaism in Russia?" *Commentary*, November 1956, p. 405.

53. Kolarz, op. cit., p. 380.

54. *Emes*, November 4, 1922.

55. *Yidn in f.s.s.r.: atlas fun kartogramen un diagramen* (Moscow-Kharkov-Minsk, 1930), p. 81.

56. *A yor arbet fun der r.k.p. in der yiddisher svive* (Moscow: Central Board of Jewish Sections of the Russian Communist Party, 1924), p. 61.

57. Schwarz, p. 102.

58. Agurskii, *Di yiddishe kommissariatn*, p. 21.
59. *Bolshaia sovetskaia entsiklopediia*, Vol. 24, (1932), p. 338.
60. H. S. Linfield, *The Communal Organization of the Jews in Soviet Russia* (New York, 1925), p. 6.
61. *Af di vegn tsu der naier shul* (Moscow, 1924), No. 8, p. 7.
62. S. Dimanshtein (ed.), *Yidn in FSSR, zamelbukh* (Moscow: Emes Publishing House, 1935), p. 259.
63. *Af di vegn tsu der naier shul*, op. cit.
64. Lestchinsky, *Dos sovetsihe yidntum*, p. 356.
65. Central Statistical Office of the Ukrainian SSR, *Statistika ukrainy*, Series VII (Education), Vol. V, Issue 1 (Serial No. 71), p. 50.
66. "Yiddishe shuln in mizrakh europa," *Algemeine entsiklopedie*, Series "Yidn" (New York: World Jewish Culture Congress, 1950), vol. III, column 387.
67. Dimanshtein, op. cit., p. 260-261.
68. M. Kiper, "15 yor," *Roiter Velt*, No. 7-8 (1932).
69. Dardak, op. cit., p. 160.
70. N. Kasteliansky, "Dos yiddishe shulvezn in ratn farband," *Di yiddishe moderne shul oif der velt* (Philadelphia: Workmen's Circle School Committee, 1935), p. 254.
71. Dimanshtein, op. cit.
72. The Soviet government never did establish a Yiddish university although some Jewish Communists had advocated this in Minsk in 1919 and 1920 (Elias Schulman, *The Fate of Soviet Jewry* [New York: Jewish Labor Committee, n.d.], p. 8).
73. White Russian Soviet Socialist Republic, Jewish Section of the Pedagogical Faculty, *Shriftn fun veisrusishn universitet* (Minsk: Jewish Section of the Pedagogical Faculty, 1929), p. 157.
74. Dimanshtein, op. cit., p. 260.
75. Ibid., p. 265.
76. C. Szmeruk, "Yiddish Publications in the USSR," *Yad Vashem Studies on the European Jewish Catastrophe and Resistance* (Jerusalem, 1960), p. 111.

77. At its beginning the White Russian Academy was known as the Institute for White Russian Culture. Its name was later changed to the White Russian Academy of Sciences (Alfred A. Greenbaum, *Jewish Scholarship in Soviet Russia,* 1918-1941 [Boston, 1959], pp. 108, 23).

78. The outstanding scholarly periodical of the Jewish division of the White Russian Academy of Sciences in this period was the *Tsaitshrift.* It contained many outstanding articles and studies which made important contributions to certain aspects of Jewish history and culture. The field of investigation was narrow and many subjects were taboo, but within the limits set for it important work was done. See *Tsaitshrift,* vols. I-V, Minsk, 1926-1931.

79. All-Ukrainian Academy of Sciences, Department for Jewish Culture, Literary and Philosophical Sections, *Shriftn,* vol. I (1928), 3.

80. Dimanshtein, op. cit., p. 126.

81. For a brief discussion of the uniqueness of Ukrainian Jewish history see the introduction to Philip Friedman, "Geshikhte fun der yidn in ukraine," *Yidn in ukraine* (New York: Ukrainian Jewish Memorial Society, 1961), vol. I, pp. 1-69.

82. Archives of the Yivo Institute for Jewish Research, File No. 3030, Document No. 105989.

83. Dimanshtein, op. cit., p. 127.

84. One of the former aspirants of the Kiev Institute has described it in the following words: "The Kiev Scientific Research Institute for Jewish culture of the Ukrainian scientific academy was the highest institution of learning in the entire thousand-year history of the Yiddish language. The institute was the highest achievement of the scientific sphere in the 'Yiddish Empire.' It was the crown of Yiddish culture in Soviet Russia.

   "The Institute employed more than 190 worker-professors, scientific workers, aspirants, research assistants, bibliographers, archivists, cataloguers, and bookbinders. Among them were many famous scholars" (Alexander Pomerantz, *Di sovetishe haruge malchus* [Buenos Aires: Argentine Branch of Yivo, 1962], p. 44).

85. *Visnshaft un revolutsie* (Kiev: Publishing House of the Ukrainian Academy of Sciences, 1934), No. 1-2, 138.
86. Ibid., p. 133-134, 137-138.
87. Ibid., p. 141, 142-149.
88. Ibid., p. 150.
89. For 1922-1931 see Dardak; for 1932 and 1933 see Dimanshtein, p. 262.
90. *Emes*, June 24, 1937.
91. For 1924, see *Af di vegn tsu der naier shul* (Moscow, 1924), No. 8; for 1926 and 1927, Central Statistical Office of the Ukrainian SSR, *Statistika Ukrainy*, Series VII (Education), vol. VI, Issue 1 (Serial No. 95), 10; vol. VII, Issue 1 (Serial No. 131), 20; For 1928, 1930, and 1931, see M. Kiper, "15 Yor," *Roiter Velt*, 1932, No. 7-8; for 1931, Dimanshtein, p. 262; for 1935, D. Mats, "Na Vysokom Podyeme (O Rabote Sredi Natsionalnykh Menshinstv Ukrainy)," *Revolutsiya i natsionalnosti*, June 1935, 60.
92. Figures for 1923, 1928, and 1931 are from Y. Kantor, *Natsionalnoie stroitelstvo sredi evreev v SSSR* (Moscow, 1923), pp. 170, 172; for 1924, *Af di vegn tsu der naier shul* (Moscow, 1924), No. 8; for 1926, *Proletarisher gedank* (Moscow), March 1927, p. 43; *Yidn in FSSR; Atlas fun kartogrames un diagramen*, p. 81.
93. *Proletarisher Gedank* (Moscow), March 1927, p. 43.
94. *Emes*, November 26, 1932. There has been much written on the subject of Jewish colonization in the Crimea and southern Russia. Some of it is of a propagandistic nature. The book by Y. Kantor, *Natsionalnoie stroitelstvo sredi evreev v SSSR*, is one of the best works on the subject published in the USSR itself.
95. Schwarz, op. cit., p. 146.

96. S. Klitenik, *Di kultur arbet tsvishn di yiddishe arbetndike inem ratn farband* (Moscow: Central Publishing House, 1931), p. 10.

97. Dimanshtein, op. cit., p. 259.

98. P. Rozenfeld, *Tsvei kulturn, tsvei sakhaklen* (Moscow: Emes Publishing House, 1932), pp. 34, 36.

99. Dardak, op. cit., p. 161.

100. *Natsionalnaia politika VKP(B) v tsifrakh* (Moscow, 1930), pp. 278-279.

101. Nathan Eck, "The Educational Institutions of Polish Jewry," *Jewish Social Studies*, vol. IX (1947), 6, 11.

102. Miriam Eisenstein, *Jewish Schools in Poland, 1919-1939* (New York: King's Crown Press, Press, Columbia University, 1950), pp. 30, 35, 46-47.

103. Aryeh Tartakover, "Yidishe politik un yidishe kultur in poiln tsvishn di tsvei velt milkhomes," *Algemeine entsiklopedie*, Series "Yidn" (New York: World Jewish Culture Congress, 1950), vol. VI, pp. 147-164 ff.

104. For a description of the vigorous cultural life of the Jewish minorities in the Baltic states between the two world wars, see three articles by Joseph Gar in vol. VI (1950) of the *Algemeine entsiklopedie*, Series "Yidn," entitled "Lebn un umkum fun di yidn in Lite," pp. 330-375; "Lebn un umkum fun di yidn in Letland," pp. 375-394; and "Lebn un umkum fun di yidn in Estland," pp. 395-404.

105. John A. Armstrong, *Ideology, Politics and Government in the Soviet Union* (New York: Frederick Praeger, 1962), p. 121.

106. William Henry Chamberlin, *Soviet Russia. A Living Record and a History* (Boston: Little, Brown & Co., 1933), p. 220-221.

107. "Yiddishe shuln in mizrakh europa," *Algemeine entsiklopedie*, Series "Yidn," vol. III, columns 388-389.

108. Kantor, op. cit., p. 173.

109. M. Kiper, *10 yor oktiaber revolutsie, di oktiaber revolutsie un di yidishe arbetndike fun ukraine* (Kiev: "Kultur Lige," 1927), p. 75.

110. Armstrong, op. cit., p. 120.

111. Armstrong, op. cit., p. 121.

112. Lestchinsky. op. cit., *Dos sovetishe yidntum*, p. 342.

113. Schwarz, p. 137;.Zevi Scharfstein, *Toldot Hakhinukh Beyisrael Bedorot Haakharonim* (New York: Ogen, 1949), vol. III, p. 102; S. L. Kirschenbaum, *Divrei Yimei Am Yisrael Beshnot 1936-1951. Skira Historit* (Tel Aviv: Dvir, 1956), p. 21.

114. "Ukrainskaia SSR," *Bolshaia sovetskaia entsiklopediia*, Supplement SSSR" (1947), column 1821.

115. Yehoshua A. Gilboa, *The Black Years of Soviet Jewry, 1939-1953* (Boston: Little, Brown & Company, 1971), p. 20.

116. *Emes*, June 30, 1934.

117. Ibid., August 17, 1935.

118. Ibid., August 23, 1935.

119. Ibid., September 2, 1935.

120. Ibid., November 15, 1935.

121. Ibid., March 28, 1936.

122. Kantor, pp. 194, 28.

123. Dimanshtein, op. cit., p. 253.

124. *Emes*, August 4, 1936.

125. Ibid., May 22, 1937.

126. Ibid., May 27, 1937.

127. Ibid., June 17, 1937.

128. Ibid., June 24, 1937.

129. Ibid., July 6, 1937.

130. *Shtern*, August 17, 1937.

131. For a description of the Malachovka children's colony, see Zalman Aranov and F. Shpitalnik, *Malachovker kinder kolonie* (Moscow: Emes Publishing House, 1932), 48 pp.

132. *Emes*, September 5, 1937.
133. Ibid., August 30, 1938.
134. Lestchinsky, *Dos sovetishe yidntum*, p. 341.
135. "Yiddishe shuln in mizrakh europa," column 388. The Russian unit of measurement for printed matter is a printed sheet of either 36,000 or 40,000 units of print, corresponding to about 5,000 to 6,000 words in English (Schwarz, p. 147). The average size of textbooks in this period, therefore, was approximately 8.8 sheets, or 44,000 to 52,000 words.
136. This is clear from an examination of the data in several articles by A. Finkelstein: "Di bikher produktsie funem farlag 'Emes' farn tsveitn finfyor, 1933-1937," *Sovetish*, (1939) vols. 7-8, 416-427; "Di yiddishe bikher produktsie funem ukrmeluchenatzmindfarlag farn tsveitn finfyor, 1933-1937," *Literarishe almanak*, (1939) vols. 9-10, 528-542; and "Di yiddishe bikher produktsie fun veismeluchefarlag farn tsveitn finfyor, 1933-1937," *Shtern*(Minsk), 1939, No. 7, 81-91.
137. Khana Shmeruk (ed.), *Pirsumim Yehudiim Bebrit Hamoetzot, 1917-1960* (Jerusalem: Historical Society of Israel, 1961), p. cxix.
138. Schwarz, pp. 135-137.
139. Eck, pp. 15-16. Besides Eck's excellent article in English, the Jewish school system in interwar Poland has been treated in Eisenstein; in A. Tartakover, "Batei Hasefer shel Hatsibur Hayhudi Bepolin," *Pisma Instytutu Nauk Judistycznych* (Warsaw, 1931); in Chaim Ormian, *Hamakhshava Hakhinukhit shel Yahdut Polaniya* (Tel Aviv: Yavneh, 1939); and in J. Zineman (ed.), *Almanach szkolnictwa zydowskiego w Polsce* (Warsaw, 1938), vol. I.
140. L. Zinger, *Dos banaite folk*, op. cit., p. 36.
141. Joseph Stalin, *Marxism and the National Question* (New York: International Publishers, 1937), p. 209.
142. Alexander V. Yurchenko, "Genocide through Destruction

of National Culture and Sense of Nationality," *Genocide in the USSR* (New York: Institute for the Study of the USSR, 1958), p. 12.

143. R. Smal-Stocki, *The Nationality Problem of the Soviet Union and Russian Communist Imperialism* (Milwaukee: Marquette University Press, 1952), p. 135.

144. Ibid., p. 144.

145. Ibid., 145.

146. Judah Rosenthal, "Hahistoriografia Hayehudit Berussia Hasovietit," *Sefer Shimon Dubnow* (London and Jerusalem: Ararat Publishing Co., 1954), p. 201.

147. Abraham G. Duker, "Evreiskaia Starina: A Bibliography of the Russian-Jewish Historical Periodical," *Hebrew Union College Annual* (Cincinnati, 1932), vol. VIII-IX, 526.

148. Greenbaum, Chap. III *et passim.*

149. *Bolshaia sovetskaia entsiklopediia* (1st ed., 1932), Vol. 24, p. 338.

150. B. Z. Goldberg, *The Jewish Problem in the Soviet Union* (New York: Crown Publishers, 1961), p. 253.

151. Gregory Aronson, *Di yiddishe problem in soviet russland* (New York: Farlag Vekker, 1944), p. 123.

152. Gregory Aronson, *Soviet Russia and the Jews* (New York: The American Jewish League Against Communism, 1949), p. 26.

153. Aronson, *Di yiddishe problem*, p. 124.

154. *Folksshtimme* (Warsaw), January 26, 1957. Alexander Pomerantz has written that the Kiev Institute was closed in 1936 shortly after he received the degree of Candidate of Sciences. Hardly any of the distinguished academic staff remained alive. (Alexander Pomerantz, p. 45).

155. *Morgen Freiheit* (New York), December 12, 1956.

156. Schulman, p. 10.

Chapter 6

The Curriculum of the Soviet Communist School in Yiddish

The Soviet School Program of the 1920s and Early Yiddish Education

THE YIDDISH SCHOOLS in the Soviet Union were Soviet government schools and thus had no independent curriculum. Like all the other schools of the minority nationalities they were governed by the slogan "National in form, socialist in content"[1] which, in effect, meant that the curriculum of the general Russian schools was used in the language of the minority.

The only national subject in the curriculum of national minority schools was language. It is extremely difficult to tell how much time was devoted to these subjects in the 1920s because Soviet schools did not have definite subject programs.[2] It was a period of progressive educational experiments in the USSR. The system of study was known as the "Complex Method," the Soviet version of the project method. The Complex was simply a center of interest. In the elementary schools the major Complex was Children's Life. More specifically the Complexes were Nature, Work, and Society, first as they manifested themselves and functioned in the small world of the child and later in the larger world. In the elementary grades, these complexes were not divided into subjects but into a series of problems, each helping and leading to a solution of the next and together forming a harmonious unit. The Complex of Work was studied along with Nature and was followed by the Complex of Society because, according to Soviet educational theorists, the formations of society are based on the conditions of labor.[3]

The following is a verbatim description of the official program of the first four grades of the Soviet Unified Labor School as adopted by the educational authorities of the Russian Federation on March 5, 1923. (The upper grades are given in much greater detail.)

Outline of Program for School of the First Level (8-12 years)[4]

1. First year
   a. *Nature and man.* Seasons of the year.
   b. *Work.* Daily work of the family in the country and the city.
   c. *Society.* The family and the school.
2. Second year
   a. *Nature and man.* Air, water, the sun. Plants and domestic animals and their needs.
   b. *Work.* The work of the village and of the part of the city in which the child lives.
   c. *Society.* The administrative institutions of the city and the village.

3. Third year
   a. *Nature and man.* Elementary notions of physics and chemistry. Local nature. The life of the human organism.
   b. *Work.* Economy of the region.
   c. *Society.* The administrative institutions of the region.
4. Fourth year
   a. *Nature and man.* Geography of Russia and other countries. The life of the human body.
   b. *Work.* The national economy of the Soviet Union and of other countries.
   c. *Society.* Organization of the state of the Soviet Union and of other countries. Pictures of the past life of the human race.

We can obtain a practical understanding of the program by examining one of the widely used Yiddish fourth-grade textbooks of the time, *Arbets kinder* by Y. Bakst and Y. Grinberg (Moscow, 1928). It was published in a fairly extensive edition of 10,000 and also came out in a third-grade edition of 12,000.[5] The book is arranged according to the program of studies given above. Although it clearly attempts to inculcate Communist ideology, it does so subtly, without preaching or blatant propaganda. In this respect it differs remarkably from *Literature Lernbuch farn 4th Shulyor* (published in 1933, after a basic change in school policy), which is aggressively propagandistic.[6]

Considerable space is devoted, as in the plan of studies, to the geography of the Soviet Union, which is taught inductively. There is almost no direct teaching of the type of geographic facts that are usually presented in an American geography class (where such classes still exist). The material consists of literary selections of a fairly high quality. Periodic questions show that "geography" is really social studies of the type favored by many progressive educators of the period.[7]

Let us examine the section on worker protection in order to gain an insight into the method. First there are several short pieces by such important Yiddish writers as Abraham Reisin and Sholom Aleichem. But the questions which follow are not based exclusively on the reading material; they require original investigations by the student and personal observations. After being taken on an excursion to a local factory, the student is asked the following questions: To whom did the factory belong before the revolution and to whom does it belong now? What kind of help does the worker receive when he is sick? What kind of help does the female worker receive after she has a child? From where is the help received? What measures are taken against accidents and to preserve the health of the worker? How much vacation does the worker receive and how many go to rest homes? Of what ages are the workers and how many hours does each age group work? To what trade union do the workers belong? What commissions does the union have and what does each do?[8]

These questions communicate their point of view subtly and, from a pedagogical point of view, quite effectively. The students divide into groups and write a collective composition entitled "The Life of the Worker — Then and Now," each group covering a different aspect of the subject. They are urged to use ideas not only from the stories in the book but also from their excursion and their parents.[9]

This 1928 textbook deals with the situation of the Jews, which 1930s texts rarely, if ever, discussed. The students are told to find out how Jews lived under the Czarist regime and to compare their residence rights, educational level and employment situation then with their conditions under the Soviet regime. The assignment is designed to show the Soviet regime in its best light in relationship to the Jews; the areas in which conditions have worsened are ignored. The deprivation of cultural freedom is not mentioned. Nevertheless, the Jewish question is recognized, albeit in a limited fashion, and is judged worthy of inclusion in the Yiddish language textbook.[10]

Later in the book there is a fairly straightforward description of the Jewish population of the Soviet Union and its social position. Like most of the material on the Jews which appeared in Soviet literature, whether in Yiddish or in Russian, it is apologetic in tone but vigorously refutes many anti-Semitic canards and lists the Jews' positive accomplishments.[11]

All courses in the Yiddish schools were taught in Yiddish. Yiddish literature was included, but it was not taught as a separate subject and the standard was very low. The growth of the Yiddish school system came at a time when the entire Soviet school system repudiated technical information, the learning of reading and writing, positive experience in mathematics, and factual information in general.[12]

Readers were furnished with a supplement to the "Workbook" for the purpose of literature study. Typical of this type of book was the *Arbet un kamf* (Work and Struggle) series of Oislender, Bakst, and Friedland. Intended for the fourth, fifth, and sixth grades, it consisted of five "notebooks."[13] Many of the sections were translations into Yiddish and most of the original Yiddish writers included were Soviet writers. Almost no Yiddish writers from outside the Soviet Union were included, although most of the great Yiddish writers of the time lived in Poland or the United States.

There were few official school programs in language

before the change in educational direction in 1931. In the Ukraine, where most of the Yiddish schools were located, not a single program of the People's Commissariat of Education devoted specifically to Yiddish language and literature was published before 1932. After that year, eight were published. In White Russia three government programs devoted to Yiddish literature were issued, but here too more appeared in the 1930s.[14]

The Effect of the Change in Soviet School Policy After 1931 on Yiddish Schools

The Soviet school system officially abandoned progressivism in 1931. Industrialization and the implementation of the five-year plan created a need for trained manpower that the older system could not meet. On November 5, 1931 a resolution of the Central Committee of the Communist Party of the Soviet Union on the subject was published in *Pravda* and *Izvestia.* It was followed by a decree of the Peoples Commissariat of Education of the RSFSR on November 15, 1931:

> The resolution of the Central Committee of the Communist Party demands a shift of our work in the realm of educational construction. This shift should consist in concentrating the primary attention of all the organs of the people's education on the raising of the quality of the labor of the school to the maximum; and the basic task in the struggle of the polytechnic school should be the liquidation of the basic defect of the school at this

moment: that the education in the school does not give a sufficient volume of knowledge in the disciplines of general education, and also solves unsatisfactorily the problem of preparation for the technicums and higher schools of completely educated men possessing a good foundation in the sciences (physics, chemistry, mathematics, the native tongue, geography and the like).[15]

The change of emphasis in the curriculum after 1931 soon manifested itself in students' reading material. Before 1931 the readers were usually called "workbook" or "helpbook"; after 1931 they were actually labelled as readers.[16] Before 1933 the reading material was usually organized as an adjunct, an ancillary aspect of the Complex; after 1933 literature was taught as a subject and the texts were organized on this basis.

An example of the later type of textbook was *Literatur: lernbuch farn 4tn shulyor*, published in 1933 in an edition of 30,000, one of the largest printings of a Yiddish textbook in the Soviet Union.[17] Because of its wide use, one can safely assume that it reflected Yiddish language education in this period. Its contrast with the early texts is apparent from only a cursory examination. It is organized according to patterns more appropriate to the study of literature than as an adjunct to social studies. All selections of individual authors are grouped together under three headings: Pre-October Literature, Soviet Literature, and Proletarian Literature of Capitalist Countries. (The earlier texts were organized according to such themes as Nature and Man, Work, and Society.) The selections of one author were not grouped together but could be included under the three different headings. As mentioned earlier, the later volumes were also much more aggressively propagandistic in favor of the Soviet regime and against Jewish nationalism.

A widely used sixth-grade text published in the Ukraine during the later period in an edition of 13,550 is another example of the newer tendency in book publishing and teaching.[18] It contains 229 pages and consists of groups of selections of eleven authors, eight of whom wrote in Yiddish. (The selections of the remaining three were translated into Yiddish.) Each author is introduced by a short but thorough biography, which includes a total picture of his work in addition to extensive comment and evaluation of his writings in regard to Communism and the Soviet regime.

The National Content of the Yiddish Schools

In order to have a basis of comparison when discussing Soviet Yiddish schools, it is useful to describe the curriculum of Polish Jewish schools, which, although frequently harassed by the Polish government,[19] can be taken as a model of what Jewish-operated schools in Russia would have been like if they had been permitted to exist.

The various types of Jewish schools of Poland between the world wars were quite dissimilar in structure and philosophy. The main systems were the Cysho-Yiddish secular schools sponsored by the anti-Zionist socialist Bund and the left-wing Zionist socialists; Tarbut — Hebrew language secular schools sponsored by the Zionist organization; Yavneh — Hebrew language schools of the orthodox religious Zionists; and Chorev — sponsored by the Agudat Yisrael, ultra-orthodox religious anti-Zionists. We shall not dwell here on the orthodox or ultra-orthodox schools because it can be assumed that their curricula were dominated by a traditional Jewish religious program, but instead shall concentrate on the modern secular Hebrew schools of the Tarbut. They are a better example than the Cysho since Tarbut was three times as large as Cysho and much stronger: under conditions of freedom it would probably have built a very large system in Russia.

Religion was only taught in the Polish Tarbut schools as an historical subject. The Bible had a very special place in the curriculum: it was primarily studied not for information on religious life and practice, but rather as a literary and cultural document and a source of moral values with which the student should be acquainted.

Modern Hebrew literature held a very important place in the Polish Tarbut school. Such major poets and writers as Peretz Smolenskin, Chaim Bialik, Saul Tchernchovksy, Achad Haam, David Frishman, and Zalman Schneour were studied. The national element in the work of the different literary figures was examined and students were required to memorize poems having national content.

The great European literary culture was also emphasized. The ideological leaders of the Hebrew schools were modern men who did not view Jewish culture as ghetto-based; they saw it instead as a melding together of Jewish tradition and European humanism.

In addition to the study of Hebrew language and literature, the Bible, the Talmud, Jewish history, and cultural geography of Palestine — which together amounted to about one-third of the total program — Polish language and literature, foreign languages (German and Latin), the physical sciences, and general history were stressed. Mickiewicz, Slowacki, Krasinkski in Polish literature; Schiller and Goethe

in German; Ovid, Cicero, Horace, and Virgil in Latin literature — these were some of the masters whose prose and
poetry were read and analyzed for grammatical structure,
poetic form, and style. Again, ethics, philosophy, and
psychology — in America usually taught in college rather
than high school — were included in the last year of the
Tarbut gymnasiums. On the whole, the Tarbut program
offered an intensive study of the humanities. The growing
interest in the natural and physical sciences was a response to
the industrial and agricultural growth of Palestine which
created a need for people with a sound background in the
sciences.

The Palestinian element was integral to the Tarbut
School. Its students were encouraged to participate in the
Jewish National Fund to help redeem land in the developing
Jewish homeland. This fund was a symbol of a new way of life
embracing pioneering, acquisition of land, and collectivism;
hence, the introduction and intensification of that activity
within the school had great emotional effects on the young.

Jews and other national minorities have never considered language alone as the exclusive ingredient of a truly
national school, although its importance is undeniable. To
serve a national purpose a school must teach the history of the
people, its literature, geography, folklore, and national
status. We shall examine the curriculum of the Soviet Yiddish
school to see if and in what manner these subjects were
taught. No course in Jewish history was ever offered in the
Yiddish schools of Soviet Russia, not even after the school
reform of 1931 which elevated Russian history to a position
of great importance and allowed the history of the local
dominant minority nationality to be studied.[20] Only in the
teacher training institutions was Jewish history studied and

here it was done in an extraordinarily distorted way. In the Yiddish section of the pedagogical faculty of the White Russian State University at Minsk there were courses offered in "The Social Movement Among the Jews," "History of the Jews in Lithuania, the Ukraine, and White Russia," and "History of the Jews in Russia and the USSR in the 19th and 20th Centuries."[21] Thus Jewish history was restricted to Russia in an effort to cut off Russian Jews from Jews in other countries. It should be remembered that the Jews were one of the few Soviet national minorities (the largest one) a majority of whose members lived outside the borders of the USSR.

In the 1920s this distortion of Jewish history in the Minsk University curriculum was slightly mitigated by the inclusion of brief courses in Hebrew and "Old Hebrew Literature."[21] However, by 1929 these courses were dropped in favor of "Economic History of the Jews in Russia."[22]

In the 1920s and early 1930s the Yiddish sections of the White Russian and Ukrainian Academies of Sciences had historical sections which did extensive research into the history of the various socialist and radical movements among the Russian Jews. This was probably the most important contribution of Soviet Yiddish historiography to the literature on Jewish history, but unavoidably it led the historians into sensitive areas concerning the Bund. After the Revolution the remnants of the Bund in Poland, Lithuania, and Latvia had been greatly weakened by being cut off from the great mass of its members in the Soviet Union. By the early 1930s the Bund parties in these countries had become very important, both in the Jewish community and in the general political life of the nations.[23] They were also anti-Communist, certainly in part because of the suppression of their movement within the Soviet Union. When Soviet Jewish historiography began to focus on an anti-Communist movement, it was suppressed. Thus most of the limited amount of scholarly material published after the early 1930s was in such politically noncontroversial subjects as linguistics.[24] Of course, even this was suspect as research in Yiddish linguistics involved study of its Hebrew origins. So we see that even the narrow field of Jewish history covered in the teacher training institutions became officially intolerable and was eliminated.

An American observer in 1920 gives an interesting account of how Jewish history was treated in the Soviet Yiddish school:

> I must amplify what I wrote earlier when I said that history was studied in the Soviet Yiddish schools. There is no specific subject called history but only the conducting of historical conversations. They do not begin from ancient times and go to our age but start from the present and go to the past.
> This is actually a very good way to familiarize a child with his history. However, they begin Jewish history in 1928 and end it with October 1917. I spoke to children in the last class who had no idea of what kind of history Jews had gone through before the October Revolution. In my conversations with them it came out that before October 1917 Jews had had no history.[25]

Literature, then, was the only "Jewish" subject in the curriculum of the Soviet Yiddish school. The only literature studied, however, was Yiddish literature. Measuring the exact importance of Yiddish in relationship to Hebrew is not an easy task. Certainly the Hebrew literary historians and critics of the early twentieth century underrated the significance of Yiddish literature. Joseph Klausner, author of a well-known history of modern Hebrew literature, spoke scornfully of Yiddish as a "jargon." Achad Haam, the great Zionist theorist and Hebrew essayist, who is one of the creators of modern Hebrew prose style, wrote in the same tone:

> The Jargon, like all the other languages which the Jews have employed at different times, never has been and never will be regarded by the nation as anything but an external and temporary medium of intercourse: nor can its literature live any longer than the language itself. So soon as the Jargon ceases to be spoken, it will be forgotten, and its literature with it; and then nobody will claim for it, on the ground of national sentiment, what our best men have always claimed for Hebrew — that it should be an obligatory subject of study.[26]

The general encyclopedia in Yiddish was no more objective on this score: it devoted 110 columns to a description of modern Yiddish literature and only 24 to modern Hebrew literature.[27]

We may accept as an objective statement on this subject the definitive history of Jewish literature since the year 1000 by the Russian-Jewish scholar Sergei Tzinberg. Tzinberg was one of the pre-revolutionary Jewish scholars who did not leave Russia after the Revolution. In the late 1920s, when he could no longer publish in the Soviet Union, he sent his manuscripts abroad. His *magnum opus* was a history of Jewish literature from the liturgical poets in Spain in the early middle ages to the Haskala of the late nineteenth century. He succeeded in sending to Vilna, the great cultural center of Eastern European Jewry, twelve volumes which were published there in Yiddish in the mid-1930s.[28] The series was immediately acclaimed as the outstanding work which treated all facets of Jewish literature objectively. The Yiddishists, who had been slighted in other Jewish literary histories, especially praised it. In 1956, when it was first published in Israel in a Hebrew translation with additional notes and commentary, the work soon earned the same esteem that it had had in Yiddish literary circles in Eastern Europe. It is fair then to state that Tzinberg's volumes are the outstanding work of scholarship on Jewish literary history and it has been so accepted by all the different factions in Jewish literary scholarship.

In the Hebrew edition (superior to the earlier edition because of the added notes), the survey of Yiddish literature constitutes one whole volume out of the six. Yiddish literature is considered an important element in Jewish literary culture, but certainly only a minor factor compared to Hebrew. Of course, the era of the greatest productivity in Yiddish literature occurred after the last period that Tzinberg described.[29] If Tzinberg had been able to complete his great work up to the post World War I period, he certainly would have included much more about modern Yiddish literature. But this would not have changed his basic premise: that Hebrew literature was by far the most important part of the Jewish literary heritage.

Thus the only "Jewish" subject in the curriculum of the Soviet Yiddish school, literature, was restricted to one sector of the Jewish literary heritage. We must now examine the Yiddish literature taught to see to what extent it was representative of major Yiddish literature. By examining the authors included in the curriculum, the selections chosen from these authors, and the manner in which these authors and selections were taught, we can understand to what extent Jewish national culture was transmitted to the pupils.

Authors Studied in the Soviet Yiddish School

The inclusion of certain authors is not in itself significant. The selections used may be quite unrepresentative and may have been chosen to suit the government's ideological convenience. And even if typical stories, poems, novels, and plays by important writers were included, they may not have been taught in a spirit of legitimate and humane Jewish nationalism. The spirit, manner, and framework in which they were taught warrant analysis.

First, in order to inquire into the authors studied, we shall examine six textbooks and one course of study. They represent material from the three publishing centers of Yiddish pedagogical literature — Moscow, Minsk, and Kharkov-Kiev; a wide variety of dates ranging from 1926 to 1940; and levels from grades four to ten. I have selected seven items that are representative in terms of place of publication, date of publication and grade level.

Item 1[30]
*A fourth-grade literature textbook
published in Minsk in 1933.*
Authors included:

Mendele Mocher Sforim	Haim Orland
Y.L. Peretz	Avraham Abtchuk
Morris Vintchevsky	Moshe Kulbak
David Edelstadt	Note Lurie
Yosef Bovshover	Peretz Markish
David Bergelson	David Hofstein
Itzik Feffer	Aaron Kushnirov
Izzy Charik	Daniel Meirovitch
Chaim Gildin	Ezra Feninberg

Item 2[31]

A literary chrestomathy for the fourth, fifth, and
sixth grades published in Moscow in 1926.
Authors included:

S. Rosin   Mendele Mocher Sforim
Sholem Asch   Sholom Aleichem
Morris Rosenfeld   Izzy Charik
Y.Y. Singer   Y.M. Weissenberg
Yona Rosenfeld   Yankel Levin

Item 3[32]

A program of studies for Yiddish
and Yiddish literature for grades five, six,
and seven published in Minsk in 1928.
Suggested authors;

David Hofstein   Yoseph Bovshover
Y. Raboy   Asher Schwartzman
Itzik Feffer   I.M. Weissenberg
Joseph Opatoshu   Itzik Kipnis
Sholom Aleichem   Halper Leivick
Izzy Charik   Aaron Kushnirov
Y.L. Peretz   D. Levinson
Sholem Asch   S. Etinger
Peretz Markish   A. Oksenfeld
Morris Vintchevsky   Y.Y. Linetzky
Abraham Reisin   M. Gordon
Mendele Mocher Sforim S. Ansky
S.S. Frug   David Bergelson
                  David Einhorn

Item 4[33]

*A literary chrestomathy for the sixth grade
published in Kiev in 1933.*

Authors included:

Mendele Mocher Sforim
Y.Y. Linetzky
Sholom Aleichem
Y.L. Peretz

David Pinsky
Morris Vintchevsky
David Edelstadt
Yosef Bovshover

Item 5[34]

*A literary chrestomathy for the tenth grade
published in Kiev in 1940.*

Authors included:

Asher Schwartzman
David Hofstein
Leib Kvitko
Peretz Markish

Itzik Feffer
Haim Orland
Shimon Halkin
David Bergelson

Item 6[35]

*A literary chrestomathy for the seventh grade
published in Kiev in 1936.*

Authors included:

Asher Schwartzman
David Hofstein
Peretz Markish
David Bergelson

Haim Orland
Itzik Feffer
Izzy Charik
Note Lurie

Item 7[36]

A literary chrestomathy for the ninth grade
published in Kiev in 1937.
Authors included:

Morris Vintchevsky	Y.L. Peretz
David Edelstadt	Sholom Aleichem
Yosef Bovshover	I.M. Weissenberg
Morris Rosenfeld	

As we can see from these lists, there is a complete absence of many important Hebrew writers who have also made substantial contributions to Yiddish literature, for example, Y.L.B. Katzenelson, Y.Y. Katznelson, Y. Bershadsky, David Frishman, M.Y. Berdyczewski, Yehuda Steinberg, Y.D. Berkowitz, and Chaim Nachman Bialik.[37] Although these men wrote primarily in Hebrew, their Yiddish works are among the most important in the language. The acknowledged master of Yiddish literature, Sholom Aleichem, who is claimed by every literary and political faction, called Bialik "our Jewish national poet."[38] To teach Yiddish literature while omitting Bialik, Berkowitz, and the others is to neglect a significant part of the writings in the language. A few omissions might be considered permissible, but the absence of every one can only be deliberate; the government wished to exclude writers associated with Hebrew because of its identification with Zionism.

　　Moreover, there seems to be a basic difference between the criteria of inclusion in the 1930s and in the 1940s. In the earlier years a considerable number of non-Communist Yiddish writers living outside the Soviet Union were included; in the 1930s almost none were. In Item 4 there seems to be an

exception to this rule: David Pinsky, a socialist who was active
in the labor Zionist movement for the greater part of his life,
is included. However, the students are expressly warned not
to be contaminated by him. The biographical introduction to
his writings in Item Four reads: "In the 1890s Pinsky deeply
immersed himself in the labor movement. In this period he
published many stories on the life of the workers. . . . In the
beginning of the twentieth century Pinsky's writings departed
from their proletarian and revolutionary motif and became
nationalistic and reactionary. Pinsky is now found in the camp
of the social-fascist nationalist writers."[39]

The great classic trio of Yiddish literature — Sholom
Aleichem (Shalom Rabinowitz), Mendele Mocher Sforim
(Shalom Abramowitz), and Yehuda Leib Peretz — all wrote
and lived in the Russian Empire and died at almost the same
time (in 1915, 1916, and 1917).[40] Their inclusion in textbooks and courses of study gave a strong ring of authenticity
to the curriculum. Since they all died before the October
Revolution, they were particularly suitable for the government's purposes.

It is noteworthy that in the tenth-grade reader published
in 1940, one of the last anthologies in Yiddish to be published
for school use, one does not find a single writer who lived
outside the Soviet Union or wrote primarily before the Bolshevik Revolution.

In order to further evaluate the curricula, we may
examine two anthologies of Yiddish poetry recently published in Israel in Hebrew translation.[41] Both are distinguished collections by leading critics, meant to be standard
works for the educated Hebrew-reading public. We also use
two prose anthologies, one published in Israel in Hebrew
translation and intended for use in senior high schools and the

other published in the United States in English translation.[42] The work published in the USA is co-edited by one of the most important living Yiddish literary critics, Eliezer Greenberg. A total of 122 authors are included in these anthologies; we can assume that all writers of real stature are represented. If a writer not included was studied in the Soviet Yiddish schools, he must have been chosen for reasons other than literary ones. However, if a writer was included in one of the four anthologies and was not included in the Soviet schools curricula, this is not in itself evidence of political or ideological motives, since school anthologies cannot include all good writers. Nevertheless, if there is a pattern in the omissions, it suggests ideological criteria.

Examination of the list of authors used in Soviet schools in items 1-7 above shows that most of them are included in the four anthologies recently published in Israel and the United States. In item 1, 11 out of 18 are included; in item 2, 8 out of 10; in item 3, 20 of 28; in item 4, 6 of 8; in item 5, 7 of 8; in item 6, 6 of 8; and in item 7, 5 of 7. We may conclude that the quality of writer used was high.

Two qualifications—one minor, one major—must be made with regard to this verdict. Some authors used in the Soviet schools but not included in any of the four anthologies were clearly chosen for the Soviet curriculum because they were radicals. Yosef Bovshover and David Edelstadt, both competent poets, were nonetheless much less gifted than many of the others included; but both wrote proletarian verses.

The major qualification is that many very important Yiddish writers found in the four recently published anthologies were not studied in the Soviet Yiddish schools. Among them are the most important figures in the history of

Yiddish literature: Moshe Leib Halperin, Mani Leib, Itzik Manger, Lamed Shapiro, Isaac Bashevis Singer, Zalman Schneour, Moshe Nadir, Jacob Glatstein, Yehoash, and Abraham Liessin. To omit Mani Leib, Moshe Leib Halperin, Itzik Manger, and Zalman Schneour and include David Hofstein, Shimon Halkin, Asher Schwartzman, and Leib Kvitko could only have been done because the latter four were Yiddish writers resident in the Soviet Union sympathetic to Communism and the former four were not.

Representativeness of the Selections Chosen

How representative were the selections of the authors which were studied? We have seen that although some important writers were omitted, the list included was considerable. Let us examine the selections chosen from Y.L. Peretz, Sholom Aleichem, and Mendele Mocher Sforim. Peretz and Mendele were both critics of the Jewish society of their time which, of course, endeared them to the Jewish Communists and caused them to be widely read in the schools. For example, one Peretz story used frequently in anthologies and readers was "Dos Shtreimel" (The Fur Hat),[43] one of the very few stories by Peretz attacking a Chassidic rabbi. The Rabbi never appears anywhere without his enormous fur hat which is the insignia of his position. In the story the furrier is engaged in a monologue in which he tells of his great pleasure in making the Rabbi's hat. He feels that he is responsible for the Rabbi's importance since the cap makes the Rabbi. He relates the transformation of a common mortal into an awe-inspiring interpreter of God's will on earth. No important occurrence in life, no birth, marriage, or death, can take place without the approval of the man who wears that fur hat. It is the hat, not the man or his wisdom, that sanctions and legalizes his various acts. Were it not for the hat, it would not be possible to tell right from wrong. This fine bit of sarcasm attacks not only the Chassidim but also our whole social system and its conventional lies.

The Soviets used "The Fur Hat" and other articles and stories critical of Jewish life of the period, not to preserve or understand Jewish culture — which might be considered the aim of studying a national minority literature — but rather to indoctrinate children in the principles of Soviet Communism. The picture given of Peretz in Soviet Yiddish school literature is exclusively that of a critic of the society he lived in. Peretz, of course, was a social critic. But he was also, as one literary historian has recently written ". . . the Jewish Pindar. He revived faltering Jewish hearts and strengthened enfeebled Jewish hands."[44] He believed in the modernization and rejuvenation of Jewish life so that the Jew could take his place as an equal among the peoples of the world with a strong contribution to make to its future: "I am not advocating that we shut ourselves up in a spiritual ghetto. But we should get out as Jews, with our own spiritual treasures. We should interchange, give and take, but not beg."[45]

The Soviet Yiddish school literature did not include any of the numerous essays and articles written in this vein. To have done so would have been to contradict the Soviet version of Jewishness, which entailed giving up Jewishness in favor of an "internationalist" Soviet society. Even during the bitter pogroms of the early twentieth century, when Jewish spirits were at a low ebb, Peretz did not advocate sacrificing Jewish identity for some amorphous proletarian future. He wrote:

Working for one's own hearth and kinsmen does not mean abandoning the banner of humanity-at-large. Today everybody must plow, sow, and cultivate his own bit of land, although — or rather because — we hope for a morrow in which there will be a common granary for mankind. To this granary all will bring their grain, their entire produce, and from this granary each person will be fed alike, without regard to his ancestry or the color of his skin.

We Jews have not suffered these thousands of years in order now to forget our own civilization. We want to and we have to continue our own way of life, so that we may later unite with the company of mankind as equal partners with equal rights and equal shares.[46]

Although Peretz was a reformer, he feared the revolutionary movement spreading over the Russian Empire. In passages which certainly did not appear in Soviet school readers, he wrote:

My heart is with you.

My eye cannot have its fill of your flaming flag. My ear never tires of listening to your sonorous song. . . .

When you clench your fists at those who would stifle the free word in your throat and still the burning protest on your lips — I rejoice; I pray to God to sharpen your teeth. Yea, when you march upon Sodom ready to rend and tear, my soul is with you. Sureness of your victory fills me with warmth and makes me drunk as with old wine.

And yet. . .

And yet I have my fear of you.

I fear the oppressed who are victorious lest they turn into oppressors, and every oppressor sins against the human spirit.

Is there not already talk among you that humanity must
march like an army at the front and that you will beat for
it the drum to keep it in step and pace?
And yet humanity is not an army. . . .
I have my fear of you.
As victors, you could turn into bureaucrats, doling out to
each his bit as to the poor in a poorhouse, apportioning
to each his work as to the imprisoned in a prison-pen.[47]

Sholom Aleichem's work was also distorted of the true
significance by means of judicious selection. The Soviets used
his work extensively but not representatively. Although the
Soviet Yiddish textbooks and courses of study cited above
included many selections from Sholom Aleichem, they were
almost entirely from the volumes of stories of his famous
characters: Tevye the dairyman, Motel the cantor's son, and
Menachem Mendel. These are Sholom Aleichem's best-
known characters but they represent only a fraction of his
total output. Many volumes of his collected works were
wholly composed of stories about the various Jewish religious
holidays or included quite a few stories of that nature.[48] These
religious holidays were one of the characteristic features of
Jewish life in Eastern Europe: full of symbolic customs and
folkways, they were a rich expression of Jewish community
feelings and were vividly depicted in Jewish literature. A
subject which so dominated the pattern of people's life would
have to be dealt with in the writings of such a man as Sholom
Aleichem, who was so concerned with the everyday feelings
of his people. Yet his delightful and frequently uproarious
stories of holiday events were seldom included in the Soviet
school anthologies, even though the Soviets paid him great
homage in theory.[49]

The selections from Mendele Mocher Sforim were more

representative. But some restrictions were made. The biographical information in one anthology pointed out that "in his earlier works Mendele fought and unmercifully exposed the fraudulent leaders of the Jewish community, but the works which he wrote at the end of his life bristle with a nationalist-chauvinist character."[50] These "nationalist-chauvinist" works were not printed for the students to read.

The basic tone of Mendele's writing was much more suitable for Soviet purposes than that of Sholom Aleichem or Peretz. Mendele's caustic satire was a wholesale attack against the entire organized Jewish community.[51] Taken out of context, it could be seen as a broadside against Jewish life in general, which it surely was not. Mendele wanted reform through greater enlightenment and a more modern school system, but he certainly did not wish to demolish Jewish culture or hold it up to shame as the Soviets did.

If we compare the Soviet Yiddish school curriculum with the literature curriculum of the Israeli high school (published by the Ministry of Education), we can see how the former was distorted.[52] The Israeli high school curriculum also includes a generous and much more representative selection of the writings of Mendele, Peretz, and Sholom Aleichem.[53] For instance, one of the two required volumes of Sholom Aleichem is the collection of holiday stories. There does not appear to be the zealous effort to show that the essence of the work of these authors is their role as "critics" of Jewish society.

Basically the Yiddish literature used in the Soviet schools, with the exception of a small amount devoted to the classicists, consisted of material written since 1917. If material written before 1917 appeared it was something that could serve as background for what the Communists had begun in

1917. An example of this is the Soviet Yiddish writer David Bergelson, possibly the greatest novelist who ever wrote in Yiddish. Bergelson wrote both before and after the revolution, but most of his work which was included was material from his Soviet period. One prerevolutionary work often extracted was *Noch Alemen* (The End of Everything),[54] a picture of a patrician Jewish family's disintegration in the wake of a conflict between bourgeois luxury and a search for more enduring values. This work was used to show the pre-revolutionary decadence of Jewish life which the Bolshevik regime eliminated.

Literature which did not serve the Soviet purpose was ignored only in the case of the Jews. The Ukrainian Communists did not disown their national poet Franko because of his collaboration with reactionaries and his ultra-nationalism.[55] On the contrary, they gave his works greater prominence than their literary merit warranted.[56] But the Jewish Communists banned the works of the Jewish national poet Bialik and maligned him, even after his death, as a fascist who "blessed the emergence of Hitler." The Islamic peoples in the Soviet Union were free, and in fact encouraged, to celebrate the anniversary of the eleventh-century physician, philosopher and religious scholar, Avicenna (Ibn Sina), who wrote in Arabic. But Soviet Jews did not dare observe the anniversary of the twelfth-century physician, philosopher, and religious scholar, Maimonides, who wrote both in Arabic and Hebrew.[57]

Method of Presentation of Literary Material

In order to scrutinize the manner in which literature was taught, we shall consider the classroom atmosphere; the organization of material in the course of study; pedagogical literature; and instruction and suggestions to the teacher in the textbooks, as well as the exercises and questions after the selections.

A fascinating report made by a prominent American Jewish community worker in 1929 sheds light on the atmosphere in which literature was taught:

> I once sat in a class when literature was being studied. The study of this subject made a very strange impression on me. I heard how the teacher spoke about Sholom Aleichem. However, it was not Sholom Aleichem the artist, the humorist, the classicist. No, the teacher was naming Sholom Aleichem's type Menachem Mendel as a means to understand that the Jews never wanted to work and that they lived from air or on the backs of the peasant and the rest of the Russian population.
> If this had not been a Yiddish class and a Jewish teacher I could have the impression that the teacher was an anti-Semite, a hater of Jews. He spoke fervidly in an extremely bitter manner about every type that Sholom Aleichem described so warmly and with such great pain. The teacher did not even find it necessary to point out the political and social conditions from where Sholom Aleichem's Menachem Mendel was a sacrifice. He did not even present the terrible role that Russian Czarism had played in crippling Jewish life in Russia.[58]

The courses of study arranged Yiddish literature in a distorted way. For example, the literature curriculum of the seventh grade in a second-level course of study listed seven subjects for the semester's work:

1.   The idea of creation by the people: folkways, folk-tales, and proverbs.

2.   A short review of Haskala literature until the liberation of the serfs.
3.   The Haskala movement after the liberation of the peasants.
4.   The development of capitalism.
5.   The development of the Jewish workers movement and the first revolution of 1905.
6.   Between the first and second revolutions.
7.   A review of current Yiddish prose in Soviet Russia.[59]

Up to and including point 3, this is a perfectly reasonable organization of the development of Yiddish literature. Points 4 to 7, however, represent minor sidelights in the mainstream of Yiddish literary development. This Soviet curriculum failed to mention crucial issues such as Jewish nationalism and the great conflict between traditional Jewish life and the modern world.

This period is treated quite differently today in the high schools of the left-wing, radical socialist kibbutzim of the United Workers Party (Mapam) in Israel. The Mapam's curricula represent a genuine effort of a radical socialist yet Zionist group to make a synthesis between general history taught in a Marxist vein and Jewish history.

High School Curriculum of Kibbutzim
of the Hashomer Hatzair in Israel (Humanistika)[60]
Grade 11
Victory of Bourgeoisie and Beginnings
of Proletarian War – 126 hours

1.   Social, economic, and spiritual ferment in eighteenth century; extension of absolutism and remnants of feudalism;

sharpening of class conflict; Encyclopedists; Rousseau; development of science and technology.

2. United States; geography of United States; settlement in United States in eighteenth century; Declaration of Independence and causes; War of Independence and development of United States; liberation of slaves; Civil War and causes; United States as manufacturing power.

3. French Revolution: (a) from Rights of Man to Civil War; (b) Jacobin dictatorship;(c) Thermidor; (d) England and Germany in the period of the French Revolution.

4. Reaction and progress; geography; Napoleon; conditions in Europe; restoration; reading in neoclassicist literature; *Sturm und Drang*; art; romanticism.

5. Beginnings of proletariat and its theory; industrial revolution; chartist movement; Utopians; 1848; Marx-Engels; Communist Manifesto; First International.

6. Beginnings of Central European states.

7. Literature and art — late romanticism and realism — Heine, Balzac, Flaubert, Pushkin.

8. Paris Commune.

9. Conclusions.

The Jewish Problem and Its Solution – 110 hours

1. The Emancipation period — economic and legal changes of Jews in eighteenth century; Haskala in Western Europe; science of Judaism; Neo-Orthodoxy; the Jews and industrial capitalism.

2. Jews of Eastern Europe; economic life under Czarism; Haskala; Chassidism; Jewish community and class structure.

3. Literature — Jewish crisis in mirror of literature; Y.L. Gordon, Mendele Mocher Sforim.

4. Anti-Semitism.

5. Solutions: assimilation, immigration, autonomy; territorialism.

6. Zionism: Smolenskin: "Auto-emancipation"; Hibath

Zion; Moses Hess; Achad Haam; political Zionism; socialist
Zionism, immigration to Palestine and settlement; new Jewish
community in Palestine.
7. Conclusions.

In this curriculum Jewish history does not disappear, but
is autonomous within the framework of general history. The
Soviet curriculum studied Sholom Aleichem and Y.L. Peretz
in the context of "the development of capitalism" whereas
they can only be understood and appreciated if read in the
light of the development of the Jewish problem in Eastern
Europe, a problem that was, of course, greatly influenced by
industrial development and urbanization.

To determine how individual stories were taught, we can
examine two fourth-grade readers, one published in Moscow
in 1928 and the other in Minsk in 1933. In both questions
appear having little to do with the story itself which are clearly
intended for Communist indoctrination.

In the earlier book there was less blatant effort to distort
the story for propaganda purposes. The story is used as a
means of acculturating people into Communist society, but
this is done by emphasizing aspects of the story, which while
not really germane, are nevertheless present to some degree.
In the 1930s there was a blatant effort to suppress the essence
of the story itself for indoctrination purposes.

Even in the earlier books there is some effort to use the
stories in a manner unrelated to their real meaning. In the
delightful children's story "Tzvei Veltn" (Two Worlds) by
Sholom Aleichem there is an effort to use the story as an
example of the Jewish life lived in the Russian ghetto, but
instead it is cited by the Soviets as an example of the evil life
the Jews lived before the October Revolution. At the end of
the story children are asked such questions as "What is there

[in this story] from the old life and what from the new?" "How does the new fight with the old?": an unreconcilable conflict between the new and the old is suggested.[61] Leading Jewish political and literary historians — Tzinberg, Klausner, Dubnow — do not feel that modern Jewish life mandates a complete break with the past or that the present is all good and the past all bad. They would feel, as would most Jewish social and political philosophers, that modern Jewish life and institutions have developed from the past. In the course of that development, they would argue, much that is good has endured and much that is no longer relevant has been forsaken.

The Soviet Communists take a different view. For them the pre-Soviet period was all evil. It was unthinkable to assign value to prerevolutionary Jewish life. This attitude in effect alienated the Jews from Jewishness and facilitated their assimilation into Russian life. One writer commented: "This presentation could only discourage a Jew's interest in Yiddish. If he recognized it as a distortion, he would be outraged by the defamation; if he assumed it to be truthful depiction, he would wish to forget his antecedents. Either reaction would be conducive to assimilation."[62]

In the 1930s the textbooks were much more aggressively propagandistic. In the 1933 Minsk fourth-grade textbook practically every story is accompanied by leading questions, having little relation to the story, which serve to indoctrinate the student. The first story is "Chapers" by Mendele Mocher Sforim, a tale of young Jewish conscripts in the early nineteenth-century Russian army. The story shows an aspect of the suffering endured by the Jews in Czarist Russia in their struggle for legal and national rights. The Russians did not take into account at all the right of the Jews to exist as Jews, regarding it as "reactionary"; they did condemn the persecution of the Jews as people. At the end of the story "Chapers" the children are asked to "compare the life of the poor children in those days with the life of the workers' children in the Soviet Union."[63] The pupils are not asked about Jewish children but about "workers' " children, the implication being, of course, that the problem of the Jews was not a national one but an economic one, and that the problem was now solved. In actual fact, the Jews always struggled for national rights as well as for economic and civil rights. After the abdication of Czar Nicholas II and the Provisional Government's proclamation abolishing discriminatin because of race or religion, all the organized Jewish parties decided to call an All-Russian Jewish convention; they wished to participate as Jews in the new Russia that was to be. The preparatory committee for the convention issued the following proclamation to the Jewish communities which cogently expresses Jewish feeling on the subject:

> Citizens, Jews! The Jewish people in Russia now faces an event which has no parallel in Jewish history for two thousand years. Not only has the Jew as an individual, as a citizen, acquired equality of rights — which also has happened in other counties — but the Jewish nation looks forward to the possibility of securing national rights. Never and nowhere have the Jews lived through such a serious, responsible moment as the present — responsible to the present and the future generations.[64]

"Chapers" is followed by a selection from Sholom Aleichem's book of stories about Motel the cantor's son who travelled with his family to America. At the end of the selection the pupils are asked "Compare Motel with our Young

Pioneers. With what interests does each one of them live?" Another story by Peretz, "Di Levone Dertzeilt" (A Tale Told by the Moon), is followed by such pointed questions as "How do children live in capitalistic cities?"[65] In this manner, the Soviets used these famous Yiddish stories, not to examine Jewish life, but to imbue Jewish children with Soviet ideology.

Professional literature and pedagogical material was published in Yiddish, although to a limited extent. From 1924 to 1928 *Af di vegn tzu der naier shul* (On the Road to the New School) was issued as a pedagogical monthly by the Central Jewish Bureaus of the Peoples Commissariats of Education of the RSFSR, the Ukrainian SSR, and the White Russian SSR, and from 1928 to 1937 *Ratenbildung* (Soviet Education), also a pedagogical monthly, was issued by the Ukrainian Commissariat.[66] From time to time separate bulletins or brochures on various educational problems or issues contained explicit articles on the treatment of Jewish subjects from a Communist angle. Typical of such articles was one which appeared in *Ratenbildung* in 1929. It discussed suitable material for dramatic circles in small town Yiddish schools. The author refers to several recent Yiddish plays that are suitable for the effort to form the new Soviet man. But the author expresses regret that many classic Yiddish plays, while quite suitable for children, are not adequate for the contemporary purposes of the school.[67]

It is clear, then, that although the Soviets frequently used the leading Yiddish writers in their schools, the material was distorted to serve political rather than literary ends.

In evaluating Soviet Yiddish schools, Jewish writers outside the Soviet Union have never considered them as truly Jewish. For example, Simon Dubnow wrote that "the special school for Jews had no Jewishness in it except the language of instruction. Children were taught the Bolshevist creed and had planted in their hearts a feeling of class hatred even for their bourgeois fathers. The belief in Marxism according to the version of Lenin came in place of every national promise of Judaism."[68]

An active Russian Zionist who has long resided in Israel has written:

> Unlike the educational and cultural activities of the territorial peoples of Russia, however, educational activity among the Jews was completely dissociated from any connection with the past, the language or the tradition of Jewry. All educational, cultural and information activities in Yiddish for which considerable sums were granted from Government resources, were conducted from the very beginning on strictly Soviet lines, without any link with Jewish cultural and spiritual sources and treasures.[69]

The Soviets aimed at such a severance from the past. According to the Soviet slogan of "National in Form, Socialist in Content" they tried to make the Soviet Yiddish school a purely Soviet school with no Jewish content. The curriculum made no effort to cultivate and develop Jewish life; in fact, it persistently attempted to uproot Jewish traditions. Several factors may have served to thwart the Communist goal of using the school to assimilate Jews into Soviet society. First, the student body was composed entirely of Jews. The very fact that Jews were together in the same school, regardless of the curriculum, may have served to increase Jewish self-awareness and identity. Secondly, even though the curriculum contained the barest minimum of Jewish content, a Jewish language was used. After all, most of the ordinary speech and language activity of any nation does not consist of specific national content. Ordinary day-to-day communication in the national language serves as a nationally reinforcing factor; it is possible that the use of Yiddish itself retarded assimilation. Finally, the conscious effort in the schools to distort the essence of the minimal part of the curriculum that was devoted to Jewish content may not have had the desired effect. Anyone who has ever been active in education knows that children do not always learn exactly what their teachers want them to learn. By vigorously denying the Jewish aspects of Yiddish literature, the educators may well have caused the children to examine that literature more closely. But it is also possible that the Soviets succeeded in making the Jewish students antagonistic to their own tradition: reading about Jewish merchants and *luftmenschen* may have inspired revulsion rather than reverence for Jewish life and culture before the Revolution. In any case, the Yiddish schools were probably not an important factor in maintaining national consciousness. The truth is that assimilation was greatest when the schools were at their peak. In 1926, 72 percent of Soviet Jews gave Yiddish as their primary language; in 1939 only 41 percent did.[70] Some argue that without the Yiddish schools the drop might have been even sharper; but how much sharper could it have been?

General Conclusions

What observations can be made about the efficacy of the Soviet minority program and its system expressed in the slogan "National in form, socialist in content"? In the Introduction we stated that the durability of minority cultures has to be evaluated with reference to the minority's population and its degree of territorial concentration. Because of these factors, we could not expect the Jews to be in as strong a position as the Ukrainians or Georgians. Does the experience of the Jews mean that national minorities with no territorial concentration are bound to be assimilated? The Jewish experience in Russia —Czarist and Soviet — shows that a national minority scattered among other peoples can retain its own identity if it is determined to do so and if it is allowed to do so. As we have shown, the Jews entered the Soviet period with an extraordinarily rich educational tradition. From the beginning of their immigration into medieval Poland from the German states to their entry into the Czarist Empire in the three partitions of Poland, the Jews had a comprehensive system of universal education unequaled anywhere in the world. At the end of the nineteenth century, when the traditional system became inadequate, new forms were devised to harmonize the traditional with the modern. When the Czar was overthrown and the Provisional Government established, the atmosphere of freedom brought about an enormous burst of creative activity. Had this atmosphere endured, the Jews would certainly have built strong independent educational and cultural institutions. In Lithuania, Latvia, and Estonia, where the Jews were given unlimited freedom and government aid, they built a network of Hebrew and Yiddish schools which most Jewish children attended. In Poland and Rumania, where there was less freedom and little if any government aid, but no actual suppression, sizeable systems were established and a substantial minority of Jewish children attended them. The Jews of the Soviet Union would have done the same had they been permitted to do so: Jewish schools in the Soviet Union were a victim not of assimilation, but of totalitarianism.

Notes

1. A. Pinkevich, *Science and Education in the USSR* (New York: G.P. Putnam's Sons, 1935), p. 153.
2. For a description of the philosophy guiding Soviet schools in the 1920s see Albert P. Pinkevitch, *The New Education in the Soviet Republic*, tr. by Nucia Perlmutter, George Counts (ed.) (New York: The John Day Company, 1929).
3. Lucy L.W. Wilson, *The New Schools in the New Russia* (New York: Vanguard Press, 1928), pp. 65-66.
4. Scott Nearing, *Education in Soviet Russia* (New York: International Publishers, 1926), pp. 94-95.
5. Y. Anilovitch and M. Yoffe (eds.), "Yiddishe lernbicher un pedagogic, 1900-1930 (Bibliografie)," *Shriftn far psikhologie un pedagogik* (Vilna, 1933), vol. I, pp. 478, 479.
6. Y. Ravin and V. Shatz, *Literatur: lernbukh·farn 4tn shulyor* (Minsk: White Russian State Publishing House, National Minorities Section, 1933.)
7. See Harold Rugg (ed.), *Democracy and the Curriculum: The Life and Program of the American School*, Third Yearbook of the John Dewey Society (New York: D. Appleton-Century Company, 1939). At one place we are given the school program of Santa Barbara, California (pp. 491-492). It shows remarkable similarity to the program of the Soviet schools

251

in the 1920s. Of course, Soviet schools had a little more blatant direction.

8. Y. Bakst and Y. Grinberg, *Arbets kinder* (Moscow: Shul un Bukh, 1928), p. 46.
9. Ibid.
10. Ibid., p. 141.
11. Ibid., pp. 173-174.
12. "Yiddishe shuln in mizrakh europa," *Algemeine entsiklopedie*, Series "Yidn," (New York: World Jewish Culture Congress, 1950), vol. III, column 387.
13. The series was published in Moscow in 1926 and consisted of seven parts published in five volumes.
14. Khana Shmeruk (ed.), *Pirsumim Yehudiim Bebrit Hamoetsot, 1917-1960* (Jerusalem: Historical Society of Israel, 1961), pp. 265-267, 285-286.
15. Quoted in Maurice J. Shore, *Soviet Education* (New York: Philosophical Library, 1947), p. 1919.
16. Shmeruk, op. cit., pp. 265-267.
17. Ravin and Shatz, p. 176. It was probably the largest printing of a fourth-grade textbook. There were a few books of a similar or slightly larger printing for other grades or levels.
18. A. Velednitzky et al. (eds.), *Literarishe khrestomatie farn 6tn lernyor* (Kharkov-Kiev: State Publishing House for National Minorities Literature, 1933).
19. The best single volume on the Jewish schools in Poland between the two world wars is Miriam Eisenstein, *Jewish Schools in Poland, 1919-1939* (New York: King's Crown Press, Columbia University, 1950). The material in this section dealing with the curriculum in Tarbuth-sponsored schools is from this work, pp. 42-44.
20. "Yiddishe shuln in mizrakh europa," columns 387-388.
21. *Iberblik fun limudim*, p. 87. "Old Hebrew Literature" was probably the Bible.
22. *Shriftn fun veisrusishn melukhe universitet*, p. 157.
23. For the history of the Polish Bund see J.S. Hertz, *Geshikhte*

fun a yugnt (New York: Farlag "Unzer Tzait," 1946), and H.L. Poznansky, *Zikhroines fun a bundist* (Warsaw: Druk Grafia, 1938), 2 vols.

24. An excellent study of Jewish scholarly research in the Soviet Union is Alfred A. Greenbaum, *Jewish Scholarship in Soviet Russia , 1918-1941* (Boston, 1959).

25. N. Chanin, *Soviet russland: vi ikh hob ir gezen* (New York: Farlag Vekker, 1929), p. 98.

26. Achad Haam, *Selected Essays,* translated from the Hebrew by Leon Simon (Philadelphia: Jewish Publication Society of America, 1948), p. 283.

27. *Algemeine entsiklopedie*, Series "Yidn" (New York: World Jewish Culture Congress, 1950), vol. III.

28. A Hebrew translation of Tzinberg was recently published in Israel with expanded notes and bibliography: Yisrael Tzinberg, *Toldot Sifrut Yisrael* (Tel Aviv: Sifriat Poàlim, 1956-1960), 6 vols.

29. Two good accounts in English of the rise of Yiddish literature are A.A. Roback, *The Story of Yiddish Literature* (New York: Yiddish Scientific Institute, 1940), and Sol Liptzin, *The Flowering of Yiddish Literature* (New York: Thomas Yoseloff, 1963).

30. Ravin and Shatz, op. cit.

31. N. Oislender et al., *Arbet un kamf: literarishe khrestomatie farn 4tn, 5tn un 6tn shulyor*, Notebook 1, Part 2 (Moscow: Central Publishing House, 1926), 67 pp.

32. White Russian Soviet Socialist Republic, Peoples Commissariat of Education, *Program fun yiddish un literatur far der zibnyoriker shul, ovntshuln far arbeter yugnt, ovntshuln fun hechern tip* (Minsk: State Publishing House, 1928), 46 pp.

33. Velednitzky et al., 230 pp.

34. S. Horovitz, *Literarishe farn 10tn klass fun der mitelshul* (Kiev-Kharkov: Ukrainian State Publishing House, National Minorities Section, 1936), 190 pp.

35. A. Holdes, *Khrestomatie far literatur farn 7tn klass fun der*

mitelshul (Kiev-Kharkov: Ukrainian State Publishing House, National Minorities Section, 1936), 190 pp.

36. A. Holdes, *Literarishe khrestomatie farn 9tn klass fun der mitelshul* (Kiev: Ukrainian State Publishing House, National Minorities Section, 1937), 192 pp.

37. Extensive articles on the literary works of these authors with accompanying bibliographies are to be found in Zalman Reizin, *Leksikon fun der yiddisher literatur, presse, un filologie* (Vilna: B. Kletzkin Publishing House, 1928) 4 vols.

38. Vol. 12 of Sholom Aleichem's collected works, which is devoted to short pieces on various writers, carries an interesting article on his relations with Bialik, whom Sholom Aleichem calls the "greatest of our poets" (Sholom Aleichem, *Ale verk* [New York, 1923], vol. XII, p. 101). Another reason why the Soviets did not print this article was that in it Sholom Aleichem mentions that he was a delegate to the 1907 Zionist Congress at The Hague. He describes his meeting with Bialik at the Congress. It might have been embarrassing for the Jewish Communists to admit that Sholom Aleichem, whom they hailed as a man of the people, was actually a delegate to a Zionist Congress.

39. Velednitzky et al., op. cit., p. 146.

40. Peretz and Mendele are equally important figures in Hebrew literature. For articles on their works see Reizin's *Leksikon*, which contains bibliographies of their writings in Hebrew.

41. Shimshon Meltzer (ed.), *Al Naharot* (Jerusalem: Mosad Bialik, 1956); and Moshe Basok (ed.), *Mivkhar Shirat Yiddish* (Tel Aviv: Hakkibutz Hameuchad, 1963).

42. *Lakat Sipurim Mesifrut Yiddish* (Tel Aviv: Moshe Neumann, 1957), and Irving Howe and Eliezer Greenberg, *A Treasury of Yiddish Stories* (New York: Viking Press, 1954).

43. It was included in N. Oislender and Y. Bakst, *Arbet un kamf: literarishe khrestomatie*, Notebook 3, Section 4 (Moscow: Central Publishing House, 1926); Y. Bakst and Y. Grinberg, *Arbets kinder* (Moscow: Shul un Bukh, 1928); and Ukrainian

Soviet Socialist Republic, People's Commissariat of Education, *Programmen farn tzveitn kontzenter fun shtotishe, shtetlishe un dorfishe arbetshuln* (Kiev: "Kultur Lige," 1927).

44. Liptzin, *The Flowering of Yiddish Literature,* p. 116.

45. Sol Liptzin (ed.), *Peretz* (Yivo Bilingual Series) (New York: Yiddish Scientific Institute—Yivo, 1947), p. 378.

46. Ibid., pp. 340, 336.

47. Ibid., p. 278.

48. Sholom Aleichem's works have been translated into most of the major languages in the world in many editions. They were frequently published in the Soviet Union in Yiddish in children's editions, but his volume devoted entirely to holiday stories was not published. See Shmeruk, p. 262.

49. In 1948 the Soviet Union began to publish the collected works of Sholom Aleichem in Yiddish in 20 volumes. Publication ceased shortly thereafter because of the general suppression of publication in Yiddish. From the prospectus of the series it is impossible to tell with certainty if they intended to publish the holiday stories. In 1961 his collected works were published in Russian translation. The book of holiday stories and other items were omitted. (Sholom Aleichem, *Sobranie sochinenii* [Moscow, 1961], 6 vols.

50. Ravin and Shatz, op. cit., p. 5.

51. For an article on Mendele Mocher Sforim, see Sol Liptzin, *The Flowering of Yiddish Literature*, pp. 20-32.

52. Although the suggested curriculum for secondary schools published by the Ministry of Education is not binding, most have either adopted it or follow a variation very similar inasmuch as the matriculation examinations are based upon it (Moshe Avidor, *Education in Israel* [Jerusalem: Youth and Hechalutz Department of the Zionist Organization, 1957], p. 76).

53. Ministry of Education and Culture, Department for Secondary Education, *Hatzaot Letakhnit Limud Bebeit Hasefer Hatikhon* (Jerusalem: The Government Printer, 1956).

54. It was included in the official reading list in the programs for secondary schools of both the Ukraine and White Russia (Ukrainian Soviet Socialist Republic, People's Commissariat of Education, *Program farn tzveitn kontzenter fun shtotishe, shtetlshe un dorfishe arbetshuln* [Kiev: Kultur Lige, 1927], p. 208; White Russian Soviet Socialist Republic, People's Commissariat of Education, *Program fun yiddish un literature far der zibnyoriker shul* [Minsk: State Publishing House, 1928], p. 34).

55. The state University in Lvov is called the Ivan Franko State University in Lvov (Central Statistical Board of the USSR, *Kulturnoe stroitelstvo SSSR* [Moscow State Statistical Publishing House, 1956], p. 244.

56. B.Z. Goldberg, *The Jewish Problem in the Soviet Union* (New York: Crown Publishers, Inc., 1961), p. 27.

57. Ibid., p. 28.

58. Chanin, op. cit., p. 100.

59. White Russian Soviet Socialist Republic, People's Commissariat of Education, *Program fun yiddish un literatur far der zibnyoriker shul*, p. 40. It should be noted that this was a period when some limited attention was paid to earlier literature. Later on, even this was eliminated.

60. Melford E. Spiro, *Children of the Kibbutz* (Cambridge, Mass.: Harvard University Press, 1958), pp. 481-483.

61. Y. Bakst and Y. Grinberg, *Arbets kinder: khrestomatie un arbets bukh farn 4tn klass* (Moscow: Shul un Bukh, 1928), p. 32.

62. Judd L. Teller, *The Kremlin, the Jews, and the Middle East* (New York: Thomas Yoseloff, 1957), p. 10.

63. Ravin and Shatz, op. cit., p. 15.

64. Quoted in Salo W. Baron, *The Russian Jew Under Tsars and Soviets* (New York: The Macmillan Company, 1964), p. 200.

65. Ravin and Shatz, op. cit., pp. 25, 28.

66. Shmeruk, op. cit., pp. 337, 391.

67. M. Krugliak, "Dramkreizen in shtetl," *Ratenbildung*, Vol. II, No. 6, June 1929, 36.

68. Simon Dubnow, *Divrei Yimei Am Olam* (Tel Aviv: Dvir, 1940), vol. XI, p. 26.

69. Benjamin West, *Struggles of a Generation* (Tel Aviv: Massadah Publishing Company, 1959), p. 10.

70. Harry Lipset, "A Note on Yiddish as the Language of Soviet Jews in the Census of 1939," *The Jewish Journal of Sociology*, vol. XII, No. 1 (June 1970), 56.

Chapter 7

Yiddish Schools in Annexed Areas, 1939-1940

THE YIDDISH SCHOOLS which were opened in areas annexed to the Soviet Union in 1939-1940, and which are properly not a part of the mainstream of the history of Yiddish schools in the USSR, warrant separate treatment.

On September 17, 1939, Soviet troops invaded Poland and met minimal resistance: Soviet losses were only 757 dead and 1,862 wounded. By September 19 Vilna was captured and the Soviets reached the Hungarian frontier. On September 29 a Treaty of Friendship was signed with Germany which formally partitioned Poland (for the fourth time in its history), thereby adding 20,000 square kilometers and almost 13 million inhabitants, primarily non-Poles, to the USSR: seven million Ukrainians, three million Belorussians, more than one and a half million Poles, and about one and a half million Jews. The Ukrainians and Belorussians, who had suffered discrimination under Polish rule, genuinely welcomed reunification with their fellow nationals[1] in the USSR.

Additional territorial annexations followed. On June 12, 1940, a Soviet ultimatum to Lithuania was promptly accepted; three days later Soviet forces invaded the country and occupied Kovno. A new Lithuanian government was formed on June 2. On June 16 the USSR demanded a change of government in Estonia; the Estonians yielded on the 22nd. Similarly, a new Latvian cabinet was formed on June 20. On June 26 a Soviet ultimatum to Rumania demanded Bessarabia and Northern Bukovina; twenty-four hours later the Rumanians complied. On July 14 general elections were held in Estonia, Latvia, and Lithuania, and on July 21 the newly-elected assemblies unanimously voted for union with the USSR.

The annexations which added more than two million Jews to the Soviet Jewish population of about three million, had a qualitative as well as a quantitative impact. The Jewish population of the Baltic states and of Eastern Poland, Bessarabia, and Northern Bukovina was culturally and linguistically the least assimilated in Eastern Europe. Almost everyone spoke Yiddish. In Eastern Poland many Jewish children studied in various types of Jewish schools.[2] Efforts to Polonize the Jewish population had had little effect. In Central, Southern, and Western Poland, Yiddish and Hebrew culture had to compete with the prestigious and developed Polish culture. In the Baltic states and Eastern Poland, however, Yiddish and Hebrew literature were more highly developed than the local literatures and cultures; thus Jews were not drawn to the latter. In the Baltic states the great majority of Jewish children studied in Jewish schools.[3] Hence the possibility existed that the newly incorporated territories offered a strong opportunity for strengthening the declining

Yiddish culture in the Soviet Union or for building a strong network of Yiddish cultural institutions in Western Soviet Russia.

The Soviets came into these new areas with a commitment to national liberation and free cultural expression for those peoples who had suffered discrimination under the Polish regime. Opportunities were opened up to the majority Ukrainian and Belorussian population — even to the Poles, a small minority in the area.[4] But the Jewish schools and cultural facilities which the Soviets set up were clearly inadequate, especially when we consider that this was the most nationalist Jewish area in Eastern Europe and had few linguistically assimilated Jews. For example, the city of Pinsk in Belorussia, together with its surrounding towns and villages, had a very large Jewish population. An article in the Minsk Yiddish daily on August 15, 1940, claimed that since the onset of Soviet power "children have the opportunity of studying in their native language." In the 1939-40 school year, according to the paper, the Pinsk district had 486 Belorussian schools, 20 Yiddish schools, and nine Polish schools.[5] This is persuasive evidence that the "opportunity of studying in the native language" was not given to all Jews and that this small number of schools was probably due to discrimination. In Bessarabia, where there had been 50 Hebrew schools operated by the Tarbut organization before the annexation, no more than eleven Yiddish schools were open in the 1940-41 school year.[6]

The only schools permitted in the entire area were Soviet Yiddish schools. Hebrew schools sponsored by Tarbut, secular Yiddish schools, and religious Jewish schools of all types were closed. The Soviet Yiddish schools were housed in former Jewish schools of various types, a fact that was repeatedly emphasized in the local Communist Yiddish press.[7]

In the absence of any choice, the schools and other cultural institutions were opened without any great enthusiasm. The Jews did not understand Ukrainian, Belorussian, Estonian, Latvian, Lithuanian, or Moldavian, so it was impossible to require Jewish children to attend schools in these languages. A transitional period with some Yiddish schools was therefore necessary; the fact that there were no longer any Yiddish schools in the old Ukraine and Belorussia indicated that the schools were transitional, and would not be permitted to exist very long.

There is strong evidence in the Yiddish press — the two old Minsk and Kiev dailies and the new papers in the Baltic states and Bialystok — that Yiddish schools in the Soviet Union had been closed by 1940. In trying to convince the new citizens that Yiddish culture was thriving in the Soviet Union, these newspapers wrote about Yiddish theater, Yiddish literature, book publication, scientific research, and journalist, citing specific dates and place. But Yiddish schools were never mentioned. The papers referred to schools in the Jewish national districts, but did not indicate whether they were Yiddish schools. Given the Soviet desire to convince the new Jewish population that Soviet Jews were well-treated, it is inconceivable that existing Yiddish schools would not have been mentioned.[8]

Since no comprehensive statistics were published on the Yiddish schools, we can only piece together bits of information from scattered sources. Yiddish schools were quite widespread in the newly-annexed parts of Belorussia: in 1941, 60,000 children were enrolled in 150-160 Yiddish schools there.[9] Lithuania had 160 Yiddish elementary schools with

20,000 pupils and more than 500 teachers, as well as ten secondary schools with 4,500 pupils.[10] The Western Ukraine had 131 Yiddish schools,[11] including 14 in Lvov district for 7,000 pupils and 300 teachers.[12] Two of Lithuania's ten secondary schools were in Kovno; Ponevezh, Shavli, and Vilkomir each had one. There was at least one in Vilna, possibly more,[13] and Riga had 10 elementary schools.[14]

An examination of the Yiddish press in the newly organized areas reveals that the most frequently mentioned educational problem was the lack of qualified teachers. (Other problems could be more easily solved: the buildings of former religious or Zionist schools could be quickly converted for Soviet purposes; previously used curricula could — with difficulty, of course — be reissued; and textbooks could be reprinted.)

Let us examine how the teacher shortage was handled in Belorussia, Lithuania, and Latvia. In February 1941 the People's Commissariat of Education of the Belorussian SSR announced that in order to meet the shortage of 150 Yiddish teachers for newly opened elementary schools in the forthcoming school year, six-month courses would be established to prepare 60 teachers for grades 1-4. The courses to be given in Pinsk, were intended to fill the needs of all of Western Belorussia, and those accepted for the course would receive scholarships and lodging.[15]

Lithuania had more than 500 teachers for its Yiddish schools. Only a few of them had pedagogical training and teaching practice; many were young and had a poor command of spoken Yiddish. They used poor grammar or "frequently broke into Lithuanian, Russian, or other languages". A former pupil in a Yiddish elementary school in Kovno during this period confirmed to me how poorly many of the teachers spoke Yiddish.[16] Apparently the teaching personnel of the former Yiddish and Hebrew schools in Lithuania were not part of the new faculties, and the authorities were forced to hire inexperienced and unqualified people.

In the summer of 1940 four-week courses were organized for 380 teachers, more than 75 percent of the staff. They came from all over Lithuania and studied Yiddish, Yiddish literature, and political knowledge.[17] The following spring, an additional three-week summer course for 350 teachers, scheduled to begin in Vilna on June 30,[19] was announced in Kovno's Yiddish daily, *Emes*. The course was needed, stated the ministry, because many Yiddish teachers had received their pedagogical preparation in Hebrew, Polish, or Lithuanian institutions and "do not have the proper qualifications for teaching Yiddish."[20] The final reference to the course was in the June 21, 1941, issue of *Emes*, one day before the German invasion.

In Latvia the quest for Yiddish school teachers began almost immediately after the inception of Soviet rule. On July 18, 1940, the newly founded Riga Yiddish daily *Kamf* announced the formation of an organization of "progressive Yiddish teachers." One of the most serious problems facing the new organization was finding enough teachers to staff the new Yiddish schools in the fall. Registration of suitable people was to begin immediately and applicants had to fill out the following questionnaire:

1. Full name.
2. Birthdate
3. Education
   a) general
   b) special

  c) master of what languages: Yiddish, Hebrew, Latvian, Russian.

4. Pedagogical activity since May 15, 1934. When? Where? What?

5. How and when were you victimized by the regime since May 15, 1934?

6. Why were you victimized? General political reasons

7. In what organization have you been active since May 15, 1934?

8. What was your occupation after May 15, 1934? If pedagogical, tell when, where and what.

9. What is your aim for future work?

10. Address and telephone number[21]

The political nature of the questionnaire must have alarmed most of the trained teachers in the Jewish-operated schools in the Hebrew, German, and Russian languages. Possibly a very small number of Communists who taught in the Yiddish language schools (a minority of the teachers in those institutions) might have been willing to join the staff of the new schools. Most of the new teachers either had no pedagogical background and experience, or were Communists with little knowledge of Yiddish whose teaching work was a party duty. Short pedagogical courses were opened to prepare the new teachers. Subjects to be studied were Yiddish language and literature, history and political education, and pedagogy.[22] Registration for teaching was to close by August 1, 1940, only two weeks after the first announcement. (The announcement was repeated in later issues of *Kamf.*) It was first stated that the courses would begin on July 29, 1940,[23] but this was later changed to August 1, 1940.[24]

The problem of textbooks was frequently raised in the

Yiddish press. In some cases, children had to be taught without texts.[25] Before the German invasion, there were energetic attempts to cope with the problem. Standard Soviet textbooks on physics, chemistry, natural science, geometry, and trigonometry were translated into Yiddish and published by the National Minorities Divisions of the State Publishing Houses in Kiev and Minsk.[26] Books on Yiddish language and literature that had been used within the old borders were reissued;[27] and new texts were published (in June 1941 two new textbooks for the forthcoming school year were announced — a Russian-Yiddish dictionary for the elementary school and the Short Course in the History of the USSR. It was also announced that new textbooks were being prepared on the history of ancient times, the Middle Ages, modern history, and th history of the USSR.[28]

The curriculum instituted in the schools was similar to that of the Yiddish schools in the Soviet Union. Jewish history, the Jewish religion, and the Hebrew language were all eliminated. The only Jewish subject was Yiddish literature, taught in its Soviet version. Although the curriculum and programs of study were similar in nature to those that had previously been in use in the Soviet Union, they were not always identical. We are told that in the 1939-40 school year in the Western Ukraine and Western Belorussia, children studied without a program in Yiddish literature in grades 5-10. Ninth graders were to study Sholom Aleichem and Peretz, and end with the prerevolutionary writings of Bergelson. Tenth graders were to study Soviet Yiddish literature and read Bergelson's "Baim Dneper."[29]

An impressive feature of the Yiddish cultural apparatus in the newly acquired area was the department of Yiddish literature in Vilna University, under the chairmanship of

Noah Prilutsky, a known Yiddishist. The course was to last five years (the standard length for a Soviet university course), and the approach was to be that of historical materialism and Marxism-Leninism. The department was announced as operating in April 1941, and impressive plans were scheduled for the coming academic year. Courses were to be given in the following subjects: history of the Jewish people, Jewish folk-lore, Yiddish phonetics, historical grammar of the Yiddish language, Yiddish style, Yiddish morphology, history of Jewish culture, history of the Yiddish theater, and history of Jewish art.

Thirty-five students were enrolled in the spring of 1941, including graduates of gymnasiums in the Yiddish, Hebrew, Polish, and Lithuanian languages. It was expected that the students would reach several hundred in the next academic year, including some from Western Belorussia and Moscow.[30]

There was considerable local opposition to the school leaders' attempts to eliminate Jewish content: after all, the newly-annexed areas were the center of Jewish nationalism in Eastern Europe. Zionist youth movements of all varieties were very active; there was a strong feeling of Jewish nationalism, and the Soviet Jewish school system had not existed long enough to uproot it. The regime carefully watched both schools and teachers and sent spies to check on the latter. The regime repeatedly ran into difficulty concerning Jewish holidays, which were of course not observed in the schools. The children stayed home or celebrated the holidays surreptitiously. Some young people formed secret Zionist organizations.[31]

Today we can see — as some observers recognized at the time — that the Soviet Yiddish school system was a temporary means to acculturate the Jewish children into the Soviet ideology. In essence it served the same function as did the Yiddish schools in the old Soviet Union. The numbers of schools founded was minimal, and it was never intended that Yiddish schools would operate permanently. In many areas with Yiddish-speaking populations, no Yiddish schools were founded at all. The system as a whole continued to exist until the German invasion, but there were signs before then in some areas of a contraction or abolition of the schools.

Postscript

THE YIDDISH SCHOOLS in the newly annexed areas were destroyed by the German invasion. Although some Jews succeeded in escaping to the interior parts of Russia, no Yiddish schools were established there and none were reopened after the war. There were three minor exceptions, albeit of brief duration, in the case of schools which accepted students for grades 1-4 in Kovno, Vilna, and Chernovitz. These Jewish communities probably had the highest percentage of Yiddish-speaking Jews of any Jewish communities in Russia after the war (a situation which still obtained in 1959).[32] The difficulties encountered by these schools were enormous. The Soviet Yiddish paper *Eynikait* published several letters regarding the Kovno school: there were no Yiddish textbooks and the students had to write everything. A desperate appeal was made to readers to donate Yiddish books. The Kovno school had been founded in November 1944 immediately after the city was liberated. At first the school taught only those rescued from the ghetto; later, others were accepted. It had four grades and 150 pupils.[33] The testimony of a Vilna Yiddish writer who was active in setting up the school there describes a similar situation. The authorities were willing to see the school exist as a temporary expedient, but when it and the schools in Kovno and Chernovitz had served their purpose they were closed. This marked the end of Yiddish language schools in the USSR.

The absence of Yiddish schools must be seen both in the light of general Soviet minorities policy and also as a specific Jewish problem. In the 1930s a policy decision was made to reduce the system of schools for national minorities. This can be seen by examining the situation in the Ukraine, the largest Soviet Republic, which until World War II was the center of the Jewish population in the USSR. In 1927 the Soviet Ukraine had an extraordinary variety of schools in minority languages: Ukrainian, Russian, Yiddish, Polish, German, Moldavian, Bulgarian, Czech, Armenian, Tatar, Swedish, and Greek.[34] By 1940-41, except for the schools in Russian and Ukrainian, practically all the others had been closed.[35] After the war in the Ukraine only the Russian and Ukrainian schools reopened.[36] In the Soviet Union as a whole there is a wide network of schools in the languages of the major republic nationalities while there has been a drastic drop in the number of schools of the smaller non-republic nationalities. In 1967 a published study showed fifty-four languages of instruction in Soviet schools.[37]

At present there are no schools in the Yiddish language,

even though nationalities with far fewer inhabitants have school networks. To the claim that this is *prima facie* evidence of discrimination against Jews, the reply is given that the Jews are scattered and linguistically assimilated, and therefore do not want Yiddish schools. The Soviet census of 1959 listed 2,267,814 Jews in the Soviet Union, of whom only 17.9 percent gave Yiddish as their primary language. However, this figure is somewhat misleading because it is not uniform. In some areas of the USSR it is much less; in a few it is much higher.

For example, in the Moldavian republic and in Latvia, 50 percent of Jews speak Yiddish, and in Lithuania, 70 percent do. The Jewish population of Chernovitz, Kishinev, Riga, Vilna, and Kovno all have large numbers of Yiddish speakers.[38] According to Soviet law, each group of ten parents is entitled to demand that their children receive education in their mother tongue. In a letter to two American professors the Vice Minister of Education of the RSFSR stated that "persons of Jewish nationality fully enjoy the same right."[39] To maintain that in the entire Soviet Union, even in areas where a considerable portion of the Jewish population speaks Yiddish, there is not even a single group of ten parents who want a school in Yiddish is absurd; the demand may be small, but it cannot be nonexistent.

There probably will never be another system of Yiddish schools in the USSR. The regime certainly has no interest in reestablishing them, and, as the Jews become more and more linguistically assimilated, their interest in such schools will shrink even further. But the decline of Yiddish and the disappearance of Yiddish schools does not in any sense conflict with the reawakening of Jewish nationalism in the Soviet Union, a nationalism which has been sparked by the government's policies of repression. The new Jewish nationalism is expressed in Russian; its adherents, like many important Russian Jewish figures in the past, use the Russian language to proclaim their resistance to the Soviet regime and their desire to emigrate to Israel.

Notes

1. The basic information given here on the Soviet acquisition of Eastern Poland, the Baltic States, Bessarabia, and Northern Bukovina can be found in Royal Institute of International Affairs, *Chronology of the Second World War* (London: Royal Institute of International Affairs, 1947). Works containing information on the specific countries are John A. Armstrong, *Ukrainian Nationalism: 1939-1945* (New York: Columbia University Press, 1955); Nicholas P. Vakar, *Belorussia* (Cambridge, Mass.: Harvard University Press, 1956): and Ants Oras, *Baltic Eclipse* (London: Victor Gollancz Ltd., 198).

2. Miriam Eisenstein, *Jewish Schools in Poland, 1919-1939* (New York: King's Crown Press, Columbia University Press, 1950).

3. Zevi Scharfstein, *Toldot Hakhinukh Bedorot Haakharonim* (Jerusalem: Ruben Mass, 1960), vol. II, pp. 224-244 et passim.

4. Vakar, op. cit., p. 160.

5. *Oktiaber*, August 15, 1940, p. 3.

6. Benjamin West, *Struggles of a Generation* (Tel Aviv: Massadah, 1959), p. 116.

7. In *Ufboi* (Riga), March 1941, we are told that School No. 92 is

housed in the building of a former "Zionist Hebrew school." The *Bialystoker Shtern*, January 27, 1940, mentions that a complete Yiddish secondary school is being opened in a former ten-year Hebrew gymnasium. In *Emes* (Kovno), April 12, 1941, it is stated that a state vocational school is housed in a school of the ORT organization. In *Kamf* (Riga), October 12, 1940, we are told of a certain elementary school housed in the building of a school which once belonged to the "fascist" Aguda organization.

8. Descriptions of Yiddish culture in the early decades of the USSR appeared in *Kamf*, July 3, 1940, and on many other occasions in *Ufboi*, *Emes* (Kovno) and in *Oktiaber*. Descriptions of schools, frequently in great detail, without any mention of Yiddish schools appeared in *Ufboi*, May 1941; *Kamf*, July 1, July 3, July 12, and July 20, 1940; *Emes* (Kovno), January 16, 1941; and *Oktiaber* throughout September and October 1940.

9. *Ufboi*, March 1941, p. 17.

10. *Emes* (Kovno), February 26, 1941. The same statistic is also given in *Ufboi*, March 1941, p. 21.

11. S. K. Hutyansky, *Lenin i Ukrayinska Radyanska kultura* (Kiev, 1963), p. 24.

12. *Emes* (Kovno), March 14, 1941.

13. Ibid.

14. *Ufboi*, June 1941.

15. Ibid, February 1941.

16. Conversation in Tel Aviv, March 1973.

17. *Emes* (Kovno), May 24, 1941.

18. *Emes* (Kovno), April 18, 1941.

19. The course was intended for elementary school, secondary school, and vocational school teachers.

20. See, for example, a small article which appeared on June 1, 1941, in *Emes* (Kovno).

21. *Kamf*, July 18, 1940.

22. Ibid.

23. *Kamf*, July 24, 1941.
24. *Kamf*, July 28, 1941.
25. *Emes* (Kovno), May 24, 1941.
26. *Ufboi*, May 1941, and in G. Zhitz, "The Production of Book by Ukrderzhnatzmerividav Publishing House in 1939 and the Plan for 1940," *Sovetishe Literatur* (Kiev), 1941, No. 4, 152.
27. *Oktiaber* (Minsk), July 28, 1940.
28. *Ufboi*, June 1941.
29. *Oktiaber* (Minsk), July 28, 1940.
30. *Emes* (Kovno), April 11, 1941.
31. For three accounts of opposition and underground activity by students and parents, see West, pp. 116-118; Yitskhak Levin, *Aliti Mespetsia* (Tel Aviv: Am Oved, 1950), pp. 38-42; Tania Fuks, *A Vanderung Iber Okupirte Gebitn* (Buenos Aires, 1947), pp. 89-93.
32. See below for details on the rate of Yiddish speaking among the Jews of various Russian cities in the census of 1959.
33. See *Einikeit*, March 22, 1945, p. 2; April 26, 1945, p. 3.
34. Central Statistical Office of the Ukrainian SSR, *Statistika Ukrainy*, Series VII (Education), vol. VIII, issue 1 (serial no. 138), 12-13.
35. "Ukrainskaia SSR," *Bolshaia Sovetskaia Entsikopediia*, supplement "SSSR" (1947), vol. 184.
36. *Pedagogicheskii Slovar* (Moscow, 1960), II, 509. There were a handful of schools in Moldavian and Polish but these were probably in the newly annexed areas, not in the areas where schools had existed in these languages in the 1920s and 1930s. There were also schools in Hungarian, but these were in the newly annexed areas of Carpatho-Ukraine.
37. Harvey Lipset, "The Status of National Minority Languages in Soviet Education," *Soviet Studies*, XIX (1967), 183-184.
38. All the data on the population from the census of 1959 is taken from the various volumes of the results published in 16 volumes. The general title is *Itogi Vsesoiuznoi Perepisi Naseleniia 1959 goda*, with separate volumes for each republic

and one summary volume. All were issued in either 1962 or 1963. The information on the Jews from the 16 volumes of the 1959 census has been brought together in Modchay Altschuler, *Hayehudim Bemifkad Haokhlusia Bevrit Hamoetzot 1959* (Jerusalem, 1963). All tables and descriptions are also given in English.

39. So stated in a letter from the Vice Minister of Education of the RSFSR which is reproduced in Joseph B. Schechtman, *Star in Eclipse: Russian Jewry Revisited* (New York: Thomas Yoseloff, 1961), p. 151.

Bibliography

Books and Official Documents

Abramovitch, Raphael. "Geshikhte fun yidn in poiln, lite, and russland," *Algemeine entsiklopedie*, Series "Yidn." New York: World Jewish Culture Congress, 1950. Vol. 4.

————. "The Jewish Socialist Movement in Russia and Poland (1897-1919)," *The Jewish People, Past and Present.* New York: Jewish Encyclopedic Handbooks, 1948. Vol. 2.

————. *The Soviet Revolution, 1917-1939.* New York: International Universities Press, 1962.

————. and Menes, Abraham. "Di yiddishe sotsialistishe bavegung in russland and poiln," *Algemeine entsiklopedie,* Series "Yidn." New York: World Jewish Culture Congress, 1950. Vol. 3.

Abramovitz, Z. et al. (eds.). *Yalkutei Poale Zion.* Tel Aviv: M. Neumann, 1947. Vol. 1.

Achad Haam. "Medinat Hayehudim Vetsarat Hayehudim," *Al Prashat Drachim.* Berlin: Achiasaf, 1903. Vol. 2.

————. *Selected Essays.* Trans. from the Hebrew by Leon Simon. Philadelphia: Jewish Publication Society of America, 1948.

Agurskii, Samuil. *Di yiddishe kommasariatn un di yiddishe kommunistishe sektzies (protokoln, rezolutzies un dokumentn, 1918-1921).* Minsk: State Publishing House, 1928.

————. *Der yidisher arbeter in der kommunistisher bavegung, 1917-1921.* Minsk: State Publishing House, 1925.

Aharoni, Yaakov. "Bet Sefer Haivri Besaratov," *Heavar*, 9 (1962).

Altschuler, Mordchay. *Hayehudim Bemifkad Haokhlusia Bevrit Hamoetzot, 1959.* Jerusalem, 1963.

————. *Reishit Hayevsektzia, 1918-1921.* Jerusalem: Aguda Lekheker Tefutzot Yisrael, 1966.

The American Jewish Yearbook 5671. Philadelphia: Jewish Publication Society of America, 1930.

Anilovitch, Y. and Yoffe, M. (eds.). "Yiddishe lernbikher un pedagogic, 1900-1930 (Bibliografie)," *Shriftn far psikhologie un pedagogic.* Vilna, 1933. Vol. 1.

Aranov, Zalman and Shpitalnik, F. *Malachovker kinder kolonie.* Moscow: Emes Publishing House, 1932.

Arkady: zamelbuch tzum ondenk fun grinder fun bund arkady kremer. New York: Unzer Tzait, 1942.

Armstrong, John A. *Ideology, Politics and Government in the Soviet Union.* New York: Praeger, 1962.

————. *Ukrainian Nationalism: 1939-1945.* New York: Columbia University Press, 1955.

Aronson, Gregory. *Soviet Russia and the Jews.* New York: The American Jewish League against Communism, 1949.

————. *Di yiddishe problem in soviet russland.* New York: Farlag Vekker, 1944.

The Autobiography of Solomon Maimon, Translated from the German by J. Clark Murray. London: East and West Library, 1954.

Avidor, Moshe. *Education in Israel.* Jerusalem: Youth and Hechalutz Department of the Zionist Organization, 1957.

Bakst, Y. and Greenberg, Y. *Arbets kinder: khrestomatie un arbets bukh farn 4tn klass.* Moscow: Shul un Bukh, 1928.

——— . *Arbets kinder.* Moscow: Shul un Bukh, 1928.

Balaban, Meier. *Letoldot Hatenuah Hafrankit.* 2 vols. Tel Aviv: Dvir, 1934-1935.

Baron, Salo W. *The Jewish Community.* Philadelphia: Jewish Publication Society of America, 1942. Vol. 3.

——— . *The Russian Jew under Tsars and Soviets.* New York: Macmillan, 1964.

——— . *A Social and Religious History of the Jews.* New York: Columbia University Press, 1937. Vol. 2.

Baskerville, Beatrice. *The Polish Jew.* London: Macmillan, 1906.

Basok, Moshe (ed.). *Mivkhar Shirat Yiddish.* Tel Aviv: Hakibbutz Hameuchad, 1963.

Bazili, Nikolai A. *Rossiia pod sovetskoi vlastiu.* Paris: Imprimerie "Val," 1937.

Ben-Adir. "Modern Currents in Jewish Social and National Life," *The Jewish People, Past and Present.* New York: Jewish Encyclopedic Handbooks, 1948. Vol. 2.

Bernfield, Simon. "Vospitanie," *Evreiskaia Entsiklopedie.* Vol. 5.

Bloom, Solomon F. "Karl Marx and the Jews," *Jewish Social Studies,* 4 (1942).

Bolshaia Sovetskaia Entsiklopedia, Vols. 7, 24 (1932).

Borochov, Ber. "Tsu der geshichte fun poale zion," *Der yiddisher arbeter pinkas.* Warsaw: Farlag Naie Kultur, 1928.

Brutskus, Boris. *Professionalnii sostav evreiskago naseleniia rossii.* St. Petersburg, 1908.

——— . *Statistika evreiskago naseleniia.* St. Petersburg: Jewish Colonization Association, 1909.

Buchbinder, N. *Di geshikhte fun der yiddisher arbeter bavegung in russland.* Vilna: Farlag Tamer, 1931.

Cahan, Abraham. *Bleter fun mein leben.* New York, 1926.

Carr, E. H. *The Bolshevik Revolution.* London: Macmillan, 1951. Vol. 1.

Central Statistical Board of the U.S.S.R. *Kulturnoe stroitelstvo*

S.S.S.R. Moscow: State Statistical Publishing House, 1956.

Central Statistical Office of the Ukrainian SSR. *Statistika ukrainy.* Series 7 (Education), Vol. 5, Issue 1 (Serial No. 71); Vol. 6, Issue 1 (Serial No. 95); Vol. 3, Issue 1 (Serial No. 138).

Chamberlin, William Henry. *Soviet Russia, A Living Record and a History.* Boston: Little, Brown & Co., 1933.

Chanin, N. *Soviet russland: vi ikh hob ir gezen.* New York: Farlag Vekker, 1929.

Cherikowsky, A. and Nikolaevsky, B. "A briv fun Heinrich Graetz tzum Karl Marx," *Historishe shriftn*, 2 (1937).

Dardak, I. "Unzere dergreikhungen in 15 yor oktiaber afn gebit fun folk bildung," *Tsum 15 yortog fun der oktiaber revolutsie, sotsial ekonomisher zamelbukh.* Minsk: White Russian Academy of Sciences, Jewish Sector, 1932.

Dawidowicz, Lucy. "What Future for Judaism in Russia?" *Commentary*, November, 1956.

Deutscher, Isaac. *Stalin.* New York: Vintage Books, 1960.

Dimanshtein, S. (ed.). *Yidn in fssr: zamelbukh.* Moscow: Emes Publishing House, 1935.

Dinaberg, Ben-Zion. *Yiddishe geshichte.* Kiev: Mefitzei Haskalah, 1918.

Drazin, Nathan. *History of Jewish Education from 515 BCE to 220 CE.* Johns Hopkins University Studies in Education No. 29. Baltimore: The Johns Hopkins Press, 1940.

Dubnow, Simon. "Council of the Four Lands," *Jewish Encyclopedia.* Vol. 9.

———. *Divrei Yimei Am Olam.* 6th rev. ed. Tel Aviv: Dvir, 1958. Vols. 1, 4, 6.

———. "Jewish Autonomy," *Encyclopedia of the Social Sciences.* Vol. 8.

———. *Kniga zhizni.* Riga: Autora Izdevume, 1934. Vol. 1.

———. *Pisma o starom i novom evreistve.* St. Petersburg, 1907.

———. "Sudby evreev v rossii v epokhe zapadnoe 'pervoi emansipatsii' (1789-1815)," *Evreiskaia starina.* Vol. 5.

———. *Toldot Hahassidut.* 2 vols. Tel Aviv: Dvir, 1930-1932.

———. *History of the Jews in Russia and Poland.* 3 vols. Philadelphia: Jewish Publication Society of America, 1916-1920.

Duker, Abraham G. "Evreiskaia Starina: A Bibliography of the Russian-Jewish Historical Periodical," *Hebrew Union College Annual.* Cincinnati, 1932. Vol. 8-9.

Eck, Nathan. "The Educational Institutions of Polish Jewry," *Jewish Social Studies*, 9 (1947).

Efrosi, C. *Yiddishe geshichte.* Kiev: Vilna Publishing House Kletzkin, 1918.

Eisenstein, Miriam. *Jewish Schools in Poland.* New York: King's Crown Press, Columbia University, 1950.

Fainsod, Merle. *Smolensk under Soviet Rule.* Cambridge, Mass.: Harvard University Press, 1958.

Finkelstein, A. "Di bikher produktsie funem farlag 'emes' farn tsveitn finfyor, 1933-1937," *Sovetish*, 7-8 (1939).

———. Di yiddisher bikher produktsie funem ukrmeluchenatzmindfarlag farn tzveitn finfyor, 1933-1937," *Literarishe almanak*, 9-10 (1939).

———. "Di yiddisher bikher produktsie fun veismeluchefarlag farn tzveitn finfyor, 1933-1937," *Shtern* (Minsk), 7 (1939).

Fishman, Isidore. *The History of Jewish Education in Central Europe; XVI to XVII Centuries.* London: Edward Goldstein, 1944.

Frankel, Jacob. "di pioner fun di leder industrie in Lite, Chaim Frankel," *Lite.* New York, 1951.

Frederic, Dr. Otto. *Der Handelshaften Odessa.* Leipzig, 1921.

Friedlaender, Israel. *The Jews of Russia and Poland.* New York: G.P. Putnam's Sons, 1915.

Friedman, Philip. "Geshikhte fun yidn in ukraine biz suf 18tn yorhundert," *Yidn in ukraine.* New York: Ukrainian Jewish Memorial Society, 1961.

Frumkin, Esther. *Doloi ravinov.* Moscow, 1923.

Frumkin, K. "Der bund un seine gegner," *Zukumft*, 2 (1903).

Fuks, Tania. *A vanderung iber okupirte gebitn.* Buenos Aires, 1947.

Gamoran, Emanuel. *Changing Conceptions in Jewish Education.*

2 vols. New York: Macmillan, 1924.

Gergel, N. *Di lage fun yidn in russland.* Warsaw: Kultur Lige, 1929.

Gershuni, A. A. *Yahdut Berussiah Hasovietit.* Jerusalem: Mosad Harav Kook, 1961.

Gessen, I. *Evrei v Rossii.* St. Petersburg, 1906.

Gilboa, Yehoshua A. *The Black Years of Soviet Jewry, 1939-1953.* Boston: Little, Brown & Co., 1971.

Ginzberg, Louis. "The Gaon, Rabbi Elijah Vilna," *Students, Scholars, and Saints.* Philadelphia: Jewish Publication Society of America, 1928.

Gitelman, Zvi Y. *Jewish Nationality and Soviet Politics.* Princeton: Princeton University Press, 1972.

——. "The Jews," *Problems of Communism,* 16 (1967), Sept.-Oct.

Goldberg, B. Z. *The Jewish Problem in the Soviet Union.* New York: Crown Publishers, 1961.

Goldelman, Shalom. "Di yiddishe natzionale oitonomie in ukraine," *Yidn in ukraine.* New York: Ukrainian Jewish Memorial Society, 1961.

Golder, F. A. *Documents of Russian History: 1914-1917.* Trans. by Emanuel Aronsberg. New York: The Century Co., 1927.

Goldman, Guido. *Zionism under Soviet Rule.* New York: Herzl Press, 1960.

Golitsyn, N. *Istoriia russkago zakon odatelstvo o evreiakh.* St. Petersburg, 1886.

Great Britain, Board of Education. *Special Reports on Educational Subjects,* Vol. 23 (Education in Russia). London: His Majesty's Stationery Office, 1909.

Greenbaum, Alfred A. *Jewish Scholarship in Soviet Russia, 1918-1941.* Boston, 1959.

Greenbaum, Yitzchak. *Hatenuah Hatzionit Behitpatchutcha.* 4 vols. Tel Aviv: Jewish Agency for Palestine, 1928.

Greenberg, Louis. *The Jews in Russia.* New Haven: Yale University Press, 1945. Vol. 1.

Halptern, Yekhiel. *Yisrael Vehakommunizm.* Tel Aviv: Israel Labor Party, 1951.

Hannover, Nathan. *Yeven Metzulah.* New York: Bloch Publishing Co., 1950.

Harcave, Sidney. *Russia, A History.* New York: Lippincott, 1953.

Heifetz, Elias. *The Slaughter of the Jews in the Ukraine in 1919.* New York: T. Seltzer, 1921.

Hershberg, A. S. *Pinkas bialystok.* New York, 1950. Vol. 2.

Hertz, J. S. *Geshichte fun a yugnt.* New York: Farlag Unzer Tsait, 1946.

Hertzberg, Arthur (ed.). *The Zionist Idea: A Historical Analysis and Reader.* New York: Doubleday & Co., 1959.

Hirsch, Liebman. "Yiddishe emigratzie," *Algemeine entziklopedie,* Series "Yidn." New York: World Jewish Culture Congress, 1950. Vol. 1.

Holdes, A. *Khrestomatie far literatur farn 7tn klass fun der mitelshul.* Kiev: Ukrainian State Publishing House, National Minorities Section, 1936.

———. *Literarishe khrestomatie farn 9tn klass fun der mitelshul.* Kiev: Ukrainian State Publishing House, National Minorities Section, 1937.

Horovitz, S. *Literarishe khrestomatie farn 10tn klass fun der mitelshul.* Kiev-Kharkov: Ukrainian State Publishing House, National Minorities Section, 1936.

Howe, Irving and Greenberg, Eliezer. *A Treasury of Yiddish Stories.* New York: Viking Press, 1954.

Hutyansky, S. K. *Lenin i ukrayinska radyanska kultura.* Kiev, 1963.

Jabotinsky, V. *Evreiskoe vospitanie.* Odessa, 1903.

———. *Gola Vehitbollelot.* Tel Aviv, 1936.

Janowsky, Oscar. *The Jews and Minority Rights, 1898-1919.* New York: Columbia University Press, 1933.

Jewish Colonization Association. *Sbornik materialov ob ekonomicheskom polozhenii evreev v rossii.* 2 vols. St. Petersburg, 1904.

Jewish Encyclopedia. Vol. 10.

Kantor, Yakov. *Natsionalnoe stroitelstvo sredi evreev SSSR.* Moscow, 1934.

Kasteliansky, N. "Dos yiddishe shulvezn in ratn farband," *Di yiddishe moderne shul oif der velt.* Philadelphia: Workmen's Circle School Committee, 1935.

Katzir: *Kovetz Lekorot Hatenuah Hatsionit Berussia.* Tel Aviv: Massadah, 1964.

Kazdan, C. S. *Fun cheder un shkoles biz tzisho.* Mexico City: Kultur un Hilf, 1956.

————. "Yiddishe shuln in mizrach europa." *Algemeine entsiklopedie*, Series "Yidn." New York: World Jewish Culture Congress, 1950. Vol. 3.

Keep, John L. H. *The Rise of Social Democracy in Russia.* London: Oxford University Press. 1963.

Kiper, M. "15 yor," *Roiter Velt.* No. 7-8 (1932).

————. *10 yor obtiaber revolutsie un di yidishe arbetndike fun ukraine.* Kiev: Kultur Lige, 1927.

Kirzhnitz, A. *Der yiddisher arbeter chrestomatie tzu geshichte fun der yiddisher arbeter, revolutzioner, un sotzialistisher bavegung in russland.* 4 vols. Moscow: Central Publishing House, 1925-1928.

Kivin, S. "Bam vigele fun der partei," *Der yiddisher arbeter pinkas.* Warsaw: Farlag Naie Kultur, 1928.

Klauzner, Israel. *Behitorer Am.* Jerusalem: Hasifriah Hatzionit, 1962.

Klauzner, Joseph. *Kitzur Toldot Hasifrut Haivrit Hahadashah.* Tel Aviv: Joseph Sreberk Publishing House, 1954.

Klitenik, S. *Di kultur arbet tsvishn di yiddishe arbetndike inem ratn farband.* Moscow: Central Publishing House, 1931.

Kolarz, Walter. *Religion in the Soviet Union.* London: St. Martin's Press, 1961.

————. *Russia and Her Colonies.* New York: Praeger, 1952.

Koralnik, Y. "Di yidn in ukraine," *Bleter far yiddishe demografie, statistik un ekonomik.* Berlin, 1924. Vol. 1.

Kremer, Arkady. "Di grindung fun bund," *Arbeter Luach*, 3 (1922).

Krugliac, M. "Dramkreizen in shtetl," *Ratenbildung*, 2 (June 1929).

Kurzweil, Zvi. *Modern Trends in Jewish Education*. New York: Thomas Yoseloff, 1964.

Lakat Sipurim Mesifrut Yiddish. Tel Aviv: Moshe Neumann, 1957.

Landau, H. "Der onteil fun yidn in der russish-ukrainer tsuker industrie," *Shriftn for yiddishe ekonomik un statistik*. Berlin, 1928.

Laquer, Walter. *A History of Zionism*. London: Macmillan, 1972.

Lenin, V. I. *Collected Works*. Moscow: Foreign Languages Publishing House, 1961. Vols. 6, 7, 8, 11, 14, 20.

———. *The Development of Capitalism in Russia*. Trans. from the Russian. Moscow: Foreign Languages Publishing House, 1964.

———. *Questions of National Policy and Proletarian Internationalism*. Moscow, n.d.

V. I. Lenin on Youth. Moscow: Progress Publishers, 1967.

Lestshchinsky, Yaakov. "Di ekonomishe lage fun di yidn in Lite," *Lite*. New York, 1951.

———. *Di ekonomishe lage fun yidn in poiln*. Berlin, 1932.

———. "Di ekonomishe evolutsie fun yidn in 19tn un onheib 20tn yorhundrld," *Algemeine entsiklopedie*, Series "Yidn." Vol. 1.

———. "Evreiskoe naselenie rossii i evreiskii trud," *Kniga o russkom evreistve*. New York: Union of Russian Jews, 1960.

———. "Jews in the U.S.S.R. — II," *Contemporary Jewish Record*, 3 (1940).

———. "Di sotsial ekonomishe antviklung fun ukrainer yidntum," *Yidn in ukraine*. New York, 1961.

———. *Dos sovetishe yidntum*. New York: Yiddisher Kemfer, 1941.

———. *Der yiddisher arbeter in russland*. Vilna, 1906.

———. *Dos yiddishe folk in tsippern*. Berlin, 1922.

Levanda, V. *Polny Khronologicheskii Sbornik Zakonov i Ptlozhenii Kasaiushchikhsia Evreev.* St. Petersburg, 1874.

Levin, Yitskhak. *Aliti Mespetsia.* Tel Aviv: Am Oved, 1950.

Levinsohn, Isaac Ber. *Bet Yehudah.* Warsaw: M. Romm, 1878.

Levinson, Avraham. *Hatenuah Haivrit Bagolah.* Warsaw: Haeksekutiva Shel Habrit Haivrit Haolamit Belondon, 1934.

Levitan, M. *Arifmetishe oifgabn farn tzveitn un dritn lernyor.* Kiev: Vilna Publishing House Kletzkin, 1919.

Linfield, H. S. *The Communal Organization of the Jews in Soviet Russia.* New York, 1925.

Lipset, Harry. "A Note on Yiddish as the Language of Soviet Jews in the Census of 1939," *The Jewish Journal of Sociology*, 12 (1970).

———. "The Status of National Minority Languages in Soviet Education," *Soviet Studies*, 19 (1967).

Liptzin, Sol. *The Flowering of Yiddish Literature.* New York: Thomas Yoseloff, 1963.

———. (ed.). *Peretz.* Yivo Bilingual Series. New York: Yiddish Scientific Institute — Yivo, 1947.

Lyashchenko, P. D. *History of the People's Economy of the U.S.S.R.* Trans. from the Russian. New York: Macmillan, 1949.

Macartney, C. A. *National States and National Minorities.* London: Oxford University Press, 1934.

Mahler, Raphael. *Chassidut Vehahaskalah.* Merhavia: Sifriat Poalim, 1961.

Margolin, Arnold. *The Jews in Eastern Europe.* New York: T. Selzer, 1926.

Marx, Karl. *A World Without Jews.* New York: Philosophical Library, 1959.

——— and Engels, Friedrich. "Manifesto of the Communist Party," *Great Books of the Western World.* Chicago: Encyclopedia Britannica, 1952. Vol. 50.

Mats, D. "NN vysokom podyeme (O rabot srid sredi natsionalnykh menshinstve ukrainy)," *Revolutsiya i natsionalnosti*, June 1935.

Maze, Jacob. *Zichronot.* Tel Aviv, 1936.

Meltzer, Shimshon (ed.). *Al Naharot.* Jerusalem: Mosad Bialik, 1956.

The Memoirs of Count Witte. New York: Howard Fertig, 1967.

Mendelsohn, Ezra. *Class Struggle in the Pale.* London: Cambridge University Press, 1970.

Menes, Abraham. "The Jewish Socialist Movement in Russia and Poland (1870s-1897)," *The Jewish People, Past and Present.* New York: Jewish Encyclopedic Handbooks, 1948. Vol. 2.

——. "The Yeshivot in Eastern Europe," *The Jewish People, Past and Present.* New York, 1948. Vol. 2.

——. (ed.). *Der yiddisher gedank in der naier tzait.* New York: World Jewish Culture Congress, 1957.

Mill, John. *Pionern un boier.* New York: Farlag Vekker, 1946.

Ministry of Education and Culture, Department for Secondary Education. *Hatzaot Letakhnit Limud Beveit Hasefer Hatikhon.* Jerusalem: The Government Printer, 1956.

Der Mishpet ibern cheder. Vitebsk, 1922.

Morgulis, M. *Voprosy evreiskoi zhizni.* St. Petersburg, 1889.

Morris, Nathan. *Curriculum and Method in the Hebrew Class.* London: Eyre and Spottiswood, 1946.

Mysh, M. I. *Rukovodstvo k russkim zakonam o evreiakh.* St. Petersburg, 1914.

Narodnoe Khoziaistvo SSR v 1970 g. Moscow, 1971.

Natsionalnaia politika VKP (B) v tsikrakh. Moscow, 1930.

Nearing, Scott. *Education in Soviet Russia.* New York: International Publishers, 1926.

Nikitin, V. N. *Evrei zemledeltsy.* St. Petersburg, 1887.

Oislender, N. and Bakst, Y. *Arbet un kamf: literarishe khrestomatie.* Notebook 3, Section 4. Moscow: Central Publishing House. 1926.

Oislender, N. et al. *Arbet un kamf: literarishe khrestomatie farn 4tn, 5tn un 6tn shulyor.* Notebook 1, Part 2. Moscow: Central Publishing House, 1926.

Orshansky, D. *Evrei v rossii.* St. Petersburg, 1887.

Oras, Ants. *Baltic Eclipse.* London: Victor Gollancz Ltd., 1948.

Pedagogicheskii Slovar. Moscow, 1960. Vol. 2.

Philipson, David, ed. *Max Lilienthal: American Rabbi, Life and Writings.* New York: Bloch Publishing Co., 1915.

Philipson, D. *Old European Jewries.* Philadelphia: Jewish Publication Society of America, 1894.

Pines, Dan. *Hechalutz Bechor Hamapeicha.* Tel Aviv: Davar, 1938.

Pinkas Hamedinah Shel Vaad Hakehilot Harashiot Bemidinat Lite. St. Petersburg, 1909.

Pinkevich, A. *Science and Education in the U.S.S.R.* New York: G.P. Putnam's Sons, 1935.

Pinkevitch, Albert P. *The New Education in the Soviet Republic.* Translated by Nucia Perlmutter. New York: John Day, 1929.

Pinsker, Leon. *Self-Emancipation.* London, 1891.

Pinson, Koppel. "Chassidism," *Encyclopedia of the Social Sciences.* New York: Macmillan, 1933. Vol. 3.

Pipes, Richard. *The Formation of the Soviet Union: Communism and Nationalism, 1917-1923.* Cambridge, Mass.: Harvard University Press, 1954.

"Poland." *Cyclopedia of Education.* New York: Macmillan, 1924.

Pomerantz, Alexander. *Di sovetishe haruge malchus.* Buenos Aires: Argentine Branch of Yivo, 1962.

Posner, S. *Evrei v obshchei shkole.* St. Petersburg, 1914.

Rabinowitsch, Sara. *Die Organisation fun judischen Proletariats in Russland.* Karlsruhe: G. Braun, 1903.

Rabinovitch, Yitzkhak. *Mimoskva Vead Yerushalayim.* Jerusalem: Rubin Mass, 1957.

Rafaeli, Aryeh. *Bemaavak Legeulah.* Tel Aviv: Davar, 1956.

Rappard, William E. et al. *Source Book in Foreign Governments.* New York, 1937.

Ratner, M. B. "Evolutzia natzionalno-politichiskoi mysli v russkom evreistve," *Sbornik Serp.* St. Petersburg, 1908.

Ravin, Y. and Shatz, V. *Literatur: lernbukh farn 4tn shulyor.* Minsk: White Russian State Publishing House. National Minorities Section, 1933.

Reizin, Zalman. *Leksikon fun der yiddisher literatur, presse un filologie.* 4 vols. Vilna: B. Kletzkin Publishing House, 1928.

Roback, A. A. *The Story of Yiddish Literature.* New York: Yiddish Scientific Institute, 1940.

Rombach, S. "Di yidishe balemelokhes in russland in der ershter helft fun 19tn yorhundert," *Tzaitschrift,* 1 (1928).

Rosenthal, Judah. "Hahistoriografia Hayehudit Berussia Hasovietit," *Sefer Shimon Dubnow.* London and Jerusalem: Ararat Publishing Company, 1954.

Rothman, Walter. "Mendelssohn's Character and Philosophy of Religion," *Yearbook of the Central Conference of American Rabbis,* 39 (1929).

Royal Institute of International Affairs. *Chronology of the Second World War.* London: Royal Institute of International Affairs, 1947.

Rozenfeld, P. *Tsvei kulturn, tsvei sakhaklen.* Moscow: Emes Publishing House, 1932.

Rubin, Ronald (ed.). *The Unredeemed: Anti-Semitism in the Soviet Union.* Chicago: Quadrangle Books, 1968.

Rugg, Harold (ed.). *Democracy and the Curriculum: The Life and Program of the American School.* Third Yearbook of the John Dewey Society. New York: Appleton-Century, 1939.

Russia. Ministry of Public Instruction. *Izvlechenie iz vsepodaneishago otcheta za 1899.* St. Petersburg, 1901.

Russkii Arkhiv. Vol. 1 (1903).

San Donato, Prince Demidoff. *The Jewish Question in Russia.* London, 1884.

Scharfstein, Tzvi. *Toldot Hachinuch Beyisrael Bedorot Haacharonim.* New York: Ogen, 1949. Vol. 3.

Schechtman, I. *Pogromi dobrovolcheskoi armii na ukraine.* Berlin: Ostjuedisches Historisches Archiv, 1932.

Schechtman, Joseph B. *Rebel and Statesman: The Vladimir Jabotinsky Story.* New York: Thomas Yoseloff, 1956.

———. *Star in Eclipse: Russian Jewry Revisited.* New York:

Thomas Yoseloff. 1961.

Schulman, Elias. *The Fate of Soviet Jewry*. New York: Jewish Labor Committee, n.d.

Schwartz, Leo W. (ed.). *Memoirs of My People*. New York, 1943.

Schwarz, Solomon. *The Jews in the Soviet Union*. Syracuse: Syracuse University Press, 1951.

Seton-Watson, Hugh. *The Decline of Imperial Russia, 1855-1914*. New York: Praeger, 1952.

Shmeruk, C. (ed.). *Pirsumim Hayehudiim Bebrit Hamoetzot, 1917-1960*. Jerusalem: Historical Society of Israel, 1961.

Sholom Aleichem. *Ale Verk*. New York, 1923. Vol. 12.

————. *Sobranie sochinenii*. 6 vols. Moscow, 1961.

Shore, Maurice J. *Soviet Education*. New York: Philosophical Library, 1947.

Sidilkovsky, Ben-Zion. *For yiddishe kinder: an alefbeis for shuln un kinderheimer*. Odessa: Kultur Lige, 1920.

Singer, I. J. *The Brothers Ashkenazi*. Trans. from the Yiddish by Maurice Samuel. New York: Alfred A. Knopf, 1936.

Smal-Stocki, R. *The Nationality Problem of the Soviet Union and Russian Communist Imperialism*. Milwaukee: Marquette University Press, 1952.

Spiro, Melford E. *Children of the Kibbutz*. Cambridge, Mass.: Harvard University Press, 1958.

Spivak, Eliahu. *Yiddish: literarish chrestomatie for dritn shul yor*. Kiev: Kultur Lige, 1919.

Spizman, L. "Di hebraishe shulvezn in mizrakh europa," *Algemeine entsiklopedie*, Series "Yidn." New York: World Jewish Culture Congress, 1950. Vol. 3.

Stalin, Joseph. *Marxism and the National and Colonial Question*. London, n.d.

Subbotin, A. *Evreiskaia biblioteka*. Vol. 10 (1880).

Subbotin, A. P. *V cherte evreiskoi osedlosti*. St. Petersburg, 1888.

Syrkin, Marie. *Nachman Syrkin, Socialist Zionist: A Biographical Memoir*. New York: Herzl Press, 1961.

Szmeruk, C. "*Yiddish Publications in the U.S.S.R.*," *Yad Vashem Studies on the European Jewish Catastrophe and Resistance.* Jerusalem, 1960.

Szwarc, P. "Di ershte yidishe oisgabes fun der pps," *Historishe shriftn*, Vol. 1 (1937).

Tartakover, A. "Batei Hasefer shel Hatsibur Hayehudi Bepolin," *Pisma Instytutu Nauk Judistycznyck.* Warsaw, 1931.

——— . "Yidishe politik un yidishe kultur in poiln tzvishn di tsvei velt milkhomes," *Algemeine entsiklopedie*, Series "Yidn." New York: World Jewish Culture Congress, 1950. Vol. 6.

Teimanas, David Bencionas. *L'autonomie des communautés juives en pologne aux XVI et XVII siècles.* Paris: Jauve et Cie, 1933.

Teller, Judd L. *The Kremlin, the Jews, and the Middle East.* New York: Thomas Yoseloff, 1957.

Tscherikower, E. *Anti-semitism un pogromen in ukraine, 1917-1918.* Berlin: Ostjuedisches Historisches Archiv, 1923.

——— . "Kommunistisher kemfer far hebraish in Turkestan," *In der tekufe fun revolutzie.* Berlin: Ostjuedischer Historisches Arkhiv, 1924. Vol. 1.

——— . *Di ukrainer pogromen in yor 1919.* New York: Yivo Institute of Jewish Research, 1961.

Tscherikower, Ilya. "Obshchestvo dlia rasprostraneni mezhdu evreiami v rossii," *Evreiskaia Entsiklopediia*, 13 (1913).

Tzentziper, Aryeh. *Esser Shnot Redifot.* Tel Aviv: Vaad Historit Shel Brit Hibbutz Galuyot, 1930.

Tzinberg, Yisrael. *Toldot Sifrut Yisrael.* Ovak. Tel Aviv: Sifriat Poalim, 1956-60.

Ukrainian Soviet Socialist Republic, People's Commissariat of Education. *Program farn tsveitn kontsenter fun shtotishe, shtetlishe un dorfishe arbetshuln.* Kiev: Kultur Lige, 1927.

——— . *Programmen farn tsveitn kontzenter fun shtotishe, shtetlishe un dorfishe arbetshuln.* Kiev: Kultur Lige, 1927.

"Ukrainskaia S.S.R." *Bolshaia sovetskaia entsiklopediia.* "Supplement SSSR" (1947).

United Nations Commission on Human Rights, Subcommission on

Prevention of Discrimination and Protection of Minorities. *Study of Discrimination in the Matter of Religious Rights and Practices.* (Conference Room Paper No. 35, January 30, 1959). New York, 1959.

Upansky, M. "Cheder Metukan," *Russkaia shokola* (1904), May-June.

Vakar, Nicholas P. *Belorussia.* Cambridge, Mass.: Harvard University Press, 1956.

Velednitzky, A. et al. (eds.). *Literarishe khrestomatie farn 6tn lernyor.* Kharkov-Kiev: State Publishing House for National Minorities Literature, 1933.

Voltke, G. "Kheder i melamed v rossii i tsarstve polskom," *Evreiskaia entsiklopediia.* Moscow, 1913. Vol. 15.

―――. "Prosveshchenie evreev v rossii," *Evreiskaia entsiklopediia,* Vol. 13.

Weinreich, M. (ed.). *Der ershte yiddishe shprach konferenz.* Vilna: Yiddish Scientific Institute, 1931.

Weizmann, Chaim. *Trial and Error.* Philadelphia: Jewish Publication Society of America, 1949.

Wengeroff, Helene. *Memoiren einer Grossmutter.* Berlin, 1908. Vol. 1.

West, Benjamin. *Naftulei Dor.* Tel Aviv: Foreign Delegation of the Tzeirei Zion, 1946.

Wettstein, F. *Kadmoniot Mepinkasiot Yeshanim.* Cracow: Y. Fisher, 1892.

White Russian Soviet Socialist Republic, Jewish Section of the Pedagogical Faculty. *Shriftn fun veisrusishn universitet.* Minsk: Jewish Section of the Pedagogical Faculty, 1929.

White Russian Soviet Socialist Republic, People's Commissariat of Education. *Program fun yiddish un literatur for der zibnyoriker shul.* Minsk: State Publishing House, 1928.

―――. *Program fun yiddish un literatur far der zibnyoriker shul, ovntshuln far arbeter yugnt, ovntshuln fun hechern tip.* Minsk: State Publishing House, 1928.

White Russian State University. *Iberblik fun limudim.* Minsk, 1926.

Wilson, Lucy. *The New Schools in the New Russia.* New York: Vanguard Press, 1928.

Yarmolinsky, Avrahm. *The Jews and Other Minority Nationalities under the Soviets.* New York: Vanguard Press, 1928.

Yidn in f.s.s.r.: atlas fun kartogramen un diagramen. Moscow-Kharkov-Minsk, 1930.

A yor arbet fun der r.k.p. in der yiddisher svive. Moscow: Central Board of Jewish Sections of the Russian Communist Party, 1924.

Yurchenko, Alexander V. "Genocide through Destruction of National Culture and Sense of Nationality," *Genocide in the U.S.S.R.* New York: Institute for the Study of the U.S.S.R, 1958.

Zborowski, Mark. "The Place of Book-Learning in Traditional Jewish Culture," *Harvard Educational Review*, 30 (1949).

────── and Herzog, Elizabeth. *Life Is with People.* New York: International Universities Press, 1952.

Zerubavel, Y. "Fun poltava biz Krako," *Der yiddisher arbeter pinkas.* Warsaw: Farlag Naie Kultur, 1928.

Zhitlowsky, Chaim. *Der sotzialism un di natsionale frage.* Warsaw, 1935.

Zhitz, G. "The Production of Books by Ukrderzhnatzmerividav Publishing House in 1939 and the Plan for 1940," *Sovetishe Literatur* (Kiev), (1941).

Zilberfarb, M. *Dos yidishe ministerium un di yidishe avtonomie in ukraine.* Kiev: Yiddisher Folks Farlag, 1918.

Zineman, A. (ed.). *Almunach szkolnictwa zydawskiego v Polsce.* Warsaw, 1938. Vol. 1.

Zinger, L. *Dos banaite folk.* Moscow: Emes Publishing House, 1941.

Newspapers, Journals, Archives

Af di vegn tsu der naier shul. (Moscow). 1924.

All-Ukrainian Academy of Sciences, Department for Jewish Culture, Literary and Philosophical Sections. *Shriftn.* Vol. 1. (1928).

Archives of the Yivo Institute for Jewish Research.

Bialystoker Shtern, 1940.

Emes (Kovno), 1941.

Emes (Moscow), 1922-1938.

Folksshtimme (Warsaw), January 26, 1957.

Haam (Moscow), March 10, 1917.

Hashachar, 1 (1869); 10 (1880).

Kamf (Riga), 1940.

Kommunistishe Fun (Yiddish daily of the Ukrainian Komfarband).
   Kiev, 1919.

Morgen Freiheit (New York), December 12, 1956.

Oktiafer (Minsk), 1940.

Proletarisher gedank (Moscow), March 1927.

Tsaitshrift (Minsk), Vols. 1-4, 1926-1931.

Ufboi (Riga), 1941.

Der vekker (Minsk), 1921.

Visnshaft un revolutsie. Kiev: Publishing House of the Ukrainian
   Academy of Sciences, 1934.

Voskhod. 1893, Issue 13. 1894, Issue 9.

Der Yiddisher Arbeter (London), March 1899.

Index

A

Abramovich, R., 161
Achad Haam, 78, 108, 112-113, 223, 227
Achildiev, M., 135-136
Achildiev, S., 135
Agurskii S., 156, 160-161, 201
Akselrod, Z., 173
Alexander I (Tsar), 10, 101
Alexander II (Tsar), 101-102
All-Russian Convention on Education, 129
All-Russian Jewish Congress, 124
All-Ukrainian Jewish National Assembly, 82-83
All-Unions Conference of Jewish Cultural Workers, 160-161, 166, 168-169, 179
Alterman, Y., 119, 121
Annexed areas
    founding of schools in, 260-262
    language of instruction in, 260-261
    Soviet occupation of, 258-259
    teacher shortage in, 262-264
    textbooks, 264-265
    Yiddish schools in, 260-268
        curriculum, 265
Asch, S., 76
Axelrod, P., 63

B

Bakst, Y., 219
Bauer, O., 149-151
Belorussification, 183-185
Ben Yehudah, E., 105-106
Berdyczewski, M.Y., 232
Bergelson, D., 240, 265
Berkowitz, Y.D., 232
Bershadsky, Y., 232
Bialik, C.N., 78, 112, 116, 120, 223, 232, 240
Birnbaum, N., 75
Bleichroder, 19
Bolsheviks
    lack of Jewish support for, 155-156

Book publishing, 90-91, 122, 191-192
Borochov, B., 70
Bovshover, Y., 234
Brik, M., 201
Bund, 62-68, 73-74, 82, 89, 121, 151, 153,158

C

Cahan, A., 106
Central Bureaus of Jewish Education, 166
Central Rada, 81-82, 86
Chamberlin, W.H., 183-184
Chashin, A., 201
Chassidism, 44-45, 47, 102-103
Cheder, 27, 39, 44, 47-53, 76, 80, 110, 112, 162
    criticism of, 48-51
    curriculum of, 39-41, 110-111
    defense of, 51-53
    suppression of, 162-164
Cheder Metukan, 110-115
Chernovitz conference, 75-76
Chevrat Chinuch Yeladim, 80
Chevrat Talmud Torah, 40-42
Choveve Sfat Ever, 118, 124
Choveve Tzion, 107
Commissariat for Jewish National Affairs, 156, 158-159, 161, 165
    attitude toward Hebrew, 159-160
    cultural and education sections, 159-160
Community supervision over education, 39-44
Complex method, 215-217
Compulsory Yiddishization, 183-184
Council of the Four Lands, 37-38
Crown rabbis, 102
Crown schools, 102

D

Dardak, I., 180
Democratic Teachers' Federation, 90
Demyevka School, 79-80

Dimanshtein, S., 158, 165, 201
Dinaburg, B.Z., 91
Dobin, S., 90
Dubnow, S., 101, 112, 245, 247
Duma, 71-72

E

Early Jewish university students, 102
Edelstadt, D., 234
Efrosi & Co., 19
Eisenstadt, S., 122
Elijah of Vilna, 45
Epstein, Y., 115
Evening and Sabbath schools, 79

F

Fraenkels, 19
Frank, J., 44
Frankel, C., 24
Frishman, D., 223, 232
Frumkin, E., 200

G

General Yiddish cultural work, 73-74
Ginzberg, L., 51-52
Glatstein, J., 235
Goldberg, B.Z., 200
Gordon, D., 106
Gordon, S.S., 116
Gorelik, S., 74
Gorki, M., 134
Graetz, H., 147
Grazovsky, Y., 115
Greenbaum, Y., 74, 120
Greenberg, C., 122
Greenberg, E., 234
Grinberg, Y., 217
Gunzbergs, 19

H

Haemet, 61
Halkin, S., 235
Halperin, M.L., 235
Halperin, Y., 11
Hamoreh, 125-126
Hannover, N., 43
Haskala, 103-105

Hebrew revival, 105-106
Hebrew schools
    after Bolshevik revolution, 129-
        134
    suppression of, 129-136
    in Turkestan, 134-136
    in Ukraine, 125-127
    under provisional government,
        121-125
Herzl, T., 64, 71, 108-109
Hofstein, D., 133, 235

I

Ivriah, 116
Ivrit Beivrit, 115

J

Jabotinsky, V., 78, 117, 120
Jewish historical research in Russia
    173-174
Jewish nationalism, 101-107
Jewish socialism, origins, 58-64
Jews
    economic status, 15-21
    effect of industrialization upon,
        23-24
    expulsions, 10-12
    legal status, 8-13
    occupations of, 15, 24-25
    population, 5, 14
    urbanization, 20, 23-24

K

Kahanshtam, A., 125-126
Kalinin, M., 133
Katzenelson, Y.L.B., 78, 232
Katznelson, Y.Y., 232
Kautsky, K., 148-149
Kharkov Yiddish Machine-Building
    Technicum, 172-173
Khrushchev, N., 201
Kindergartens
    Hebrew, 119, 121, 129
    Yiddish, 80
Kirov, S., 200
Klauzner, J., 116, 120, 236, 245
Klitenik, S., 179

Komfarband, 132-133
Komsomol
    Jewish work, 157
Kook, A.I., 109
Kremer, A., 63, 65
Kronenbergs, 19
Kultur Lige, 89-91
Kvitko, L., 235

L

Language question, 76-78, 113, 116-117
Lassalle, F., 147
Leib, M., 235
Lenin, V.I., 127-128, 151-153, 248
Lestchinsky, J., 167, 185
Levinsohn, I.B., 103-104
Liberberg, D., 201
Lieberman, A., 61
Liessin, A., 235
Literary selections, representativeness, 229-240
Litvakoff, M., 200
Lunacharsky, A., 130-132, 134
Lvov, Prince G., 121

M

Maimon, S., 49-50
Malachovka Children's Colony, 190
Mandelstam, L.I., 45
Manger, I., 235
Mapu, A., 106
Marr, N., 133
Martov, J., 62
Marx, K., 146-149
Marxism and Leninism on the Jewish question, 127-128, 146-148, 150-155
Marxism and nationalism, 149
Maze, J., 130-131
Mefitzei Haskalah, 77-79, 110, 118, 120, 125
Melamed, 40, 48, 80
Melamed, Z., 90
Mendele Mocher Sforim, 15, 233, 235, 238-239, 245
Methods of instruction, 217-219, 221-222, 226, 240-247

Meyer & Co., 19
Mill, John, 66
Minsk Higher Pedagogical Institute, 171, 225
Mirenburg, D., 132
Mirsky, M., 201-202
Mohilever, S., 109

N

Nadir, M., 235
Nathansons, 19
National minorities, Soviet school statistics on, 181
Niger, S., 73-74, 161
Nurock brothers, 24

O

Odessa Committee, 112
Oislender, N., 219
Oldenburg, S., 133
"On Agitation," 63-64

P

Pale of Settlement, 12-14
    exceptions, 13-14
Paperna, A., 27
Pasmanik, D., 119-120
Paul I (Tsar), 8-9
Pereira Freres, 19
Peretz, Y.L., 75, 79, 233, 235-237, 239, 244, 247, 265
Persitz, S., 121-122
Pines, N., 121, 126
Pines, Y. M., 109
Pinsker, L., 107-108
Pinsky, D., 233
Poale Zion, 70-71, 73-74, 89, 91, 158
Pogroms
    of 1648-1649, 44
    of 1919, 88-89
Pokrovsky, M., 132
Poliakoffs, 18
Polish Socialist Party (P.P.S.), 63, 66
Polonization efforts, 259
Pomerantz, A., 175-176
Pre-modern education, 27-28
Prilutsky, N., 266

Progressive education, abolition of, 220-221
Progressive Yiddish Teachers Organization, 263

R

Rafalovich, 19
Ratner, M., 107
Reisin, A., 76, 218
Renner, K., 149
Rosenfeld, P., 179
Rosenthal, L., 77
Rosenzweig, F., 52-53
Rudnitzky, M., 131
Russian Zionist organization, second congress (Minsk, 1902), 113
Russian Zionist organization, seventh congress (Petrograd, 1917), 122

S

Saltzberg, I. B., 202
Schneour, Z., 223, 235
Schwartzman, A., 235
Schwarz, S., 192-196, 201
Secular education for Jews, beginnings, 60
Shabetai Zevi, 44
Shapiro, L., 235
Shklover, N., 9-10
Sholom Aleichem, 218, 232-233, 235, 238-239, 241, 244, 246, 265
Sigismund II, 7, 37
Singer, I. B., 235
Sirkes, J., 42
Skoropadski, Hetman P., 86, 125
Smidovich, P., 134
Smolensk, Yiddish cultural activity in, 157
Smolenskin, P., 104-105, 106, 223
Socialist Zionism, origins, 69-70
Sokolov, N., 116
Speransky, Count N., 10
Stalin, J., 133, 197-198
on Jewish question, 153-155
Steiglitz, 19
Steinberg, Y., 232
Strashun, A., 83

Sulzbach, 19
Syrkin, N., 69

T

Tarbut
in Poland, 222-224
in Russia, 122-123, 125-126, 130
Tchernichovsky, S., 223
Textbooks
Hebrew, 115, 126-127
Yiddish, 167, 169, 191-192, 217-219, 229-232, 245-246
Tzechanov, Y., 136
Tzeirei Tzion, 89, 122-124
Tzinberg, S., 227-228, 245
Tzuzmer, M., 127

U

Ukrainian Academy of Sciences, Jewish division, 173-176
Ukrainization, 183-185
Unified Labor School, 216-220

V

Vayter, A., 74
Vice Secretariat for Jewish Affairs, Ukraine, Education Department
curriculum, 83
structure, 82-83, 86-88
textbooks, 84
Vilna and Zhitomir rabbinical seminaries, 102
Vilna University (1941)
Yiddish courses, 266
Vladeck, B., 73

W

Wawelbergs, 19
Weinstein, R., 201
Weizmann, C., 50-51
Wengeroff, P., 26
White Russian Academy of Science, Jewish division, 173
White Russian State University at Minsk, Pedagogical Faculty, Jewish section, 171-172
Witte, S., Count, 1, 2

Y

Yehoash, 235
Yeshiva, 28, 43, 45-47, 76
  curriculum of, 43
Yevsektzia, 129-130, 134, 156-158, 165-166
Yiddish-Hebrew struggle, 76-78
Yiddish pedagogical literature, 247
Yiddish Pedagogical Technicum of Smolensk, 172
Yiddish schools
    in annexed areas, 260-268
    authors studied, 229-240
    in Baltic states, 183, 259
    curriculum, 215-217, 219-220
    decline, 173, 185-190, 192-202
    higher education in, 169-176
    national content, 222-228
    in Poland, 179-180, 183, 222
    postwar, 268-269
    statistics on, 161, 166, 168-170, 176-178, 181, 194
    in Tsarist period, 78-81
Yiddish teachers' conference (1907), 76
Yiddish teachers' conference (1916), 80

Z

Zerubavel, Y., 73
Zhitlowsky, C., 67, 75, 76, 147-148
Zilberbarb, M., 82, 125
Zionism, 65, 67, 82, 107-109, 112-113, 120, 212-224, 132, 133
Zionist Socialists (S.S.), 73
Zlatopolsky, H., 121